DATE DUE

NOV 0 6 2017

The Political Philosophy
of Thomas Paine

THE POLITICAL PHILOSOPHY OF THE
AMERICAN FOUNDERS
Garrett Ward Sheldon, Series Editor

Garrett Ward Sheldon, *The Political Philosophy of Thomas Jefferson*
Garrett Ward Sheldon, *The Political Philosophy of James Madison*
Lorraine Smith Pangle, *The Political Philosophy of Benjamin Franklin*
Jeffry H. Morrison, *The Political Philosophy of George Washington*
Jack Fruchtman Jr., *The Political Philosophy of Thomas Paine*

THE
POLITICAL PHILOSOPHY
OF
Thomas Paine

JACK FRUCHTMAN JR.

The Johns Hopkins University Press
Baltimore

© 2009 The Johns Hopkins University Press
All rights reserved. Published 2009
Printed in the United States of America on acid-free paper
2 4 6 8 9 7 5 3 1

The Johns Hopkins University Press
2715 North Charles Street
Baltimore, Maryland 21218-4363
www.press.jhu.edu

Library of Congress Cataloging-in-Publication Data

Fruchtman, Jack.
The political philosophy of Thomas Paine / Jack Fruchtman.
p.   cm. — (The political philosophy of the American founders)
Includes bibliographical references and index.
ISBN-13: 978-0-8018-9284-4 (hardcover : alk. paper)
ISBN-10: 0-8018-9284-8 (hardcover : alk. paper)
1. Paine, Thomas, 1737–1809. 2. Political science—
History—18th century.   I. Title.
JC177.A4F73 2009
320.51'2092—dc22
2008043995

A catalog record for this book is available
from the British Library.

Special discounts are available for bulk purchases of this book.
For more information, please contact Special Sales
at 410-516-6936 or specialsales@press.jhu.edu.

The Johns Hopkins University Press uses environmentally friendly book
materials, including recycled text paper that is composed of at least 30 percent
post-consumer waste, whenever possible. All of our book papers are acid-free,
and our jackets and covers are printed on paper with recycled content.

FOR

J. G. A. Pocock

CONTENTS

ACKNOWLEDGMENTS

This book, in many ways, had its origins in a conference in the spring of 2002 organized by J. G. A. Pocock, entitled "History, Theory, and the Subject of Rights, Opposition, Dissent, and Revolutionary Sympathies: Origins of the British Left, 1770–1800," held at the William Andrews Clark Memorial Library at the University of California, Los Angeles. I am especially grateful to John Pocock, of the Johns Hopkins University, for inviting me to participate in the conference. Thirty-four years ago, I had the good fortune, privilege, and opportunity to study under him at Hopkins. Since those days, he has been most generous with his time and concern. His magnificent work is an inspiration and a model to any scholar who encounters it, and his guidance and wisdom continue to be personally and professionally vital to me.

I also appreciate the insightful comments concerning my presentation at the conference expressed by James E. Bradley, of the Fuller Seminary, and Gregory Claeys, of the University of London. I thank those who remarked on my presentations at various meetings of the American Society for Eighteenth-Century Studies and especially the East-Central Society for Eighteenth-Century Studies. H. George Hahn, my colleague at Towson University, and I have long discussed Paine and other eighteenth-century figures, and his insights are always incisive. A sabbatical leave approved by my department chair, James C. Roberts, and the dean of the College of Liberal Arts at Towson University, Terry A. Cooney, allowed me to complete the manuscript. I appreciate the support and assistance of Henry Y. K. Tom, at the Johns Hopkins University Press, and Garrett Ward Sheldon, of the University of Virginia, in encouraging me to undertake this project, as well as the observations of an anonymous reader, who helped me reshape earlier ideas about Paine. I am indebted to Michael Johnston and Barbara B. Lamb, who read the manuscript with keen eyes, and for that I thank them. Finally, JoAnn Fruchtman as always offered crucial advice, encouragement, and support, and my devotion to her remains beyond words alone.

The Political Philosophy
of Thomas Paine

INTRODUCTION

AMERICANS WITH a historical sensibility have long been ambivalent about the leading figures of their founding period. On the one hand, they often grow impatient with the unfulfilled promise of the ideals presented in the Declaration of Independence and the Constitution of the United States. These documents failed to resolve the problem of slavery, they neglected the rights of women, and they dismissed Native Americans' rights to their lands as increasing numbers of Americans moved westward.[1] On the other hand, Americans have been enamored with the founding period from the First Continental Congress to the presidencies of George Washington, John Adams, and Thomas Jefferson. By the end of the twentieth and the beginning of the twenty-first centuries, they began to crave an unprecedented amount of information about those who played principal roles in America's founding era. This peculiar phenomenon, christened "Founders Chic" in 2001, has been marked by the appearance of numerous books focusing on the illustrious figures of the Revolution against Britain and the drafting of the Constitution—Washington and Jefferson, Adams, Alexander Hamilton, and Benjamin Franklin—and on less prominent figures like Gouverneur Morris and even the maligned Aaron Burr.[2] Jefferson's and Franklin's images have even graced the front cover of *Time* magazine.[3] The opportunity to study afresh the political philosophies of the notable personalities of America's founding generation enhances our understanding of their thinking about how they explained their ideas to a new emerging nation founded on novel political principles, which they thought were untried though workable, risky though exciting. The central question they posed was how to form a government that best celebrated and protected individual rights while not diminishing the community's security. The answer was their defense of the democratic republic. Their differences arose in the particular way they preferred to structure the republic to ensure and guarantee the citizens' rights and liberties.[4]

The Founders Chic phenomenon has included Thomas Paine, an Englishman by birth, an American by choice and necessity. More than any eighteenth-century political writer and activist, Paine defies easy categorization. A liberal and a radical with at times conservative economic views, Paine's contradictions make him appear to be a believing and nonbelieving Quaker, who was no pacifist. Later in life, he became a deist, holding that God's creation was all we need to know about Him, except when we detect a tincture of theism in his writings; at times, he reveals his belief in God's controlling hand in history and, as we will see, he even suggested that he himself possessed a divinely appointed role.[5] Meanwhile, Paine has been excoriated as an unreconstructed atheist and a radical, even romantic revolutionary on two continents. But just who was Thomas Paine, and what drove his thinking? Many commentators have asked this question, leading to so much attention devoted to him in academic and nonacademic circles that the study of his life and thought has become a growth industry in America, England, and France. No fewer than eight new biographies, including three in French, have appeared over the past twenty years.[6] Numerous book-length commentaries and several essays on his writings have been published in learned journals and the popular press.[7] A new Library of America edition of his works has now fixed him securely in the canon of American literature, as only writers considered genuinely "American" have their writings included among its publications.[8] At least one political pundit, who himself has extensively commented on Paine's *Rights of Man,* has recently been touted as "the Tom Paine of our troubled times," and Paine has even been cited as a precursor to the Internet; an article entitled "The Age of Paine" echoed John Adams's famous and marvelously eloquent deprecation of Paine in an 1805 letter to his friend, the physician Dr. Benjamin Water-house.⁹ Adams wrote that he was deeply offended that the era he had tried to shape was now called the Age of Reason because a wretched book by Paine (that "disastrous meteor") carried that name. Adams told Waterhouse:

> I am willing you should call this the Age of Frivolity as you do, and would not object if you had named it the Age of Folly, Vice, Frenzy, Brutality, Daemons, Buonaparte, Tom Paine, or the Age of the Burning Brand from the Bottomless Pitt, or anything but the Age of Reason. I know not whether any Man in the World had more influence on its inhabitants or affairs for the last thirty years than Tom Paine. There can be no severer Satyr on the Age. For such a mongrel between Pigg and Puppy, begotten by a wild Boar on a Bitch Wolf, never before in any Age of the World was suffered by the Poltroonery of mankind, to run through such a Career of Mischief. Call it then the Age of Paine. He deserves it much more, than the Courtezan who was consecrated the Goddess in the Temple at Paris, and whose name, Tom has given the Age. The real intellectual faculty has nothing to do with the Age the Strumpet or Tom.¹⁰

As Adams dismissed Paine two centuries ago, some contemporary scholars and writers have claimed he is overrated. Works by Pauline Maier, Joseph Ellis, and David McCullough, for example, reveal their authors' preference for Adams or Washington or Hamilton to Paine or even Jefferson.¹¹ For some, Founders Chic has become transformed into "Federalist Chic"; as Jack Rakove tells us, "Alexander Hamilton is clearly the winner in the most recent round of 'Founders Chic.' Hamilton's soberly realistic views of national security seem more suited to our age of holy terror than Thomas Jefferson's touching faith that our coasts could best be protected by gunboats."¹² Still, the fluctuations seesawing between Federalist and Republican, between Hamilton and Jefferson or Paine, constantly shift as studies come to focus on specific aspects of the life and thought of Jefferson and Madison, Franklin and the others, including of course Paine.

As an inherently fascinating iconoclastic writer and thinker, Paine was consistently convinced that he was always right and that anyone who opposed him was patently wrong and badly uninformed. He once wrote, perhaps famously, that "I have not only contributed to raise a new empire in the world, founded on a new system of government, but I have arrived at an eminence in political literature, the most difficult of all lines to succeed and excel in."[13] This is why so many commentators look first at his writing style to see how he addressed the concerns of the common people, the working poor rather than aristocrats, in language that did not require a classical education. He wrote, says Eric Foner, "in language carefully crafted to appeal to a mass audience of ordinary readers," while Sean Wilentz simply says that Paine was "the most gifted democratic writer in the English-speaking world."[14] His work possessed riveting images because his words were never like a volcano encased in solidified lava, but instead they poured forth with heat and power. When presenting his views and attacking those who disagreed with him, Paine was a passionate master literary stylist.[15] As *un homme engagé*, he was so thoroughly consumed by the political and social transformations he witnessed that he was not particularly systematic in his assessment of politics and society. His work often appears disjointed, even rambling, amounting to a stream of observations on political events or statements by others, most notably after 1790 those by Edmund Burke, which he interpreted to his own advantage, often disregarding the original speaker's intentions.

But there is more to Paine than a brilliant literary style; there is the substance of his political thought. By illuminating his thought, we can discover who he was and how he figured ideologically in the revolutionary mood of the late eighteenth century. The most recent studies have typically investigated specific aspects of Paine's thought or focused on a single work, most notably the analyses of *Common Sense* by Vikki Vickers, the *Rights of Man* by Greg Claeys and Christopher Hitchens, and *The Age of Reason* by Edward Davidson and William Scheick.[16] Although several of his minor works were first published in 1775 and although he wrote almost to the day he died, it is astonishing that his major writings flourished only over two short decades, from 1776 until 1797. Most of that work falls into one of two categories: as rejoinders to specific political or social issues or events, as in *Common Sense* and the *American Crisis* series, consisting of several articles Paine wrote from 1776 to 1783 on the war with

Britain, or as responses to a tract or event that he found to be unusually foolish, such as both parts of the *Rights of Man* and *Agrarian Justice*.[17] The exception is *The Age of Reason*, his great attack on organized religion and its unholy link to government. Even today, it may well be his best known yet most misunderstood work.

Paine was in fact a writer of contradictions. He attacked organized religion, yet remained personally a deeply religious man, even using religious or scriptural language and imagery. This is true from the long passages in *Common Sense* to all his other major works. He sometimes even wrote as if he himself were a biblical prophet, using the imagery and cadences of a country preacher. In the first harsh winter of the war in 1776, he wrote of his unambiguous reliance on God.

> I thank God, that I fear not. I see no real cause for fear. I know our situation well, and can see the way out of it. . . . By perseverance and fortitude we have the prospect of a glorious issue; by cowardice and submission, the sad choice of a variety of evils—a ravaged country—a depopulated city—habitations without safety, and slavery without hope—our homes turned into barracks and bawdy houses. . . . Look on this picture and weep over it! and if there yet remains one thoughtless wretch who believes it not, let him suffer it unlamented.[18]

Sixteen years later, he proclaimed that "when the valleys laugh and sing, it is not the farmer only, but all creation that rejoice" (*RM*, 22–27). As an eighteenth-century Jeremiah, he declared himself the tool of God Almighty to bring justice and liberty to all people everywhere.

In terms of the sources of his political thought, we might say that Paine was Lockean because he accepted the basic tenets of government by consent, the existence of rights and liberties, and ultimately the people's right to revolution.[19] And yet, he once somewhat notoriously wrote that Locke's writings themselves meant little to him. "I never read Locke, nor ever had Locke's *Second Treatise of Government* in my hand," and he once proudly wrote that he hardly ever read anything at all because he would rather think than read: "I scarcely ever quote; the reason is, I always think."[20] He reported in the *Rights of Man:* "I neither read books, nor studied other people's opinions. I thought for my-self" (219n). A friend of his, Etienne Dumont, once reported that "he believed that his book, the *Rights of Man,* would replace all the books in the world, and he said if he had the power to de-molish all the libraries in existence he would do it, because of all the errors contained in them."[21] Even late in life, Paine was de-termined that his audience would know that he had devoted his life to being "unshackled by the fable and fiction of books, by whatever invented name they may be called."[22]

Nor can we say that Paine was a classical republican by any tra-ditional definition of that ideology. He denied the efficacy of the triadic division of power in government between the one, the few, and the many, as illustrated in a separate executive and two houses of the legislature, as John Adams always argued for so vo-ciferously. He never admired the autonomous yeoman farmer who devoted his life and death to the republic, as had Thomas Jefferson. Isaac Kramnick notes that because Paine focused so much on the individual, he turned "traditional republican doc-trine . . . on its head: self-serving individuals further the com-mon good," not the community as a whole, "and public gov-ernment serves its own selfish and corrupt interest."[23] Then again, Paine strongly believed that the people must develop a public spirit that promoted their civic engagement in govern-mental decision making—through the right to vote and service in public office—and he marveled at the prospect that the United States would become a strong commercial republic based on trade and manufacturing, not agriculture. Like Alexander Hamilton, he was an urban man, not one rooted in the soil, who believed that progress occurred in the great cities where he himself resided throughout his career— places like Philadelphia and Paris.

His work on the whole displays a sound and lucid political phi-losophy based on what he thought were achievable goals: the global spread of liberal and republican ideas would destroy he-redity, rank, privilege, and injustice; the defeat of the disabling impact of corruption and influence in government would secure human liberty; and the defense of the economic and social rights of the poor would guarantee the survival of those rights in a world ruled by aristocratic parasites with their rotten placemen constantly seeking offices like mosquitoes whining around the heads of the ministry. That Paine sometimes changed his mind is unsurprising given the enormous transformative activities taking place in America and Britain and on the Continent. While he was initially attracted, for example, to a unicameral legislature, he later accepted the greater efficiency and safety of power divided into a two-house legislature.

J. G. A. Pocock reminds us of the frustration many commentators have about Thomas Paine when he wrote that Paine

> remains difficult to fit into any kind of category. *Common Sense* breathes an extraordinary hatred of English governing institutions, but it does not consistently echo any established radical vocabulary; Paine had no real place in the club of Honest Whigs to which Franklin had introduced him in London, and his use of anti-Normanism to insist that Britain did not have a constitution but rather a tyranny does not permit us to think of him (as contemporaries might have) as a New Model soldier risen from the grave. Moreover, when the Revolutionary War was over Paine returned to live under the "the royal brute of Britain" as if nothing had happened, nor was he pursued by the authorities until the very different circumstances of 1791.[24]

Part of the problem, but in no way the whole of it, is that Paine was not a particularly organized thinker or writer. He loved to sprinkle ridicule, humor, and sometimes vindictive sentiments throughout his work because so much of his writings were "attack" pieces, designed to target those whom he disliked or those who said things he despised.

Still, we can detect a general unity and consistency underlying his thought as he encountered new, rapidly changing events in America and France over his writing career from 1774 until his death thirty-five years later. Six themes in particular pervade his work, giving it clarity, coherence, and unity with a seventh attended by an important caveat:

- Faith in God as a benevolent deity who created the universe and sometimes intervened in it but who also imparted to human beings the task of improving the world through their good works
- Detestation of rank and privilege and of corruption, selfishness, and injustice in politics, commerce, and economics

- Belief in the democratic republic whose structure was not as important as the written constitution on which it was based as long as it guaranteed free and frequent elections open to all white males over twenty-one, even if they were without property
- Trust in the public-spiritedness of all citizens who devoted their lives to participating in political decision making and who were morally engaged in the affairs of the day
- Faith in a strong commercial republic, underscored by a Hamiltonian spirit, in which wealth and prosperity flourished, but not at the expense of the less fortunate, especially the poor, the elderly, and young children in need of education
- Belief in the republic's international commercial relationships founded on a strong navy composed of fast gunboats, a fair system of taxation, and a just banking system open to everyone

Most commentators concentrating on his political ideology have focused primarily on his resolute belief in the efficacy and necessity of revolution to terminate the death grip of hierarchy, rank, and privilege. For some, revolution alone defined Paine's ideal of bringing a new democratic order into being; Harvey Kaye calls Paine "the firebrand of revolution," while Isaac Kramnick terms him a "radical democrat," Maurice Ezran tells us he is "the fighter of two revolutions," and Jean Lessay simply says he was "the professor of revolutions."[25] But in fact we can detect a demonstrable shift in Paine's thinking after his release from prison in France at the end of the Reign of Terror. Thus, the seventh and final theme may run as follows:

- Faith in the efficacy of revolution until his release from prison in 1794, and thereafter a belief in reform through civic engagement and public spiritedness[26]

After his release from the Luxembourg prison, Paine advised his readers to disavow violent revolution, except in the most extreme cases. Instead, citizens should do all they could to make gradual political changes to bring about the republic, especially by expanding the franchise to all male citizens.

These seven themes are not inclusive. While they cover his political and social thought, they also pose the "Paine question" that Pocock asks us to consider, namely, just who was Thomas

Paine and what was the meaning of his ideas in terms of the eighteenth-century debate about political and social transformation, the struggle for liberty, and the fight for human rights?[27] The Paine question demands that we determine how to approach Paine's political philosophy to decide how his thought figured in Enlightenment ideas that echoed through America, England, and France at the century's end. Above all, it asks us to lay out the apparent contradictions in his thinking and to seek ways to resolve them that make sense to us and do justice to his philosophy.

What can we reasonably conclude at this preliminary stage of our inquiry? First, Paine was a man who thought seriously about religion, a man who wrote about religious matters either indirectly, as when he included biblical references in his political works like *Common Sense,* or directly, as in *The Age of Reason.* Most importantly, he made clear in his earliest essays, those published in 1775, and in *Common Sense* that he believed that God existed, that He created the universe and everything in it, and that the duty of all men was to heal the world of all the wounds caused by human weakness and failure. Paine was certainly attracted by the inner-light spirituality of the Society of Friends and the Quaker belief that every person possessed a divine spark impelling him or her to do good works for all people. Some things about the Quakers, however, repelled him. He thought Quakerism a stale, dour religion that stifled human creativity. By the time he became a deist, he was disgusted with Quaker plainness and gravity. "Though I reverence their philanthropy, I cannot help smiling at the conceit that if the taste of a Quaker could have been consulted at the Creation, what a silent and drab-colored Creation it would have been! Not a flower would have blossomed its gaieties, nor a bird been permitted to sing."[28] When it came time to fight for American independence against a powerful British imperial army and navy in the Revolutionary War, he attacked Quaker pacifism and Quaker Tories as misguided and weak willed.

Still, we are faced with a variety of other apparent contradictions about his religious background that we need to untangle. Initially educated in the teachings of the Church of England, Paine rejected the requirements of its liturgy but accepted Quaker and then later deist notions of human freedom and responsibility. At the same time, he maintained close friendships throughout his life with the most sincere and devout Christians, for example, preachers Richard Price, Joseph Priestley, and Elihu Palmer. As an adult, he never attended church services, and he even avoided Quaker meetings. Paine was, in short, a religious man who detested organized religion but who had no difficulty associating with specific individuals deeply devoted to those very religions (Price, Priestley, and Palmer were originally Presbyterians but became Unitarians late in their careers). Perhaps it was their agreement with him that church and state must be separate that made him see these men in a very different light from those who, like Burke, argued for an enduring link between the Church of England and the English government. Still, as Barry Alan Shain reminds us, Americans might well have held liberal or republican views, but they remained devotees of reformed Protestantism. Paine too built his political philosophy on the foundations of his "Protestant religiosity," which, in Shain's terms, played a vital role "in creating and nurturing a truly radical idea: that a presocial right or privilege might be so integral to the accepted goals of organized social life or essential to being fully human that it could be neither traded nor relinquished without nullifying those ends."[29] Shain did not focus specifically on Thomas Paine when he came to this conclusion. Although he was addressing what Americans in general believed at the time of the Revolution, his view applies to Paine, which is why, as Shain emphasizes and as we shall soon see, Paine was exceptionally desirous of the guarantee of religious liberty, not merely religious tolerance.

Religion was not the only element that posed a contradiction in Paine's life and thought—which brings us to the second concern in the Paine question. Like Franklin, Paine enjoyed little formal schooling, but he became one of the most popular, most articulate writers of his time, crafting phrases that were liberally quoted in the twentieth century and are still cited in the twenty-first.[30] Although he claimed not to be particularly well read, which is perhaps his anti-intellectual side, Paine frequently used classical references, signing his work "Atlanticus," "Humanus," "Comus," and other designations as well as often referring to the great heroes and writers of antiquity, Socrates, Plato, Aristotle, and Aristides.[31] He regularly cited John Locke, Jean-Jacques Rousseau, Adam Smith, Baron de Montesquieu, Voltaire, François Quesnay, Anne-Robert-Jacques Turgot, the Abbé Sieyès, and other great writers of the Enlightenment, often directly quoting them.[32] He relied on history, especially in the *Rights of Man*, and yet, in the words of Eric Foner, he was "a man with little interest in the past and unbounded optimism about the future."[33]

To assert that Paine was an Enlightenment figure in the mold of any of the men who argued on behalf of justice, liberty, and equality is hardly a remarkable statement.[34] It is, however, difficult to determine the roots of his Enlightenment political thought, that is, just how he came to be a philosophe with a revolutionary agenda to transform the world by ending slavery, torture, and tyrannies by church and state, and by promoting human freedom and natural rights, political liberty and civil justice, and with them the separation of church and state; in short, by advocating nothing less than a democratic order. He understood how and why religious liberty was so important to this order and how equality, especially political equality, equality before the law, and equality of opportunity, functioned in a genuine republic. I suspect he read far more than he let on, though that is pure speculation. He was well aware of the political positions taken by Locke, Montesquieu, Voltaire, and Rousseau. Moreover, he read the papers and obviously loved to debate the major ideas of the day, which were, as John Pocock suggests, akin to a kind of "influenza" spreading germs through the air infecting and affecting those who came into contact with them. As Jacob Talmon reminds us, "there is such a thing as a climate of ideas, as ideas in the air." Enlightenment principles permeate Paine's writings either firsthand, through his own experiences and reading, or as second nature, through what Talmon calls the creation "of a state of mind" shared by the community in which he resided.[35]

Like his French counterparts who dreamed of the end of the monarchy and the establishment of republican government, Paine was an intellectual, a philosophe, who developed new ideas and programs that he actually tried to implement.[36] He was no naive "romantic" revolutionary, as Joseph Ellis has argued. Ellis, among others, claims that Paine thought merely in terms of revolution as the only act republican-minded men need undertake, while the rest would automatically fall into place "once the last king [had been] strangled with the entrails of the last priest."[37] This statement suggests that Paine had no stomach or aptitude for the practical side of constitution making or nation building, but we know that this was not the case. Paine participated in the first American government under the Articles of Confederation, serving as the first secretary of the Committee on Foreign Affairs for Congress, and ten years later he was elected a deputy to the French National Convention and almost immediately worked on the draft of a republican constitution. He even served a second term in the Convention under the Directory. He was committed to helping build the actual republic in France, and when it failed, he was disgusted, but he remained proud of his service.

The third element in the Paine question is his personal financial status. Although he was chronically poor throughout his life, he could have easily achieved comfortable wealth had he chosen to accept his share of the profits from the sale of his successful pamphlets and books. *Common Sense* reputedly sold in the hundreds of thousands, though the actual figures are unknown, and Paine always claimed that the *Rights of Man* was the greatest bestseller of its time.[38] He chose instead never to accept any royalties for his work, and he preferred to live modestly. He implored his friends and acquaintances to give him money or a bed, the latter sometimes for long periods despite his ownership of two farms in America: one in Bordentown, New Jersey, which he eventually sold, and the other in New Rochelle, a gift to him by the State of New York after the Revolution.

Paine was more than just a bundle of contradictions in his personal life, in his theology, and in the success of his writings; the contradictions extend to politics and economics as well. This brings us to the fourth and final prong of the question. Was monarchy an evil per se or did Paine target only certain monarchs, those he thought were personally stacked against him? In 1775, his detestation for the British monarchy was so intense that he wanted to do everything possible to demolish it. Yet within a short time, we find him extolling the French monarchy as "enlightened" because of its support of the American cause and then later through its ability to transform itself into a constitutional monarchy during the early phases of the French Revolution. The French government of course had its own reasons for supporting the Americans against England, long a traditional enemy, especially in 1763, after France's devastating defeat in the Seven Years' War. In the fast-moving events of 1789 and 1790, Louis XVI was undoubtedly frightened when he made a series of compromises and undertook retreats to save the monarchy and himself. Despite Paine's deep hatred for monarchy everywhere, not just in Britain, Paine saw only the good in Louis. Still, Louis was a king, so why did he not receive the same harsh treatment as George III? Was there something qualitatively different about him and his aristocratic minions that they could admire the rustic Benjamin Franklin during his diplomatic mission to France in 1776?[39] Was there an underlying appreciation of political reform among French nobles when they openly celebrated the success of the American victory, or, we should correctly say, Franco-American victory, with numerous *fêtes* on the thirteenth of each month along with drinks accompanied by thirteen toasts?[40] These are questions to which we will return in chapter 4.

Moreover, just as Paine was skeptical of priests and organized religion but associated with the likes of Price, Priestley, and Palmer, how could this self-professed man of the common people so easily be connected with wealthy manufacturers like Robert Morris or the French aristocrats in the Royal Academy of Sciences? In addition, he fiercely supported the Bank of North America, a bastion of established commercial wealth, just as Hamilton later so powerfully promoted the Bank of the United States. Did Paine abandon those whom he claimed to support, the poor and unrepresented, or did he have a different view about how best to improve the economic and financial condition of the poor? What gave him, in effect, what I wish to call his "Hamiltonian spirit" in light of his revolutionary activism? These questions are addressed in chapter 5.

After helping to resolve the debate over the bank by supporting it wholeheartedly and after attacking the British monarchy so stridently in *Common Sense* and other writings, Paine, as Pocock pointed out above, surprisingly chose to return to London in 1787. Paine's own explanation seems gratuitous, though believable: first, he claimed he wanted the Royal Society of London to endorse his design of an iron bridge without piers so that it might one day span the river Thames; second, though he accepted none of the profits from the sale of his work, he grew frustrated with the parsimoniousness of the United States Congress and the states when they refused to compensate him for his writing services on behalf of the American cause; and third, he declared that he wanted to see his parents once again. But if the monarchy, especially George III himself, and aristocratic privilege were as revolting as he claimed they were, purely on moral and emotional grounds he should never have been able to return to an irrevocably corrupt England.

Although Thomas Paine never set out to write a formal political philosophy, we may discern in his whole body of work a consistency and coherence in his political and social thought. As a keen observer and ardent participant in the key events of his time, he commented on the unfolding, world-changing moments, which included two major revolutions and the development of a new nation, the United States, under its written constitution. Paine's work demonstrates that he was more than a political commentator and social critic, though he was no trained philosopher with a university education. He was often not particularly rigorous in his argumentation, frequently using sneering ridicule, personal invective, and entertaining humor to score points at the expense of those whom he thought were scoundrels and mountebanks. He certainly used hard evidence and sound theoretical principles, but only when he thought they played to his advantage. If the facts failed to fit his argument, he often discounted or ignored them. If a theory proved him wrong, he simply rejected it or even denied its existence as a rational principle. It is no wonder that at times his books, pamphlets, and essays appear impressionistic and shallow to many of his readers. Despite his sometimes biting, sometimes hilarious, sometimes discourteous style, the seven themes laid out above offer answers to who Paine was and how his ideas fit into the opposition movement in England and America in the last quarter of the century. The present study explores the evolution of Paine's political thought as it poured from his pen, making him into the era's pre-eminent philosopher of political and social transformation.

CHAPTER 1

PAINE'S POLITICAL THOUGHT

IN HISTORICAL CONTEXT

LIKE MANY eighteenth-century intellectuals with little formal education, Thomas Paine developed a political philosophy as a reaction to the individuals he encountered and the events that occurred around him. As a rootless, often solitary, wanderer, Paine's political philosophy was unequivocally shaped by his experiences in the small towns and hamlets in which he resided throughout the Midlands.[1] He lived in places like Dover, Sandwich, Alford, and Lewes from the time of his birth in Thetford in 1737 until his penniless arrival in Philadelphia thirty-seven years later. These experiences in his early years imparted important lessons in social class. As the son of a maker of stays for women's corsets who entered the craft himself, Paine learned early on to fight to improve the lot of the common people, the poor, those whom monarchs and aristocrats, men of undeserved privilege and enormous wealth, oppressed and exploited.[2]

Paine's life in the country town of Thetford in Norfolk, England, perhaps exposed him to his first repellent political spectacle. Located about ninety miles north of London, Thetford was dominated by the aristocratic Grafton family. The third duke, far more liberal than his predecessors, served as the king's prime minister from 1767 to 1770, but George III dismissed him when Grafton suggested that the Americans might be granted independence. The Graftons controlled the elections, the patronage, all the contracts and licenses, and just about everything else in the borough. Thirty electors, all under the sway of the powerful family, supported the two members of Parliament. One of them was always a Grafton. For seventy years, beginning in 1733, Thetford had no contested elections. The electors and everyone else simply did what was expected of them. Perhaps young Thomas recalled these earliest experiences when he wrote of the importance of engaging in a spirited public criticism of governmental authority as a decisive check on absolute power.

Paine's more specific interest in politics dates from his experiences as he traveled throughout southern England, the Midlands, and London, though we cannot say for certain because the documentation about his early life is meager. He visited London at least twice before he was thirty, and there he met many scientists, including Franklin, and others interested in public affairs. He married at a young age, but his wife died in childbirth, as did the infant. Biographer John Keane has speculated that Paine's political imagination was sharpened when he was a Methodist preacher in Dover and Sandwich in the 1760s, though Keane offers no hard evidence beyond thin speculation about this mysterious ministry.[3] Perhaps the plain-speaking style of the Methodist preacher and the Methodist appeal to the emotions concerning universal salvation gave Paine some early experience in addressing the social and political ills of the day. Methodism and Paine seem, however, to be a poor mix. Surely Methodism's emphasis on social justice may have been tempting to the young man, but it also emphasizes a rigid, relentless personal self-discipline and self-help, and its moralism tends toward political conservatism. These features do not sound like Thomas Paine.

FORMATIVE POLITICAL EXPERIENCE

The first appearance of his interest in politics likely came in the Sussex town of Lewes, where Paine was directly engaged in political discussion and debate, beginning in 1768. He probably thought at the time that his rootless years were over, feeling that his life mirrored that of a carpenter bee going from window to window smacking up against the glass until it finally found the wood into which it could bore its hole. At thirty-two, he took lodgings above the dry goods shop of Samuel and Esther Ollive, who lived there with their daughter, Elizabeth, who became Paine's second wife. A lively and hardly Methodist redoubt, Lewes boasted a coffeehouse for discussion and debate, a theater that played comic opera and Shakespeare, a lending library, a large Dissenting community, and, most important for Paine's political education, a large oak-paneled tavern called the White Hart Inn. As the main attraction for the town's social life, it was a drinking establishment and a hotel for travelers. The hotel's stables housed about a hundred horses. The town, with a population of some four thousand inhabitants, included Paine's excise service area during his second and final tour as a tax collector.

Lewes had a long tradition of self-government. Its townspeople had supported the Puritans during the English Revolution. One of its two members of Parliament, Colonel Anthony Shapley, had signed Charles I's death warrant in 1649. It was also a leading center of Cromwellian politics. This background translated into a town with distinct republican sympathies, which were not quashed when the monarchy was restored in 1660. The only dark blot on the town's underlying public spirit was the still-existing Norman castle that dominated the hillside overlooking the skyline, yet another reminder to Paine, when he later wrote *Common Sense*, of the dreadful nature of tyrannical government.[4] While its local self-governing council, known as the Society of Twelve, was declared illegal in 1663, it was fortuitously re-established the year Paine arrived, immediately following the death of Thomas Pelham-Holles, the duke of Newcastle, who oversaw the entire region. The duty of the society was to manage routine town affairs day-to-day: to make sure the streets were kept clean, to capture stray dogs and cats, pigs and cows, and to appoint various town officials, like the clerks of the market and, most importantly, two constables. Obviously well connected, Samuel Ollive, Paine's father-in-law, was one of the constables, and soon Paine, most likely through Ollive's influence, became a member of the Society of Twelve.

Here Paine's political education first took shape. While the society often met in the town hall, it more often than not met at the tavern, where the members discussed the financial and political matters of the moment, such as taxes, mortgages, and other town questions. The society was accountable to no one. It was not an elected body, but a self-perpetuating oligarchy of the most prominent citizens. Paine's participation gave him a sense that he was no longer the lower-middle-class craftsman whose career until that time had been shabbily unspectacular. If it did anything, it made him into the bourgeois political writer that Isaac Kramnick makes him out to be.[5] It also taught him the crucial importance of having local voices, even if unelected, involved in political decision-making, especially when the danger of aristocratic tyranny, in this case the next duke of Newcastle, loomed—recalling, perhaps, his earlier Thetford years, when he had witnessed the power of the Graftons.

As a member of the Twelve and a frequent visitor to the White Hart, Paine was also introduced to a social or drinking club, known locally as the Headstrong Club, a group of prominent local men who gathered weekly to partake of plates of oysters and jugs of ale and lager, port, brandy, and Madeira while they discussed the issues of the day. Paine quickly grew to enjoy the political debates, the oysters, the ale, and the brandy, if not necessarily in that order. For six years, from 1768 to 1774, he might well have discussed and argued with his friends about Britain's deteriorating relationship with its American cousins. We do not know for sure because there are no surviving records of the club. Nor do we know how much they talked about John Wilkes and his troubles with Parliament at the time. We do know that in 1770 Wilkes passed through Lewes and may even have stopped at the White Hart, in which case Paine may even have met him. The townspeople surely knew that Wilkes had been elected three times to Parliament and three times rejected, though he had soundly defeated his opponent, Colonel Henry Luttrell, who was eventually seated. They understood that this was not a local issue merely for Middlesex, but one that asked the more important questions concerning the rights of Englishmen, such as free speech and voting rights. When Wilkes entered the town, he was greeted with the ringing of church bells. Moreover, the local newspaper, the *Sussex Weekly Advertiser,* was known as a republican sheet that made no bones about its detestation of aristocratic privilege and its support for Wilkes. Its publisher, William Lee, was a member of the Headstrong Club and Paine's close friend.[6]

When the debate, along with the drinking, became so intense

that it was difficult to hear who was saying what, one person was named the most articulate orator of the evening. The winner received a prize, known as the Headstrong Book, and Paine won the prize more often than any other man. One of Paine's earliest sympathetic biographers, Clio Rickman, said that the book—the same one was passed around every time—was "no other than an old Greek Homer, which was sent the morning after a debate vehemently maintained to the most obstinate haranguer of the club."[7] A messenger delivered the book the next morning because it was presumed that the winner most likely wound up stone drunk in a gutter somewhere in town.[8] It is ironic that Paine's prize was a work in Greek, given his disdain for what he later called the "dead" languages. "As there is nothing new to be learned from the dead languages, all the useful books being already translated," he later wrote, "the languages are become useless, and the time expended in teaching and learning them is wasted." And this included Greek. "The difficulty of learning the dead languages does not arise from any superior abstruseness in the languages themselves, but in their being *dead,* and the pronunciation entirely lost. The best Greek linguist that now exists does not understand Greek so well as a Grecian plowman did or Grecian milkmaid" (*AR*, 1:491–92). Paine never learned to speak any language other than English, including French, despite his nearly fifteen-year residency in Paris. Living or dead languages did not matter to him. He learned how to write with perfect phrasing, cadence, and rhythm. In France, others translated his words for him.

Paine's friend William Lee, the newspaper publisher, admired the tenacious young man, calling him "a shrewd and sensible fellow" who possessed an unusual "depth" of understanding politics. In a parody of a funeral oration, Lee wrote the following:

> Immortal PAINE! while mighty reasoners jar,
> We crown thee General of the Headstrong War;
> Thy logic vanquish'd error, and thy mind
> No bounds, but those of right and truth, confined.
> Thy soul of fire must sure ascend the sky,
> Immortal PAINE, thy fame can never die;
> For men like thee their names must ever save
> From the black edicts of the tyrant grave.[9]

Still, Paine wrote virtually nothing during this period, except an appeal to Parliament on behalf of the excise men's salaries, but it was not published for the general public until years later. John Keane speculates that Paine's writing career began in earnest in Lewes because "there is evidence, weighed here carefully for the first time, that he made time to practice the art of pushing words around a page—with considerable effect."[10] Now, Paine might well have made time to practice his writing skills, but Keane provides no documentation that Paine wrote any of the anonymous pieces that appeared in Lee's paper. The only thing we can say for certain is that Paine wrote mostly bad poetry there and the petition to Parliament.[11] The important thing that his life in Lewes did more than anything was to instruct him in politics and political debate. There, he truly earned his spurs as the general of the Headstrong War. Lewes did not, however, provide him with happiness. After Parliament rejected his petition on behalf of the taxmen, he returned to Lewes to learn that he had been dismissed from the excise a second time—he had abandoned his post without permission. Having married the young Elizabeth Ollive, he tried his hand at running his now-deceased father-in-law's dry goods store. When it failed, his marriage was over. The couple separated, Paine left for London, and the two never saw each other again.[12]

Despite the disappointments that his Lewes experience held for him, this period was the most formative in the development of his political thought. Paine had perhaps won the local war of the headstrong at the White Hart, and he had perhaps proved that he could go to London to compete in the major league of Parliament, even if he lost. With his interest in science he had earlier met the great American scientist and diplomat Franklin, then in England as the agent for Pennsylvania.[13] James Ferguson, a scientist and friend of Paine's father-in law, was Franklin's neighbor on Craven Street, in London. He undoubtedly made the introduction (Paine had earlier purchased a set of globes from Ferguson). When Paine decided to abandon England for America, he took with him a letter of introduction from Franklin, who later became so enamored with Paine that he referred to him as his "political adopted son."[14] Paine made a positive impression.[15] Franklin's suggestions in his letter that Paine could become an assistant schoolmaster, an assistant surveyor, or a clerk were not bad ideas because these were not unpleasant occupations. Certainly Paine had experience in two of them. Franklin would not have known about the man's soon-to-be revealed facility with words. As a skilled craftsman with a strong class-consciousness and many interests, Paine demonstrated little interest in actually writing about politics, with the sole exception of his parliamentary address. Thanks to Franklin's generous letter, Paine became a fixture in the literary and political milieu of Philadelphia after his arrival in November 1774.

Finding a residence on the corner of Market and Front Streets directly across from the slave market, a sight that he found utterly repulsive, he frequented the Library Company, founded by Franklin in 1731, and a variety of bookshops, where he browsed through the stacks and made a few purchases, including Priestley's new work on his experiments involving different kinds of air.[16] Next door to his residence was the bookshop and printing company of Robert Aitken, who was beginning a new enterprise, the *Pennsylvania Magazine*. Paine was soon writing for it and became its editor. From this moment, Paine's name became familiar to David Rittenhouse, Benjamin Rush, John and Samuel Adams, and Thomas Jefferson, as well as Franklin, all of whom by 1775 were already talking about America's separation from England and meeting in Philadelphia in an illegal extra-parliamentary session of a Continental Congress. Soon Paine's words would explode onto the world with *Common Sense*, his first major publication, which was both eye opening and revolutionary. It also marked the beginning of his extraordinary writing career. For the next ten years, we can detect the discernible shift in his thought as he moved from his early Quaker views and adherence to Lockean individualism to his deist ideology and his more mature Rousseauist ideas of community. This is not to suggest he gave up on Locke's principles of consent and liberty and focused only on Rousseau. It was, rather, the melding of the two, which took place during his years in France after 1787, when he added to his commitment to Lockean liberalism a newly realized devotion to the ideal of community as a means to guarantee the people's financial protection and social security.

QUAKERISM AND LOCKE, DEISM AND ROUSSEAU

From his youth to his maturity, Paine passed through two major intellectual and religious stages that directly affected his political thought. First, as a Dissenter, in his case as a Quaker, he embraced radical individualism. Second, as an inveterate deist, he adopted a social communitarian approach emphasizing government's responsibility to the less fortunate members of society. The enormously influential John Locke strongly figures in the first phase, which took shape largely in England and America and lasted approximately until his arrival in Paris in 1787. In the first period, we observe Paine's keen focus on the principles of government by consent, individual liberty based on natural rights derived from natural law, and the idea that revolutionary change must be undertaken to persuade those in power that they have oppressed their people for too long. Indeed, he never gave up on these ideals, and in that sense he remained a lifelong Lockean thinker and writer, even when he encountered the more expansive social and nationalistic ideals of Jean-Jacques Rousseau.

As a Quaker, Paine firmly fitted into the Dissenting tradition. He was not a Dissenter in the narrow meaning of the term because he did not subscribe to any of the three major Dissenting sects, historically by convention identified in the General Body of Protestant Dissenting Ministers (1771) as Presbyterians, Baptists, and Independents (Congregationalists). Nor did he ever consciously identify himself as a "Dissenter." Historians have, however, long recognized the Quakers, or Society of Friends, as part of the Dissenting sects because they suffered under the same social and political disabilities as did other Nonconformists. For this reason we may locate Paine in the Dissenting order when he adopted his father's Quaker beliefs, founded on the principles set forth by George Fox in 1647 in England. Fox was inspired to declare that every individual, either male or female possesses the inner light of salvation.[17] After the restoration of the monarchy in 1660, the Quakers were persecuted because of their pacifism and refusal to pay taxes to the Church of England, their rejection of the priesthood, and their opposition to Anglican ritual. Most meaningful to Paine, they declined to pay homage to any man, including the king, even going so far as to refuse to remove their hats when appearing before him or any other mere mortal.[18]

On the other hand, Paine was certainly no Dissenter along the lines of a Richard Price or a Joseph Priestley, who, as preachers, had been formally trained in the Presbyterian tradition in the English dissenting academies. These institutions had been established especially for those who refused to belong to the Anglican Church and were thus prohibited from attending the universities at Oxford or Cambridge. In their professional careers, Price and Priestley led congregations or taught in the academies, and sometimes did both. They denied the Church's Trinitarianism and were founders of modern Unitarianism. They believed in the revelations and teachings of their Lord Jesus and in the miracles he wrought to prove God's divine will. Price believed that Jesus was a divine being, a matter over which Priestley often and spiritedly disagreed.[19] Unlike Price and Priestley, Paine denied the existence of miracles and revelation, an important factor in his distinctive version of Dissent and later deism. As a boy, he was confirmed in the Church of England because his mother, Francis Pain (Thomas added the *e* a year after his arrival in America), dominated the marriage. Ten years her husband's senior, she came from a more prominent family: her father was a lawyer by profession. During Thomas's youth, her religious influence may well have outpaced that of her Quaker staymaker husband, or perhaps Joseph Pain was not much concerned about his son's early religious beliefs. We do not know for certain. As soon as he was able, young Thomas, at thirteen, apprenticed to his father to learn the trade. He eventually became a master staymaker, but he was a terrible businessman. He also found that the tenets of the Society of Friends, the religion of his father, were far more congenial to his way of thinking than the theological mysteries promulgated by the Church of England.

Paine remained a Quaker until he rejected his own peculiar nonpacifist version of Quakerism and became a deist, a perspective that matched his political and social policy positions in the second stage of his political and social thought, when he resided mainly in France.[20] There, Rousseau, along with the continuing presence of Lockean ideas, profoundly influenced his thinking. Rousseau stimulated him to advocate not only political but also social reform. While responding to Burke in part 2 of the *Rights of Man*, Paine took aim at the impoverished condition of the people and determined that political liberty alone was insufficient if social conditions did not also improve. Social policy must include the government's financial support for the poor and the elderly in what was an early-modern version of the contemporary welfare state. Paine's deism became the underlying philosophical and theological foundation supporting his social policy ideas, a foundation based on his continued rejection of revelation but, more importantly, relying on natural religion, with its emphasis on reason and science. His religion worshipped God's universe as a divine creation in which men possessed the duty to fulfill God's moral precepts. In so doing, they discovered that their responsibility was to improve the world by undertaking successful social and political transformations.[21] Paine's faith included the promise of a benevolent afterlife for people who accomplished these good deeds. Paine's greatest mentor, Benjamin Franklin, and many other leaders of the American founding were also deists and often held similar beliefs.[22]

Paine's religious views in this period reflected the position of several deist predecessors, such as John Toland and Anthony Collins, Thomas Woolston and Peter Annet, all of whom argued that true religion was founded on human reason, not faith, and that individual liberty precluded the hierarchy demanded by organized Christian churches.[23] A person's rational faculty could easily expose miraculous stories as mere myths. "In Deism our reason and our belief become happily united," Paine proclaimed. "The wonderful structure of the universe, and everything we behold in the system of the creation, prove to us, far better than books can do, the existence of a God, and at the same time proclaim His greatness." Paine denounced the idea that miracles recounted true stories of God's manifestations on earth. Such stories had no place in a person's faith. "It is by our reason that we are enabled to contemplate God in His works, and imitate Him in His way." We must not therefore follow the so-called teachings of false prophets to formulate our life's work. Our duty is to improve the world, just as God the creator has instructed us. "When we see His care and goodness extended over all His creatures, it teaches us our duty toward each other, while it calls forth our gratitude to Him. It is by forgetting God in His works, and running after the books of pretended revelation, that man has wandered from the straight path of duty and happiness, and become by turns the victim of doubt and the dupe of delusion."[24]

By the late eighteenth century, deists promoted free expression, religious liberty, and political and social reform, if not revolutionary action to achieve them. They also placed the agency of change in the hands of human beings, not in some distant deity who rules the universe and oversaw human accomplishments.[25] Paine's most mature work outlining his deism was of course *The Age of Reason,* two volumes that many people unfamiliar with his other writings know came from his pen. Over time, it has faced the most considerable charge that it reflected a man who ridiculed religion for purely political reasons—a not wholly inaccurate charge, but certainly a misleading one.[26] With the appearance of the first part of *The Age of Reason* in 1794, and the second a year later, Paine's enemies were convinced that he was indisputably an atheist, or at least they depicted him that way. But despite John Adams's view of Paine as "profligate and impious" ("let the blackguard Paine say what he will [about the Christian religion]—it is goodness itself to man"), Paine was never a nonbeliever.[27] His writings were always God-centered, overflowing with his ebullient faith in inevitable progress resulting from human ingenuity, science, and reason. God had created the universe but did not demand anything more of human beings than that they observe his magnificent creation and imitate His good works. Paine's motivations were based on his faith that his role in the world was God-given: he was to spread the gospel of democratic freedom and human rights everywhere. Yes, he affirmed, we live in "the age of reason" and in an "age of revolution," but these were the means by which we would realize on earth what God demanded: the end of slavery in all its forms; the downfall of corrupt and evil governments overrun by serpent monarchs and devil aristocrats; and government assistance to the poor and less unfortunate so that their lives would improve.

Despite his confirmation in the Anglican Church by the Bishop of Norfolk, Paine's early religious training was not extensive, but he somehow managed to acquire the ability to quote long biblical passages from memory, a skill that remained with him throughout his life. He claimed that he had drafted the second part of *The Age of Reason* without access to a Bible while imprisoned in France during the Reign of Terror. As a deeply religious man of a nontraditional, nonconventional sort and with his deep distrust of what he called the foolish superstitions and fabulous fabrications of Judaism and Christianity, he grew to hate the Bible, not only because he thought it contained ridiculous stories, but also because it perverted a person's true view of God and God's creation.[28] In his earliest publications, he affirmed his belief in God as both creator and intervener in human affairs. Paine's deism, while radical in the sense that it made him a strong advocate for political transformation and social welfare, presumed that God might also intervene in the world. Many passages in his 1775 essays in the *Pennsylvania Magazine*, in *Common Sense* the following year, and then in his *American Crisis* essays suggest an abiding faith in God's watchfulness over the Americans and God's unwavering support of the American cause. We even find it, somewhat amazingly, in his most radical political work, the *Rights of Man*. His deist faith after 1794, however, marked a distinctive shift in his religious sensibilities, away from God as a meddler in human affairs to a more rationalist approach to God.[29]

Eighteenth-century deism, which Paine called a "pure and simple profession," was not "organized" in that it possessed no liturgy, ministry, hierarchy, or sanctuary. Nor did all deists share the same sentiments or beliefs. Still, its major tenet extolled each individual human being as a child of God the creator. As Paine put it, "it is only in the CREATION that all our ideas and conceptions of a *Word of God* can unite. The Creation speaks a universal language, independently of human speech or human language, multiplied and various as they be. It is an ever-existing original, which every man can read. . . . It preaches to all nations and to all worlds; and this *Word of God* reveals to man all that is necessary for man to know of God." For Paine, "the true Deist has but one Deity, and his religion consists in contemplating the power, wisdom and benignity of the Deity in His works, and *in endeavoring to imitate Him in everything moral, scientifical and mechanical*" (*AR*, 1:483, 498, emphasis added). This is why Paine proclaimed in at least two places his belief that "every religion is good that teaches man to be good." To emphasize this point, he made the remark twice in the *Rights of Man*, which he completed just as he was in the midst of composing his attack on organized religion in the first part of *The Age of Reason* (*RM*, 260, 270).

We begin, then, with a focus on Paine's religious faith, on which he based the central tenets of his political and social thought.

CHAPTER 2

FAITH AND REASON, HUMAN NATURE
AND SOCIABILITY

Paine's faith that God is a benevolent creator provided a firm moral foundation for his political thought, a faith evident as early as *Common Sense* and running throughout his writings over the next three decades. Despite his own repeated assertion of his faith, a historic controversy has raged over whether his theology actually figures at all in his politics.[1] Some commentators have argued that Paine used religion purely for rhetorical purposes to appear sympathetic to his readers as a way to persuade them of the truths of his argument.[2] Others have argued, along with Theodore Roosevelt's famous characterization, that we might dismiss his profession of faith because he really was "a filthy little atheist."[3] The way to cut through this controversy is to understand Paine's distinction between established organized religions, especially those religions linked to government, and an individual's private religious faith, which he claimed was a right inherent in every human being. His most controversial work, *The Age of Reason*, comprised his harshest evaluation of organized religion, and yet, like all of Paine's writing, we find here a careful attempt to set forth his belief in God, which was consistent throughout his life. Priests, he thought, had designed organized religions to blunt human reason as a trap to trick people into believing that God speaks only through them. Catholic or Protestant, they were nothing more, in the words of Jonathan Israel, than "manipulators of popular credulity and vendors of magical formulae couched in incomprehensible terminology."[4]

Indeed, all established formal religions—Judaism, Christianity, or Islam—attempt to control their followers so their adherents will not think for themselves.[5]

Paine first argued this point as early as 1776. John Adams recorded in his diary that Paine told him of his plan sometime in the future to write formally about organized religion, but Paine thought "it will be best to postpone it to the latter part of life." Adams wrote that even then he suspected that Paine was an atheist who hated Christianity, noting that such aspiration to write about religion was "daring impudence." The "profligate and impious" Paine, he declared, "could not write about Christianity, which was the religion of wisdom, virtue, equity, and humanity. Let the blackguard Paine say what he will. It is resignation to God—it is goodness itself to man."[6] Adams distinguished himself from Paine when he said that he was a serious self-identified Christian and that no greater religion than Christianity existed in the world. Yet, for Paine, a person could believe in God without the dangerous trappings of a religious order or organized religion. Just a year later, he wrote that "a man may be religiously happy without *modes*," meaning that religious faith was a private matter without the mediation of a church.[7] All organized religions are "no other than human inventions, set up to terrify and enslave mankind, and monopolize power and profit" (*AR*, 1:464).

As a result of statements like this one, for two centuries Paine has been branded an atheist. His theological views were attacked in his own time not just by John Adams but also by many leading authorities, such as Gilbert Wakefield, Samuel Adams, and Thomas Erskine, the lawyer who defended him when he was tried for sedition for libeling the king and thus committing treason for publishing the second part of the *Rights of Man*. Even more ruthless than John Adams's vitriol against Paine was Erskine's attack. When Paine heard that Erskine had prosecuted Thomas Williams, a London publisher and bookseller, arrested for selling copies of *The Age of Reason*, he summarized his religious position with these words: "Mr. Erskine is very little acquainted with theological subjects, if he does not know there is such a thing as a *sincere* and *religious* belief that the Bible is not the Word of God. . . . It is not infidelity. . . . It is a pure religious belief, founded on the idea of the perfection of the Creator."[8]

GOD AND POLITICAL TRANSFORMATION

This idea—man's faith in the "idea of the perfection of the Creator"—permeates Paine's writings from the beginning.[9] More importantly, because his faith in God was consistent throughout his life, his shift from Quakerism to deism was seamless. He made this clear when he wrote, plainly enough in *The Age of Reason:* "I believe in one God, and no more; and I hope for happiness beyond this life."[10] Quakerism was particularly appealing because of its emphasis on individual faith, unencumbered by hierarchies of popes, bishops, and priests. He thus refused to follow the strictures of any particular church because, as he put it so memorably, "my own mind is my own church" (1:464). Deism, like Quakerism, emphasizes individual faith, but it also presupposes that deists possess a rational outlook focused on God's works. True faith does not arrive when a person studies the chapters and verses written by someone who claims to speak for or report the word of God. A person learns religion "out of the action of his own mind," by reflecting on what he sees and knows of his world. The Christian religion and its theology are, under Paine's sharp analytical scalpel, nothing more than extensions of pagan mythology. Christianity and paganism demand that their followers believe in divine revelation, something he claimed no man could prove because revelation was made only to a few people and sometimes to just one person without any witness's testimony. Everyone either believed it on the basis of hearsay or rejected it. Doubting Thomas was correct not to believe in the resurrection because he never saw it: "*So neither will I,* and the reason is equally as good for me, and for every other person, as for Thomas" (1:468, 506).[11]

Paine's religious views gave meaning to his writings, just as Franklin's deism infused the great polymath's political thought, and a comparison of the two writers is worth making here. Writing in 1785, Franklin echoed views that he had held for sixty years when he mused about the afterlife. "Finding myself to exist in the World, I believe shall, in some Shape or other, always exist; and, with all the inconveniences human Life is liable to, I shall not object to a new Edition of mine; hoping, however, that the

Errata of the last may be corrected."[12] For Franklin, the driving force of religion placed the burden on human beings to improve the world, write good constitutions, and build good republics and to allow people to reach their greatest potential: these principles all underscore his political principles.[13] Like Franklin, Paine too was driven by his own personal religious precepts. He described monarchs and aristocrats as saboteurs of the human race. We find him often dubbing them "savages," "brutes," "parasites," "serpent-worms," and even "monsters." Monarchs and aristocrats were inhuman. He carefully distinguished between the natural humanity of the people from the unnatural condition of their rulers. The latter figuratively and literally consumed them because those without titles and hereditary places "are begotten to be devoured. They are thrown to the cannibal for prey, and the natural parent prepares the unnatural repast" (*RM*, 82).

In a more jocular mood, Paine, while feeling as deeply negative as ever about kings and nobles, might offer a more humorous analogy of these denatured creatures. "We have to imagine," he wrote in 1792 on the eve of the convening of the French National Convention "that, as in the case of racehorses, a prince has certain peculiar characteristics that destined him for the throne, just as the courser has certain physical qualities which destine him for the race-track. But in the case of the noble race of Andalusian steeds, certain precautions are taken to insure its genuineness. Surely, in the cases of princes, except when similar precautions are adopted, no matter how much they violate the laws of decency, it is impossible discover whether the offspring of a queen is a legitimate prince or a bastard."[14] God never created such a being because He is pure perfection Himself (masculine, when Paine spoke of God, or feminine, when he referred to Providence).[15] The Bible was "so manifestly obscure, disorderly, and contradictory" that it cannot "be His work. I can write a better book myself."[16]

As a Quaker, Paine distinguished between those who manifested God's spirit, or an Inner Light, and those who did not.[17] The severest criticism he laid against monarchs and aristocrats, besides vividly imagining them as cannibals and worms, was that they were relapsed papists. This image, emerging in Protestant historical thought, was a traditionally vicious attack on one's enemies when the Pope was first identified as the Anti-Christ, an association long attributed to Martin Luther.[18] Paine did not include Jesus or even the Anti-Christ in his analysis because Jesus was a mere man, a symbol of goodness and virtue, not a godly or holy superman. Kings and lords were different. They arose as a result of the ungodly extension of popery. He exclaimed in *Common Sense* that "the Almighty, hath here entered his protest against monarchial government is true, or the scripture is false. And a man hath good reason to believe that there is as much of king-craft, as priest-craft in withholding the scripture from the public in Popish countries. For monarchy in every instance is the Popery of government." Despite the king's attempt to call himself the "parent" or "father" of his country, he "and his parasites" want to achieve their "low papistical design of gaining an unfair bias on the credulous weakness of our minds" (76, 84). Sixteen years later, when Paine attacked Burke and his assault on the French Revolution, he claimed that Burke's views had "shortened his journey to Rome." Burke will be so sorry when he sees that "arbitrary power, the power of the Pope, and the Bastille, are pulled down." Indeed, "monarchy . . . is the popery of government; a thing kept up to amuse the ignorant, and quiet them into taxes" (*RM*, 43, 51, 184).[19]

But the Americans need not worry because "the Almighty" himself had taken precautions to open in America "a sanctuary to the persecuted" (*CS*, 87). In other words, Paine wrote, God was on the Americans' side in their struggle with Britain. Because of that support, they would inevitably win their independence and establish a republic. So if the war effort was going poorly, as it did most of the time, Americans should petition God for help, and He would intervene. In the first *American Crisis* paper, he reiterated this point when he noted that God intervened because He never left men "unsupportedly to perish," especially when they "have so earnestly and so repeatedly sought to avoid the calamities of war." God would never give "us up to the care of devils."[20] This was what Paine meant when he said that "the hand of providence has cast us into one common lot," as if to suggest that the American cause of liberty was divinely inspired, which he in fact thought it was.[21] This is also the meaning of his reference to providential inaction when he wrote General Nathanael Greene about the treasonous Benedict Arnold: "But why if Providence had the management of the whole did she let Arnold escape?" he demanded.[22] He surely knew the answer himself. While it would have been important for the Americans to have executed Arnold for treason, it was a specific event, and not a world-shattering one like American independence from Britain.

This is why Paine could say with absolute confidence that "the cause of America is the cause of all mankind." While freedom was "hunted round the globe," only America had received "the fugitive" to "prepare in time an asylum for mankind." Americans were as yet untouched by the vicissitudes of tyranny and had it in their power to create the world over again and to fulfill God's will to form that purist, most perfect constitution the world had yet seen. This is also why "the Almighty hath implanted in us these unextinguishable [sic] feelings for good and wise and purposes" (*CS*, 63, 100, 99). Years later, just before his death in 1809, Paine expressed the same thought when he remarked that in his opinion, "those whose lives have been spent in doing good, and endeavoring to make their fellow-mortals happy, for this is the only way in which we can serve God, *will be happy hereafter*. . . . I gratefully know that He has given me a large share of that divine gift."[23] With the exception of *Common Sense*, Paine's religious beliefs were never founded on scripture, but only on his own personal faith in God. In his great pamphlet, he focused on how scripture, which ranked monarchy "as one of the sins of the Jews," directly exposed this strategy. He devoted several paragraphs to this subject by showing how the scripture argued that "the Almighty" condemned monarchy (*CS*, 73, 75). But after *Common Sense*, while he essentially left social and political changes to human agency, we find that he still continued to believe in God's intervention in human affairs—just in more limited ways.

As a deist, Paine was far more skeptical about using scripture than he was as a Quaker because he now found that the stories and allegories of the Bible mirrored the decrees of monarchs for their loathsomeness. According to Paine, the scriptures destroy the human mind as an independent and autonomous vessel of knowledge because they were, as John Turner notes, "filled with fables, legends, stories, romances, theatrical farces, absurdities, quibbles, contradictions and lies, all of them perpetuated by the unholy trinity of Mystery, Miracle and Prophecy on behalf of Power and Privilege."[24] His analysis of Mary and the Immaculate Conception is a case in point. Because the story flew in the face of natural processes, it had to be false. "Were any girl," he huffed, "that is now with child to say, and even to swear it, that she was gotten with child by a ghost, and that an angel told her so, would she be believed? Certainly she would not. Why, then, are we to believe the same thing of another girl, whom we never saw, told by nobody knows who, nor when nor where? How strange and inconsistent" (*AR*, 1:574).[25] After his return to America in 1802, he slightly tempered his view of Mary when he concluded that she had "never said" how Jesus was conceived. "All the evidence of it is that the book of Matthew says that Joseph dreamed an angel told him so." Even then, Paine was not about to allow the story to be simply left there as the gospel truth. He continued on, using his finest ridicule: "Had an old maid two or three hundred years of age brought forth a child it would have been much better presumptive evidence of a supernatural conception than Matthew's story of Joseph's dream about his young wife."[26]

Priests, bishops, and popes were no better than monarchs and aristocrats, who enslaved human beings. The shackles they forged around men's minds and souls must be destroyed. Where Paine the Quaker was apt to use biblical scripture directly, Paine the deist preferred to focus, not on biblical passages, but on his perception of God's will, acting through individual men to improve the world. Paine's deism was far more complex and rich than his Quaker outlook. Paine held that as creator, God was indwelling in all human beings, a belief in an immanent deity he shared with Spinoza. Paine approvingly cited Spinoza in *The Age of Reason* because of Spinoza's harsh attack on the Christian claim of biblical infallibility and Spinoza's advocacy of religious liberty.[27] Despite their separation in time (Spinoza lived one hundred years before Paine) and nationality (Spinoza was Dutch), they held many views in common, including an abiding belief in democracy, which entailed the elimination of monarchy, aristocracy, and ecclesiastical authority and the establishment of free expression, and the separation of church and state. Spinoza had written that he held "an opinion about God and Nature very different from that which Modern Christians are wont to defend. For I maintain that God is, as they say, the immanent cause of all things, but not the transeunt *[sic]* cause. . . . I assert that all things live and move in God."[28]

This spark of universal godliness indwelling in all men led Lewis Feuer to note that "Spinoza was the first political philosopher of modern times to avow himself a democrat." [29] Jonathan Israel goes even farther: Spinoza was, he argues, the founder of modern liberalism. "By prioritizing freedom of the individual, and of expression . . . Spinoza in fact cleared a much wider space for liberty and human rights, than did Locke, and cut a historically more direct, and ultimately more important, path towards modern western individualism."[30] Because God's material creation contained the divine, human beings must realize their duty to Him and to each other. For Spinoza as it was for Paine, "the greatest good of those who seek virtue is common to all, and can be enjoyed by all equally."[31] And both emphasized the power of human reason and man's duty to interpret scripture without the mediation of priests and bishops. These ideas are evident in Paine's writings in two ways. First, human beings must understand that they possess the power to observe that the universe was God's creation. Second, God had conveyed to His people the gift of reason to understand those observations. These two principles, highly Spinozistic in their outlook, formed the underlying foundation of Paine's religious faith, and they underlay his moral and political thought. Both thinkers were liberal and democratic in their shared belief in the equality God had given to all men to know that His presence was manifested in everyone, not only an Elect Few—either those granted salvation in Calvinist thought or the monarchs and aristocrats in the political realm who controlled the lives of their subjects. This was why Spinoza could argue so favorably for the democratic republic, the state he thought was "most natural" to man and the one that "approaches most closely to the freedom nature bestows on every person."[32] With this emphasis on nature and liberty and democracy, Paine, and for that matter Rousseau, could not have said it better.[33]

All religions, Paine thought, begin therefore with a similar belief in God. From that belief, the deists did not develop a religion founded on the tales rooted in the Jewish Scriptures, the Christian Bible, or the Islamic Koran. Rather, God brought harmony to his creation so that "the farmer of the field, though he cannot calculate eclipses, is as sensible of it as the philosophical astronomer. He sees the God of order in every part of the visible universe."[34] While God was not a personal deity to whom men could petition forgiveness, wealth, or health, neither did He abandon men to their dismal lot. God eternally dwelled within, and when He sometimes intervened, He did so in generalized ways. When Paine attacked monarchy in either its hereditary or elective form, he wrote that "it finally amounts to an accusation upon Providence, as if she had let to man no other choice with respect to government than between two evils" (*RM*, 173).[35] The choices were far wider than hereditary and elective monarchs. The best choice was the democratic republic with elections for all offices, factors that would make it very different from the English model of a republic with king. The people would not choose one if they were truly free to do so.

Religion thus occupies an important place in society only when grounded on the right principles and beliefs. Toward the end of the *Rights of Man*, Paine injected a personal note, something he often did, to inform his readers that he was a man of the people and not someone above them. He tried to be as candid as he could, noting that he was motivated, not to earn a fortune by selling his pamphlets, but to let his readers know that he wrote with "an open and disinterested language, dictated by no passion but that of humanity." His goal was to tell the truth as he saw it and to make judgments based on that perceived truth. His conclusion was simple and straight: "My religion is to do good." He then added that this belief could be transformed into a universal principle, which suggests that as long as religion teaches human beings to be good and to perform good works, it is a good religion, "and I know of none that instructs him to be bad" (228, 260, 270). True revelation, "the word of God," dwelled within God's creation. God "speaketh universally to man" because God's creation "speaks a universal language," "an ever-existing original, which every man can read."

Do we want to contemplate His power? We see it in the immensity of the creation. Do we want to contemplate His wisdom? We see it in the unchangeable order by which the incomprehensible whole is governed. Do we want to contemplate His munificence? We see it in the abundance with which He fills the earth. Do we want to contemplate His mercy? We see it in His not withholding that abundance even from the unthankful. In fine, do we want to know what God is? Search not the book called the Scripture, which any human hand might make, but the Scripture called the creation.

If we want answers to the cosmic questions of life, death, and faith, we must study the universe and its science and nature. "The human mind," he noted, "has a natural disposition to scientific knowledge and to the things connected to it" (*AR*, 1:482–84, 492). This is where true faith lay. He claimed to have obtained a good moral education because his father was a Quaker. This had allowed him to engage in the study of science and politics, including the later American cause against Britain. He had learned that he alone could teach himself that "the pure and simple profession of Deism" meant the study of the works of Providence: "That which is called natural philosophy is properly a divine study. It is the study of God through His works. It is the best study, by which we can arrive at a knowledge of His existence, and the only one by which we can gain a glimpse of His perfection."[36] Although he revered the philanthropy of the Quakers, even "Adam, if ever there were such a man, was created a Deist" (1:496, 498, 512).

Because Paine envisioned Providence as an all-encompassing, nurturing she-goddess of nature, he imagined that the immensity of the universe proved that there are many worlds like his own. She would have left open the possibility of creating "a plurality of worlds, at least as numerous as what we call stars" (*AR*, 1:499). Like Nature's God depicted by Jefferson in the Declaration of Independence, Paine's Providence was the First Cause, the giver of all life. Once Providence had created the universe, She left it up to the people to improve the world under Her guiding hand and did not bequeath the responsibility to those denatured monsters and worms in the guise of kings and aristocrats who controlled their daily lives. That God is the creator of the universe is absolutely known to everyone: "Every child born into the world must be considered as deriving its existence from God. The world is as new to him as it was to the first man that existed" (*RM,* 66). Christianity has no true foundation in the universe, except as it blinds men to God's true creation. Imagine, he demanded of his readers, that if they believed in a savior like Jesus, "a virtuous and an amiable man," who preached and practiced a "morality . . . of the most benevolent kind," they would find a plurality of Eves, apples, serpents, and redeemers throughout the universe. Such a belief required the faithful to envision a cavalcade of traveling shows starring Jesus: "In this case, the person who is irreverently called the Son of God, and sometimes God Himself, would have nothing else to do than to travel from world to world, in an endless succession of deaths, with scarcely a momentary interval of life" (*AR,* 1:467, 504).

Aside from this obvious ridicule, Paine's point was that human beings naturally possess reason, and if they use it, they follow Providence's challenge to improve the world by creating democracies worldwide. Virtuous citizens everywhere, not only in America, must work together to create democratic constitutions (*CS,* 120). Such ideas frightened men like John Adams, who feared the term *democrat* or any of its variants, even the word *democracy* itself, which was not used in America in a positive sense until the 1820s and 1830s.[37] Lord Bolingbroke noted that "absolute monarchy is tyranny; but absolute democracy is tyranny and anarchy both."[38] Later, when the Americans complained that the states possessed far too much power under the Articles of Confederation, especially in regard to taxing their citizens to repay war debts, they condemned the "democratical tyranny" or "democratic licentiousness" that had been unleashed in the states: "A headstrong democracy" had undermined the principles of the American Revolution when the state leaders ran rampant over federal power so that Congress enjoyed little or no authority, especially in terms of raising revenue, regulating commerce, or even carrying out a united foreign policy.[39]

Paine's vision, Adams wrote, was "so democratical, without any restraint or even an Attempt at any Equilibrium or Counterpoise, that it must produce confusion and every Evil Work."[40]

But Paine argued that in his vision of democracy, "a government by representatives" founded on reason and human rights, manifestly reflected his providential view of life and politics.[41] Monarchy did not do so, nor did aristocracy or the priesthood. Paine believed he was God's chosen instrument to open the eyes of his fellow citizens, first in America, then in France, finally in England, and even worldwide if possible. His 1776 argument for America to separate from the Empire gradually evolved into a global revolutionary outlook with a crusading spirit, with himself in the lead. He alone could achieve universal political and social transformation under God's authority. "Why may we not suppose," he told his readers of *Rights of Man* toward the end of part 2, "that the great Father of all is pleased with variety of devotion; and that the great offence we can act, is that by which we seek to torment and render each other miserable." And then he made an extraordinary statement about God, the divine being who had intervened to "choose" him, a late-in-life acceptance of God's intercession in human affairs. "I am fully satisfied that what I am now doing, with an endeavour to conciliate mankind, to render their condition happy, to unite nations that have hitherto been enemies, and to extirpate the horrid practice of war, and break the chains of slavery and oppression, is acceptable in his sight, and being the best service I can perform, I act it cheerfully" (*RM*, 271).

In other words, God had targeted Paine to play a special role in global affairs to transform the world in the image He had envisioned, perhaps from the moment of creation. Paine's enemies would have none of this, however, for when he finally returned to America in 1802, he was astonished by the attacks on him by the leaders of the Federalists, whom he called "the Terrorists of the New World." While they also despised him because of his fierce written assault on George Washington—who, he thought, had refused to help him when he was held for eleven months in a French prison during the Terror—they mainly condemned him as an atheist.[42] In response, he noted that "according to their outrageous piety, [Providence] must be as bad as Thomas Paine, she has protected him in all his dangers, patronized him in all his undertaking, encouraged him in all his ways, and rewarded him at last by bringing him in safety and in health to the Promised

Land:" a remarkable revelation of his perception of the she-goddess, Providence.[43] These were extraordinary statements crafted by a writer accused of atheism. He knew, however, with his usual dose of absolute confidence, that he, like Moses, possessed divine inspiration to carry out God's will to lead the people to freedom.

REASON AND HUMAN NATURE

Paine also believed God had imparted an inherent goodness and natural sociability to all human beings, a faith that distinguished him from James Madison and many other founders of the new American polity. As Madison famously noted in Federalist 51, "if men were angels, no government would be necessary," but because they were not angelic, they instituted government to force them to be virtuous, that is, to compel them to work together to seek the common good. Madison held that political institutions had to be properly developed because men were creatures of passion and seekers after self-interest. Good government could overcome men's natural passion, force them to reason, especially together, and ensure that "ambition . . . be made to counteract ambition."[44] This meant the construction of a democratic republic established along classical republican ideas, including a representative system based on separating the powers between elected executive and two legislative branches, the latter of which encompassed a small upper house and a larger lower one.[45]

Even if the people established the republic, Madison remained skeptical about its future, given men's inherent egotism and their inability to forego their individual interests for the common good. He famously noted that "in all very numerous assemblies, of whatever characters composed, passion never fails to wrest the scepter from reason. Had every Athenian citizen been a Socrates, every Athenian assembly would still have been a mob."[46] Still, the new American republic was a worthy attempt as long as the powers accorded to each branch of government guaranteed what he termed "practical security." This "security," which was "the great problem to be solved," demanded that "each [branch of government must enjoy protection] against the invasion of the others."[47] No fine calibration of the checks and balances among the separated powers could really guarantee this security. And yet, Madison thought the delegates at the Philadelphia convention had made their best efforts: "Each department should have a will of its own" so that no two departments might dominate the third; "the members of each should have as little agency as possible in the appointment of the members of the others;" and "all the appointments for the supreme executive, legislative, and judiciary magistracies, should be drawn from the same fountain of authority, the people."[48]

Paine's views about the nature of man were quite different. He knew human beings were not angels, but he also consistently argued that if left alone, they would truly want to achieve the good of all through their power to reason. He echoed Hobbes's and Locke's admiration of man's rational faculty as the way in which men best understood God's true nature. Paine's early scientific bent and his reliance on human reason to debunk organized religion provided a foundation for his thinking about politics and society. After all, it is only through "the exercise of reason that man can discover God" (*AR*, 1:484). As he noted in the *Rights of Man*, the vast political and social transformations the world was experiencing meant that "the present age will hereafter merit to be called the age of reason" because "a morning of reason" was "rising on the subject of government" (268, 208). France "attained the age of reason" once it knocked down hereditary monarchs and aristocrats.[49] In naming his work on theology "the age of reason," he emphasized the centrality of this key human faculty in his thinking, in particular, and in human nature, in general. Even in 1776, he argued that it was time for America to part from Britain, not because of the Americans' passions, but because it was a reasonable step to take. The Americans literally came to their senses in 1776 to realize that separation, their "revolution," was the lone alternative. The same regard for man's rational faculty was embedded in his comment in the *Rights of Man* that "in the enlightened countries in Europe" monarchy and aristocracy would not "continue seven years longer." American independence would soon be "accompanied by a revolution in the principles and practices of government" there as well (156, 159).

This is why he argued that revolution was now part of the "natural" course of events. He used, almost overused, the terms *nature* or *natural* to suggest that the universal turn toward revolution was brought to men's minds through their reason. Nature of course was God's creation, something that Paine reveled in as we have seen, but now he applied it to revolutionary action. "Man" has now become "what he ought. He sees his species, not with the inhuman idea of a natural enemy, but as kindred; and the example shows to the artificial world [of tyranny], that man must go back to Nature for information." Once one revolution succeeded, "it is natural to expect that a global revolution will follow" (*RM*, 160, 161). Someone like Burke, Paine's main target in part 1 of the *Rights of Man*, was emblematic of tyranny. Because Burke was a creature without the capacity to reason, Paine accused him of being "a metaphysical man," who "supposed that some must be managed by fraud, others by force, and all by some contrivance" (177). This was why Burke was unable to see that human depravity and slavery were logical consequences of his argument that kings and lords were valuable if only because they had lasted a long time. This was Paine's great condemnation of Burke's doctrine of prescription, which asserted that political institutions like kingship and nobility were good because they had flourished for hundreds of years.

In one of Paine's most famous passages, he complained that Burke's absurd position in his *Reflections* obscured reality. Metaphysics overshadowed reason. Burke's horror of "a swinish multitude" breaking into the queen's bedchamber and daring to touch her person was, for Paine, perverse. Burke had figuratively wept at such unrelenting insolence, completely ignoring the plight of the people, who felt they had no choice but to so act. Here is Burke's portrayal:

> It is now sixteen or seventeen years since I saw the queen of France, then the dauphiness of Versailles, and surely never delighted on this orb, which she hardly seemed to touch, a more delightful vision. I saw her just above the horizon, decorating and cheering the elevated sphere she just began to move it—glittering like the morning star, full of life and splendor and joy. Oh! . . . little did I dream that I should have lived to see such disaster fallen upon her in a nation of gallant men, in a nation of men of honor

and of cavaliers. I thought ten thousand swords must have leaped from their scabbards to avenge even a look that threatened her with insult. But the age of chivalry is gone. That of sophisters, economists, and calculators has succeeded; and the glory of Europe is extinguished forever.

The last two sentences of this passage include some of Burke's most famous phrases from his *Reflections*. Lost on Paine were the finer graces of nobility that Burke had identified: that "generous loyalty to rank and sex, that proud submission, that dignified obedience" that the mobs lacked even as they invaded her very person at Versailles.[50]

With Burke's anguished cry of "Oh!" Paine answered that poor Burke was deluded by the image of royalty being brought low by the unwashed poor and not by the underlying social and economic causes that had stimulated the people's outrageous behavior. Paine's image was equally riveting, and famous: "He pities the plumage, but forgets the dying bird." Burke was no natural man, but a wicked creature like kings and nobles. "Accustomed to kiss the aristocratical hand that hath purloined him from himself, he degenerates into a composition of art, and the genuine soul of nature forsakes him." He had become an artifice, a thing without human personality. Burke unjustly ignored "the real prisoner of misery, sliding into death in the silence of a dungeon" (*RM,* 51). If hereditary monarchs were evil, hereditary aristocrats, particularly those in the Lords, amounted to "an excrescence growing out of corruption." The lords were to the common people what "a regular member of the human body [is to] an ulcerated wen."[51] While "a swamp breeds serpents," Paine said, "hereditary succession breeds oppressors."[52]

SOCIABILITY AND HUMAN NATURE

For Paine, then, human beings are innately good and sociable creatures, who work best when they join with others to achieve common goals and when they are neither oppressed nor neglected by those who rule them. This inherent feature of men working together operates not only "by instinct," as he put it, but also by virtue of the "reciprocal benefits" that men realize when they work collectively for the same goals: "Man is so naturally a creature of society," he wrote, "that it is almost impossible to put him out of it" (*RM*, 164). Government is an artifice, whereas society is natural. In the opening paragraphs of *Common Sense*, he made this clear, in his well-known distinction between government and society. There, like many of his colleagues during the American founding, he argued that "government, even in its best state, is but a necessary evil; and in its worst state an intolerable one," while society is a natural condition because God never meant for men to live a solitary existence. "Government, like dress, is the badge of lost innocence; the palaces of kings are built on the ruins of the bowers of paradise" (65). Government is always an artifice, but the past proved that a few people would always control the lives of the many.[53]

The result was, as he wrote in the *Rights of Man*, that the wealthy few not only dominated the common people but also literally placed them in a state of political and social somnolence, casting them into a deep sleep. They "deaden his faculties" and "benumb" the mind so that "it descends below the stature of mental manhood" (196, 177). The people had fallen into a "drowsy unconcern," so that all they did was work, not for the good of themselves and fellow members of society, but for those who controlled government and the economy. Monarchies and aristocracies, with their tight, hammy fists around rank and privilege, had placed the common man in a deep slumber from which only the Americans and the French had so far emerged, thanks to their mighty revolutions. In England, the people remained under the spell of the prime minister, who "waves over them his sleep-compelling wand" so that "they are at once plunged in the slumber of servitude."[54]

This somnolence theme runs throughout Paine's writings. Kings and lords denature human beings, who only do the bidding of monarchs and aristocrats, those inhuman, devilish "apostate[s] from the order of mankind." They have "not only given up the proper dignity of a man, but sunk him beneath the rank of animals, and contemptibly crawl though the world like a worm." These were powerful and treasonous words because they attacked the entire English political establishment and King George III personally, as well. Paine's image of the king as a serpent-worm possessed both satanic and sexual connotations. When the devil-serpent of Genesis tempted Eve to bite the forbidden fruit, the apple served as an emblem of Satan's prodigious sexual appetite. Satan, in successfully scheming to have man and woman expelled from Paradise, was alone responsible for "the invention of monarchy" (*CS,* 72). This passage, which sequentially followed Paine's celebrated distinction between government and society, was itself followed by his equally famous condemnation of the Jews' adoption of kingship. "Nearly three thousand years passed away from the Mosaic account of the creation, till the Jews under a national delusion requested a king. . . . Monarchy is ranked in scripture as one of the sins of the Jews, for which a curse in reserve is denounced against them" (73). The devil-serpent, by enticing Eve, symbolically raped her, and in her humiliated modesty, she thought only of bringing in Adam to make it a bizarre obscene threesome. The result was monarchy, and its offshoot, aristocracy, whose noblemen were no better than kings, and the rise of "a form of government, which the word of God bears testimony against, and blood will attend to it" (80). As he later said, "titles are like circles drawn by the magician's wand, to contract the sphere of man's felicity. He lives immured within the Bastille of a word, and surveys at a distance the envied life of man," for government by hereditary title "is a mode of government that counteracts nature. It turns the progress of the human faculties upside down. . . . Its subjects age to be governed by children, and wisdom by folly" (*RM,* 80, 182–83).

Paine made this clear when he charged that "the [Brute] of B[ritain has] . . . wickedly broken through every moral and human obligation" and has also "trampled nature and conscience beneath his feet." But now, rule by the king-devil-worm was ending as the relationship between England and America was beginning to break down. "How impious is the title of *sacred majesty* applied to a worm, who in the midst of his splendor is crumbing into dust" (*CS,* 72).[55] The Americans were ever so slowly awakening from their soporific state to realize their subservient condition. "There is existing in man, a mass of sense lying in a dormant state, and which, unless something excites it to action, will descend with him, in that condition, to the grave"

(*RM*, 176). Paine's call to action in his great 1776 pamphlet was just such a means to that awakening. As he famously put it, if the Americans used their "common sense," they would "have it in [their] power to begin the world over again," as if to suggest that the Americans had slipped back to the beginning of time, to the Garden of Eden, to start afresh. "The birth-day of a new world is at hand," he proclaimed, and "the cause of America is in a great measure the cause of all mankind" (*CS*, 120, 63). As he later noted, "the present generation will appear to the future as the Adam of a new world" (*RM*, 268). Men's innate common sense told them how enslaved they had become in their time. So now, once they have awakened from their slumber, George III will have procured "for himself an universal hatred" (*CS*, 114).

If government was, then, a necessary evil, what could men do to help themselves? Like Madison, Paine thought they could construct the republic by creating the appropriate institutions to avoid the major pitfall that characterized nonrepublican governments, namely, the tendency to enslave people. The best form of government results when individuals join together to undertake collective decision-making to create good institutions, like the democratic republic's representative components. Monarchy and aristocracy stunt human beings' innate self-governing abilities. Genuine leaders, those chosen to lead through free and fair elections with a broad franchise, are the direct opposite of monarchs and aristocrats. Paine's rich imagery emphasized the inhumanity of the king, a man who greedily indulged in anthropophagical deeds so that his subjects' blood was smeared on his lips. Here Paine employed an image from antiquity quite popular in the eighteenth century, that of the god Saturn devouring his own children.[56] "Britain is the parent country, say some," he exclaimed. "Then the more shame on her conduct. Even brutes do not devour their young, nor savages make war upon their families" (*CS*, 84).[57] This could not happen in the era of revolution, when "the mind of the nation" was undergoing such a great transformation, and "the new order of things . . . naturally followed the new order of thoughts" (*RM*, 93). Until that time, the people must understand that "kings are monsters in the natural order, and what else can we expect from monsters but miseries and crimes?"[58] Paine may later have been dismayed by the

1793 words of his close friend and fellow deputy to the French National Convention, Pierre Vergniaud, a Bordeaux lawyer and leader of the moderate Girdondin faction. As the Terror was unleashed, Vergniaud used a similar image when he addressed the convention: "Citizens, it must be feared that the revolution, like Saturn, successively devouring its children, will engender, finally, only despotism with the calamities that accompany it."[59]

HOMO FABER, MAN A MAKER IN GOD'S IMAGE: LAWMAKING

According to Paine, man is a naturally talented creature who possesses the ability to build things, a trait that reflects God, who Himself is a divine creator, and that perfectly matches his sociable human nature. Because people are makers of things, their duty is to improve His creation by leaving the world better than they found it. In this way, their actions signify their nature as *homo faber*, man as a maker of things, an enduring feature of the human character. They are inventors of items for practical use, like Franklin's stove and bifocals or Paine's pierless iron bridge— Paine worked hard to design this bridge just before he left America for Paris in 1787.[60] And they best perform their creative work jointly in society, because such cooperation "encourages intercourse" and promotes virtue among the people. Paine argued that "nature created" human beings "for social life," and as a result, "she has implanted in them a system of social affections, which, though not necessary to their existence, is essential to their happiness." Indeed, "there is no period in life when this love for society ceases to act. It begins and ends with out being" (*CS*, 65; *RM*, 163). Like the social contract theorists before him, namely, Locke, Hobbes, and Rousseau, Paine considered the conditions of life before or without government establishing laws and rules for men to follow. Because of the dangers that each person poses to every other, "society will be their first thought," because they knew instinctively that God had created them to live and work together in order "to seek assistance and relief" (*CS*, 65–66). Although human beings are naturally equal in their original condition of life, through their subjugation by corrupt monarchies and nobility, they no longer enjoy their natural equality (*CS,* 71, 76, *RM,* 66). Now it is man's duty as *homo faber* to make laws in "a well-constituted republic" (*RM,* 142).

In politics, men make laws for the good of all based on sound constitutional principles. With the understanding that human beings are social creatures who possess the duty and ability to make good things, Paine suggested that they are also intrinsically creatures of compassion. "It is the nature of compassion to associate with misfortune," he said, an idea that paralleled Rousseau's comment that the human tendency to feel pity is an inherent part of human nature. In his famous 1754 *Discourse on Inequality,* Rousseau noted that human beings possess "an innate repugnance to seeing [their] fellow men suffer." While it was true that man in the natural state had to be highly egocentric to survive, he also enjoyed the capacity to feel pity for his fellow human beings when he witnessed their suffering. Pity, said Rousseau, is "a disposition that is fitting for beings that are as weak and as subject to ills as we are; a virtue all the more universal and all the more useful to man that it precedes in him any kind of reflection."[61] Adam Smith, in his 1759 *Theory of Moral Sentiments,* noted the same response when human beings see someone suffering: "By the imagination we place ourselves in his situation, we conceive ourselves enduring all the same torments" and "the plaintive voice of misery forces us almost involuntarily" to try to alleviate his pain.[62] Man's duty is to erect a republic because, as Paine put it, only heaven "was impregnable to vice." Natural compassion and natural sociability soon begin to fade when men seek to advance themselves.

It is only in properly constructed political institutions that men formulate laws to secure their "freedom and security." Government becomes, then, this "necessity . . . to supply the defect of moral virtue" (*CS,* 68, 66). The problem is that human beings were not always vigilant because they all too often became complacent—or somnolent—so those who were more powerful easily controlled them. The powerful formulated the myth of hereditary government and then dulled the human senses and forced men to follow their will. Paine hated this outcome, but he recognized that with the advent of powerful men over the weaker, "we have added that of the hereditary principle," which only worsened the social, financial, and political condition of the people (76). The Americans destroyed this possibility when they separated from England, and thirteen years later the people of France followed, when they established a constitutional monarchy based a single-house assembly. In 1792, even better, the French people had an opportunity to create a democratic republic without a king when Louis was overthrown, but that opportunity was aborted with the onset of the Terror.

Until the people established a representative assembly, they remained victimized by corruption unleashed by those who controlled government. In England, this state of affairs began with the deeds of William the Conqueror, the "chief among plunderers," a "usurper" who had with him "an armed banditti" that "certainly hath no divinity in it" (*CS,* 77–79). The problems in English government that resulted from this invasion were rooted in its creation of an overly complicated system of government with three divisions, in which the king collaborated with the nobility, in the House of Lords, to control the ordinary people, whose representatives served in the House of Commons. The people would be better off with a simpler form of government; indeed, nature requires that the simpler anything is the better it will be, a thought Paine expressed in both *Common Sense* and in one of his letters on "interesting subjects." In the former, he argued that "the more simple any thing is, the less liable it is to be disordered, and the easier to be repaired when disordered" (68). A few months later, in his *Fourth Letter on Interesting Subjects,* he added that "the forms of government are numerous, and perhaps the simplest is the best."[63]

Here Paine again followed his mentor Franklin, whom Paine called "the wisest and ablest man." *Homo faber,* man the maker, must create good legislatures if they were to make good laws. Like Franklin, he preferred unicameral lawmaking bodies elected by all men regardless of their religion or economic status: universal male suffrage with no religious tests or property qualifications.[64] The model of the good citizen was a man like Paine himself, "a man with a chest of tools, a few implements of husbandry, a few spare clothes, a bed and a few household utensils, a few articles for sale in a window, or almost any thing else he could call or even think his own." Even these few items were unimportant in determining who should vote. "It is disgraceful," he declared in 1778, that governments would make "*trifling things*" like property ownership depend on freedom and the right to vote, or the right to do anything whatsoever.[65] Almost twenty years later, he reiterated this position in arguing against the new French constitution of 1795, which required property qualifications for all male voters. In condemning this practice, he noted that "every man has a right to one vote, and not more in the choice of representatives. The rich have no more right to exclude the poor from the right of voting, or of electing and being elected, than the poor have to exclude the rich."[66]

Paine's advocacy of the single-house legislature's virtues places him well outside the sphere of classical republican theory, with its Aristotelian roots of divided power between the one, the few, and the many—the monarchical, the aristocratic, and the democratic elements of society.[67] Paine recalled Franklin telling him that if we imagine a wagon pulled in opposite directions by two teams of horses, one up front, the other in the back, "if the horses are of equal strength, the wheels of the cart, like the wheels of government, will stand still; and if the horses are strong enough, the cart will be torn to pieces."[68] To Paine's delight, the 1776 Pennsylvania constitution, "perhaps the most democratic in human history," set forth exactly what he had in mind.[69] Elected after the Declaration of Independence, the Pennsylvania convention, chaired by Franklin, developed a constitution that provided for only one house. It abolished property qualifications both for voting and for holding office, and it extended the franchise to all white males over twenty-one who had lived in the state and paid taxes there for at least a year. Although the states might have different forms of republican government, and only time would judge which among them worked best, Paine had no doubt that Pennsylvania's new document was unsurpassed. When critics attacked it, Paine immediately went into high gear to defend the constitution, although he had had no hand in drafting it. He hoped the people would at least give it a chance, "purely for the sake of discovering what ought to be retained, reformed, or rejected. . . . It is like recommending death as a cure for a disease; a remedy which few are fond of, and as few, I hope, have any opinion of the other."[70] He was equally delighted with the new Articles of Confederation, also drafted in 1776 and ratified by all the states five years later: it too was largely a result of Franklin's powerful influence and provided for a single house of Congress with no separate executive or independent judiciary.[71]

In the years immediately following the Declaration of Independence, Paine argued that a two-house legislature was irrational because it stimulated controversy, party squabbles, factions, and general discord. A legislature with just one house satisfied his basic principle, that government in its simplest form is best. If men insisted on more than one house, why, he queried, would they stop at two houses when there could be twenty? Once the number increased beyond one, the danger was that the number of political parties, or what today are called interest groups, would inevitably increase, which amounted to a recipe for disaster. The ideal form of the republic, he noted in 1776, was when there was "a large, equal and annual representation in one house *only*, the different parties, by being thus banded together, would hear each other's arguments, which advantage they cannot have if they sit in different houses."[72]

Paine's views directly conflicted with those of John Adams, who roundly condemned Pennsylvania's single-house legislature. Adams even fought his cousin Sam Adams on this issue when Sam publicly favored a single-house legislature. John deeply admired the English system, with its classical republican tripartite division of powers between the king, the Lords, and the Commons, a form of government he thought could easily be transported to American soil. With his emphasis on the need for a strong unitary executive, Adams was accused, often by Paine himself, of being a closet monarchist. In his 1776 brief pamphlet *Thoughts on Government,* Adams outlined why he thought a strong executive worked flawlessly with a two-house legislature. If the law-making body were reduced to a single house, it would become "liable to all the vices, follies, and frailties of an individual—subject to fits of humor, starts of passion, flights of enthusiasm, partialities or prejudice—and consequently productive of hasty results and absurd judgments."[73] The key danger was that assemblymen would increasingly desire greater power and vote themselves into a perpetual assembly and become tyrannical.

Even worse, Pennsylvanians, with their single legislative assembly, would soon long for the return of George III to rule America just to end the factionalism the assembly inspired.[74]

Paine would have none of this. The excellent political configurations of the 1776 Pennsylvania legislature provided two critical safeguards. First, the assembly was restrained by a bill of rights, and second, the people were required to revise their constitution every seven years, when a new constitutional convention was to rework "the constitution, and [to make] alterations, additions, or abolitions therein, if any such should be found necessary." It was a government of law, not of men or even institutions: it became "the political bible of the state" (*RM*, 187). And yet, Paine was the pragmatist as well. He recognized that he could not foresee how the new constitution would actually work in practice; he never once claimed that it was even near perfect. When it was dumped fourteen years later, in 1790, he acknowledged "that the present constitution has errors and defects," an idea "not to be doubted." He was not fully convinced, however, that it was all bad, and he immediately added that "it has some excellencies likewise."[75]

In any event, Paine knew full well, as most members of America's founding generation did, that "we are a people upon experiments, and though under one continental government, have the happy opportunity of trying variety in order to discover the best." Franklin, the quintessential dabbler in experimentation, with his electrical and other scientific experiments and his numerous inventions, commented for the entire era when he wrote that "this is the Age of Experiments," while his young protégé Paine later insisted that "we live to improve, or we live in vain."[76] The idea that all of America, even the world itself, was undergoing novel changes through man the maker was prevalent in the late eighteenth century. Paine was not alone in arguing that lawmaking was an inexact science, something with which to experiment. "All forms [of government] have failed in producing freedom and security: Therefore to object against the present constitution [of Pennsylvania], because it is a *novelty*, is to give one the best indirect reasons for trying it that has yet been given; because as all have been defective, that which shall not be so, *must be a novelty*, and that which is *not a novelty*, must be defective."[77] James Madison, too, was acutely aware of the newness of crafting the Constitution of 1787 when he noted that "the novelty of the undertaking immediately strikes us."[78]

When John Adams was posted to Paris on behalf of the United States to assist Franklin in working out the military agreement that brought France to the Americans' side in the Revolutionary War, he was appalled to see how much the French admired Franklin's 1776 Pennsylvania constitution, with its single-house legislature. Adams immediately went to great lengths to circulate copies of his Massachusetts constitution (a constitution that has proved to be the oldest written one in history),[79] which he had had so great a hand in creating, especially pointing out its two assemblies. To his apoplectic dismay and mounting anger, he was ignored. He never forgot the slight. When he wrote his three-volume *Defence of the Constitutions of the United States* in 1787, he proclaimed that the lawmaking structure of "the English Constitution is in theory the most stupendous fabric of human invention" ever to be created in history.[80] There actually could be, Adams argued, a republic with king, as the English constitutional monarchy proved (or what David Hume called the "crowned republic"), as long as independent lawmakers sat in the Lords and the Commons.[81] This statement led Jefferson to remark that "Mr. Adams had originally been a republican. The glare of royalty and nobility, during his mission to England, had made him believe their fascination a necessary ingredient in government, and Shays's rebellion, not sufficiently understood where he then was, seemed to prove that the absence of want and oppression was not a sufficient guarantee of order. His book on the American constitutions having made known his political bias, he was taken up by the monarchical federalists"[82]Adams was hardly surprised, though impressed with France's folly when he saw in 1791 that the French had adopted a constitutional monarchy with a single national assembly. That it hardly worked well became clear when factions began splitting it apart: the Girondins, the Jacobins, the Cordeliers, the Feuilliants, and the royalists, and others. This constitution lasted only one year; a national convention was elected to write a new republican constitution after Louis XVI was incarcerated in August 1792 (he was executed five months later, in January 1793).

Convinced that he was doing God's work after his election to the new National Convention in Paris, Paine was immediately appointed to serve on the drafting committee. Paine's handiwork was evident in the draft, including a single-house legislature, universal manhood suffrage with no property qualifications, universal education for all children no matter their class standing, and religious liberty.[83] Though the convention overwhelmingly passed it and though it was then ratified by the French electorate, Robespierre suspended it indefinitely just as the great Reign of Terror was getting under way in the late spring of 1793.[84]

Toward the end of his life, Paine nostalgically recalled that, although the Pennsylvania constitution in 1790 required two houses, the convention that originally created the 1776 document had had good intentions. It had distanced itself from the English government. "It formed a Constitution on the basis of honesty," he said, so its main defect was that it sometimes acted too quickly. But this defect could have been easily overcome by some means other than wholesale revision into a bicameral legislature, because "the ground-work . . . of that Constitution was good, and deserves to be resorted to."[85] The sole question was its "precipitancy"—whether its decisions had been made too quickly, without sufficient thought. He concluded that decisions during its existence had "not effectually" been made. It had failed only because the laws the assembly made were ill considered and poorly implemented.

And yet, he was also clearly upset with the outcome of the assembly debate over whether the farmers and artisans who owed huge debts during the 1780s could pay them in paper money. When the assemblymen agreed that they could, he was enraged, arguing that only gold and silver were appropriate means of exchange. "My idea of a single legislature was always founded on a hope, that whatever personal parties there might be in the state, they would all unite and agree in the general principles of good government—that these party differences would be dropped at the threshold of the state house, and the public good, or the good of the whole, would be the governing principle of the legislature within it."[86] But when it promoted a "party" agenda, namely, the printing of paper money to the detriment of specie, he perhaps began to question unicameral legislatures, which ran amok unchecked by another house in the assembly.

One thing was certain: good lawmaking bodies came only after the powerful grip of monarchy and aristocracy had been broken, and if God had a role for Thomas Paine to play, it was in revolutionary action to tear down monarchy as the first step in creating a republic based on a written constitution. He had demonstrated that whenever he went to the White Hart Inn in Lewes and when he agreed to go to Parliament to fight on behalf of himself and his colleagues in the excise service. Although he asserted that when he came to America, he only wanted to live a private life beyond the public view, to seek no political office, and to live quietly, he later remarked that "all the plans or prospects of private life (for I am not by nature fond of, or fitted for a public one and feel all occasions of it where I must act personally, a burden) all these plans, I say, were immediately disconcerted, and I was at once involved in all the troubles of the country."[87] In fact, scarcely had he set foot in America to have, as he put it several times, "the country set fire about my ears almost the moment I got into it."[88]

On his arrival in America in the fall of 1774, he said he "found the disposition of the people such that they might have been led by a thread and governed by a reed. Their suspicion was quick and penetrating, but their attachment to Britain was obstinate, and it was at that time a kind of treason to speak against [the empire]. They disliked the ministry, but they esteemed the nation. Their idea of grievance operated without resentment, and their single object was reconciliation."[89] After the bloody events at Lexington and Concord in April 1775, he knew that Britain rejected reconciliation and only wanted to subjugate the Americans. When Benjamin Rush suggested to him in the fall of 1775 that he should compose a short pamphlet advocating American separation from the empire, he leapt at the chance.

CHAPTER 3

COMMON SENSE, AUTHORITY,

AND AUTONOMY

Drawing on his faith in a creator God, Paine challenged political authority whenever he believed it interfered with individual autonomy. It is not surprising that within a year of his arrival in America he became one of the first, if not the very first, to proclaim publicly in writing that the Americans must immediately separate from the empire. Despite the pressures of his birth into a lower middle-class tradesman's family and his limited formal education of five years of schooling, he developed into a self-confident, brash young man with a distinctive sense of his own worth and a fervent desire to maintain his freedom and independence. Nor is it surprising that once the Americans had succeeded in creating an independent republican nation, he dedicated his life to promoting liberty, first in France, then in his native England, and finally, throughout the world. Arguments on behalf of individual freedom developed into consistent themes in Paine's political thought. They characterized his free-spirited life and thinking, both of which exhibited a deep self-confidence that he alone knew best how to achieve political and social reform.

In vigorously railing against heredity, rank, and privilege, the triad that formally identified how the ruling class of Britain maintained control over its subjects, Paine demanded that the Americans undertake armed revolt against British despotism. They must wait no longer because time does not prevail, either morally or politically, over principle: "Time has no more connection with, or influence upon principle, than principle has upon time." If it does, "the wrong which began a thousand years ago is as much a wrong as if it began to-day; and the right which originates to-day is as much a right as if it had the sanction of a thousand years." He used this same strategy fifteen years later to respond to Burke's fervent attack on the French Revolution.[1]

Despots possessed many ways to control the common people, but the most important foundation of tyranny rested on the formal classical education that aristocratic rulers required of their sons. The status ascribed to a classical education transformed them into gentlemen because with such learning, it was presumed that they could communicate with one another in ways that excluded those without a full mastery of the Greek and Latin authors of antiquity. Now, Paine knew full well that many of his contemporaries enjoyed a classical education. Unlike Jefferson, educated at the College of William and Mary and the founder of the University of Virginia, and Madison, a graduate of the College of New Jersey (now Princeton), Paine read neither Latin nor Greek and never fully mastered written French. The dead classical languages were useless to those who truly desired to be free from the iron grip both of the oppressors in control of politics and society and of those who ruled men's souls as well. Moreover, Paine firmly believed that Madison and Jefferson, unlike Adams, who had graduated from Harvard, were different because they were true devotees of republican principles, whereas Adams was suspect because of his admiration of Britain. A more appropriate parallel to Paine was his mentor, Benjamin Franklin, whose formal education had lasted just two years. After deciding that education was too expensive to waste on young Ben, his father apprenticed him to his older brother, James, in his Boston print shop—where Ben read everything in the place.

And yet, the two men differed in one important respect. While Franklin had an aptitude for foreign languages, Paine did not. As he wrote in the first part of *The Age of Reason,* "learning does not consist, as the schools now make it consist, in the knowledge of languages, but in the knowledge of things to which language gives names." Learning languages was something that ought merely to be reserved to "the drudgery business of a linguist." Because the classics were now available in English translation, learning antique tongues was a waste of time. He declined to learn Latin, he said, not only because it was prohibited by the Quaker faith of his father, which it was, but also because he "had no inclination to learn languages" (1:491–92, 496). He never admitted that he had no aptitude for learning languages, only that he had no interest in doing so, a feature that remained with him throughout his life. Still, he became well acquainted with the subjects in the Latin books in his Thetford grammar school, which he attended for just five years, until his father removed him to start his apprenticeship in the family trade. Although his formal education ended in 1749, his political and intellectual education continued for the rest of his life. When he came to America in the fall of 1774, he encountered the liveliest city in America, Philadelphia, where he soon was introduced to the activists for the American cause. Philadelphia was America's intellectual, political, and financial center, the seat of its Continental Congress, which included Adams, Rush, Jefferson, and Washington. It was there that Paine wrote his first important work, *Common Sense.*

"COMMON SENSE WILL TELL US"

Common Sense was more than just the first printed argument for American independence. It was a sparkling commentary, and it was treasonous. It was also a call to global revolution, even if at first it addressed only the Americans. Paine's main focus was on the continent of North America and the particular problems caused there by a vigorous British government, which wanted to ensure an uninterrupted stream of revenue from loyal colonies. In the section entitled "Thoughts on the Present State of American Affairs," we find the most quotable phrases still cited today as emblematic of the entire work. "Now is the seed time of continental union, faith and honor" or "This new world hath been the asylum for the persecuted lovers of civil and religious liberty from *every part* of Europe" or "The blood of the slain, the weeping voice of nature cries, 'TIS TIME TO PART" or "in America THE LAW IS KING." The most famous phrase is undoubtedly the one that American presidents have especially enjoyed quoting over the past two centuries, "We have every opportunity and every encouragement to form the noblest, purest constitution on the face of the earth. We have it in our power to begin the world over again. A situation, similar to the present, hath not happened since the days of Noah until now. The birth-day of a new world is at hand" (82, 84, 87, 98, 121).[2]

To *form a constitution* that was pure and noble was the enormous task the Americans faced. But if the pamphlet was on its face about America's inevitable separation from the empire, its larger purpose was a call for revolution, sanctioned by God on a global scale: an end to the British monarchy and then, indeed, to monarchy and aristocracy everywhere.[3] Before the work was published in its final form, Paine asked Franklin, Rush, and Sam Adams to review his draft (Rush provided the title).[4] Did they understand the nature of Paine's enterprise? Rush assured Paine that they all believed in separation, and he even secured the services of the Scot, Robert Bell, a printer with identical sympathies, to publish the pamphlet.[5] They suggested changes and approved it, and he sent it to Bell. And yet, they probably did not appreciate the extremism of the pamphlet the way Paine did.

His advocacy of global revolution placed him giant steps ahead of his Philadelphia, Boston, and Virginia friends, and it was the ultimate meaning of his title: *Common Sense*, making it and him far more radical and revolutionary than many commentators have acknowledged.[6] For all the simple straightforwardness, wonderful imagery, and quotable phrasing of the work, his words were designed to appeal to a global audience to motivate them to create democratic republics (in addition to America, *Common Sense* was published in England and France). Paine hated kings and aristocrats, and he made no bones about it. Kings were useless scum who preyed only on the weak, and they did virtually nothing except wreak havoc on people. Note his universal assault on monarchy as he condemned the British monarch: "In England a king hath little more to do than to make war and give away places; which in plain terms is to impoverish a nation and set it together by the ears. A pretty business indeed for a man to be allowed eight hundred thousand sterling a year for, and worshiped into the bargain! Of more worth is one honest man to society, and in *the sight of God*, than *all the crowned ruffians that ever lived*" (81). Paine saw no use whatsoever for the English Crown and neither did God—it was not merely that the Crown was useless, but that it was dangerous and perfidious because it was oppressive and went against God's own commands. The only thing worthwhile in the world of politics was that "one honest man," the virtuous citizen, a public-spirited everyman, must run his own affairs without threats from some brutish king. In fact, Paine referred to George III many times as "Pharaoh," "Savage," or "the brute of Britain" (92, 114).[7] George was no different from all other "crowned ruffians that ever lived."

Paine's vision then, clearly went beyond America: "The cause of America is in very great measure the cause of all mankind." "Many circumstances hath, and will arise, which are not local, but universal, and through which the principles of all Lovers of Mankind are affected, and in the Event of which, their Affections are interested. The laying a Country desolate with Fire and Sword, declaring War against the natural rights of all Mankind, and extirpating the defenders thereof from the Face of the Earth, is the Concern of every Man to whom Nature hath given the Power of feeling" (*CS*, 63–64). In this way, as Eric Foner has put it, "Paine transformed the struggle over the rights of Englishmen into a contest with meaning for all mankind."[8] Rejecting the polite, civil style of his excise petition, he opted for a hard-hitting and blistering assault on the throne and the nobility.[9] Revolution was the game to be played, not merely separation, even if the ensuing war left the British monarchy intact, something he hoped would not be the outcome. Many Americans who despised the manner in which the British ruled the colonies, who declared that they were deprived of their rights as Englishmen, and who demanded a say in local colonial affairs had been debating in the streets, in the taverns, in the coffeehouses, and even in their shops what future action the colonies ought to take. This included the destruction of all political and military ties with the empire. Most who advocated that step knew that the consequences would lead to war.

We can come close to pinpointing Paine's radicalizing moment. It had little to do with the repressive laws, like the Intolerable Acts or the Declaratory Act and Stamp Act, that Parliament had passed since the mid-1760s, or with what the ministry did or said. The galvanizing moment was the incident at Lexington on April 19, 1775, when shots were fired that left eight American militiamen dead and ten wounded. On that date, British Major John Pitcairn, with no orders from a superior officer, ordered his troops in six companies to fire on a crowd of some seventy Americans assembled on the green in front of the meeting house. "Lay down your arms, you damned rebels and disperse!" he is reported to have shouted. "Damn you! Why don't you lay down your arms?" Another British officer joined in the shouting, "Damn them! We will have them." And when the Americans refused, the shots rang out.[10]

Paine, having arrived in America only five months earlier, was more than merely incensed. His emotions appeared to have been mixed with sorrow, anger, and hatred. Already burned, if you will, by his failed English experiences as a rootless adult with no profession, he must have blamed everything on the miserable political and social conditions of Britain. He wrote an essay—utopian of sorts, actually—that appeared in the *Pennsylvania Magazine,* the journal he now edited, just one month after the events in Lexington. "A Dream Interpreted" told of a land that was once beautiful and idyllic, full of greenery and tranquility. Suddenly, hit by a terrible drought, everything withered as the heat burned and blackened the hills. A storm of raging fury suddenly struck and tore the land to pieces. By morning, when the dreamer (no doubt Paine himself) awoke, he was astonished to find that after the storm had abated, "the air, purged of its poisonous vapors, was fresh and healthy. The dried fountains were replenished, the waters sweet and wholesome." The world, restored to its natural goodness, had resisted the horrors of drought and storms, darkness and terror. Paine's allegory was about America and the mistreatment inflicted upon it by the empire. "In our petition to Britain we asked but for peace; but the prayer was rejected. The cause is now before a higher court, the court of providence before whom the arrogance of kings, the infidelity of ministers, the general corruption of government, and the cobweb artifice of courts, will fall confounded and ashamed."[11] Paine's ideas of a revolution under God's provenance began to crystallize as early as the spring of 1775.

Two months later, Paine ruminated over the difficult moral

and religious question of whether pacifist Quakers should participate in a defensive war against Britain. He had a ready answer: "I am thus far a Quaker, that I would gladly agree with all the world to lay aside the use of arms, and settle matters by negotiation; but unless the whole will, the matter ends, and I take up my musket and thank heaven he has put it in my power." Already news of Bunker (or, more accurately, Breed's) Hill had arrived in Philadelphia just as the Continental Congress appointed Washington commander-in-chief of American forces and voted to use arms, if necessary, against Britain. Still, at this moment, many Americans desired reconciliation, not war. Note this remarkable and lively conclusion by Joseph Ellis concerning the horrible winter of 1777–78, when American troops were dying of disease, starvation, and the cold while stationed at Valley Forge. "If we could draw a map of the adjoining counties [in Pennsylvania] and color the pro-British areas red and the pro-American areas blue, the result would resemble a random pattern of red and blue patches, but the largest area would need to be colored purple, reflecting a population that remained equivocal: Quakers who were conscience-bound to a posture of neutrality; lukewarm patriots or loyalists whose allegiance shifted in accord with the military balance of power in their neighborhoods; and a substantial segment of indifferent citizens who just wanted the war to go somewhere else and allow them to get on with their lives."[12] Paine, however, was not indifferent: writing in July of 1775, he noted that "whoever considers the unprincipled enemy we have to cope with, will not hesitate to declare that nothing but arms or miracles can reduce them to reason and moderation. They have lost sight of the limits of humanity. The portrait of a parent red with the blood of her children is a picture fit only for the galleries of the infernals."[13] Again, his image of Saturn in the guise of the king of England brutally consuming his American children made Paine's point of a corrupt, denatured, dehumanized beast of a king, a monster, who had to be destroyed. He would repeat these images six months later in *Common Sense*.

To make his point more flamboyantly, Paine likened England's enthrallment of the Americans to a master's enslavement of black people. He focused on the miseries suffered by black slaves in the Caribbean islands and in America and more particularly on the slave trade, especially on how British slave captains and their men "ravaged the shores of Africa, robbing it of its unoffending inhabitants to cultivate her stolen dominions in the West." He concluded: When I reflect on these [horrors], I hesitate not for a moment to believe that the Almighty will finally separate America from Britain. Call it independence or what you will, if it is the cause of God and humanity it will go on."[14] Unafraid to use the word *independence* in public and even in a publication, he argued that independence meant more than separation. God was on the American side. Reconciliation with England, with the Americans preserving their right of self-government, would therefore fail, despite the hope of many Americans for reconciliation. The only solution was for Britain to accept the Americans' terms, but Paine did not wish for that outcome. War was inevitable between virtuous Americans and a corrupt government composed of an unholy alliance between the monarchy and Parliament. Both must be destroyed because the only difference between the governments of England and France was a matter of degree, not kind: the rise of the Parliament after the 1649 execution of Charles I "hath made kings more subtle—not more just" (*CS*, 71).

Paine's position paralleled the approach expressed by many Protestant Dissenters.[15] If God demanded that America separate from Britain, it also required men to destroy monarchy, rank, and privilege everywhere around the globe. Recall in the previous paragraphs Paine's reference to the role of the "Almighty" in human affairs and his assertion that he was a Quaker who believed in the necessity of arms in a defensive war. As he described it in the first part of *Common Sense,* monarchy began when the Jews defied divine commands and adopted the heathen institution of kingship. "Jewish royalty," as he put it, was the beginning of political impudence when the Jews created the worst antireligious idol that they could have designed. It was nothing less than "the most prosperous invention of the Devil" himself. The Jews, the people who had prided themselves on being the first to believe in a single benevolent God, adopted monarchy, the most venal institution, and they had to face the gravest consequences. "For the will of the Almighty, as declared by Gideon and the prophet Samuel, expressly disapproves of government by kings."

Kingship "so impiously invades the prerogative of heaven." Monarchy was a crime for which they have suffered many times over by their history of persecution and death. Paine here entered a biblical quotation of Brobdingnagian length, commenting like a Jewish Talmudist as he went along. The scriptural passages, all attacking the Jews for having a king to rule over them, proved the single most important point that Paine made in this section, namely, that "monarchy in every instance is Popery in government"—undoubtedly, again, the most grievous charge he could make in America or England, with their strong Protestant traditions (72–73, 76).

The practice of hereditary succession among aristocrats was as corrupt as monarchy. Either way, the usurpation of power "opened the door to the *foolish*, the *wicked*, and the *improper*, it hath the nature of oppression." Kings, whose "whole character" was "absurd and useless," grew insolent when their power was unassailable, their minds easily poisoned by the thought that they were untouchable and that they could do anything they wanted whenever they wanted. Monarchs were inevitably thrown into battle against those who wished to succeed them or conquer their territory. Throughout history monarchy and hereditary succession have left the world torn apart "in blood and ashes." God, in his own words, long disapproved of this form of government and would continue to do so, as "blood [shed by kings against their people] will attend to it." England was a case in point, but it was just one case among many. The English monarchy had already "eaten out the virtue of the house of commons." It was now intent on subduing the Americans. His conclusion was once again simple and straightforward: there could be no republican virtue as long as monarchy reigned. The Americans' only recourse was to end it quickly because, after all, "common sense will tell us" that there could be no other conclusion (*CS,* 69, 79, 80–81, 105). His argument possessed the power of what Winthrop Jordan has rightly called "the killing of the king."[16] In an open letter to Viscount William Howe, the commander of British ground forces in America, a letter that appeared as the second *Crisis* paper, Paine declared his deep animosity in heated words: "If I have any where expressed myself over-warmly, 'tis from a fixed, immovable hatred I have to cruel men and cruel measures. I have likewise an aversion to monarchy, as being too debasing to the dignity of man."[17]

The third edition of *Common Sense* is the most important because of its short address to the Quakers highly reminiscent of his 1775 essay "Thoughts on Defensive War." In that essay, Paine had argued that pacifism no longer worked in light of the scale of British tyranny. The wealthiest Quakers hoped matters would not come to an armed struggle because they were genuinely pacifist and also because many of them had an enduring loyalty to the Crown. They believed that it was their duty "to pray for the king . . . in a government which God is pleased to set over us."[18] Paine was appalled, even disgusted, by their ill-advised weakness in the face of tyranny and even more by their obsequious subordination to a corrupt regime, as he noted in *Common Sense*. Sam Adams, Franklin, and Rush never saw this part of the pamphlet until after its publication, so it is difficult to determine just what they would have thought about it, and there is no record of their having commented on it. So Paine wrote freely and for himself. "We view our enemies in the characters of Highwaymen and Housebreakers, and having no defence for ourselves in the civil law, are obliged to punish them by the military one, and apply the sword." The words of John Locke's *Second Treatise* echo in this passage, words that Jefferson later imitated in the opening lines of the Declaration of Independence. Locke had written that most people were cautious and conservative when it came to changing their form of government, even when that government was abusive. But when it became tyrannical and the people "made miserable," they must take their grievances to the government and demand changes. But when lawmakers ignored the entreaties of their people, after "a long train of abuses, prevarications and artifices, all tending the same way," Locke famously wrote, then and only then would they have the right, even the duty, "to rouze themselves, and endeavour to put the rule into such hands which may secure to them the ends for which government was at first erected."[19] This statement sets forth the classic Lockean notion of the natural right to revolution.[20]

If America were now transformed into a state of nature, why would some people refuse to obey this natural law to rise in revolution? Americans were beyond the law, that is, simply put, out-laws. This condition therefore required them to take the law into their own hands because the civil law for them no longer existed, and God demanded it. They must apply force against force as the only way to destroy "all the murdering miscreants who are act-ing in authority under HIM whom ye profess to serve" (*CS*, 124). Paine blamed his own fellow religionists, the Quakers, declaring that if they were truly honest men, these "Tory" Quakers, they would tell the royal brute that he was doomed to an eternal life in hell. Calling them Tories was an insulting moniker. "What is a Tory?" he asked a bit later that year. "Every Tory is a coward; for servile, slavish, self-interested fear is the foundation of Tory-ism; and a man under such influence, though he may be cruel, never can be brave."[21] When many Quakers refused to partici-pate in the war against Britain, he derided "the present race of Quakers," who "have artfully changed themselves into a differ-ent sort of people to what they used to be, and yet have the ad-dress to persuade each other that they are not altered; like anti-quated virgins, they see not the havoc deformity has made upon them, but pleasantly mistaking wrinkles for dimples, conceive themselves yet lovely and wonder at the stupid world for not ad-miring them." He knew that the Quakers, led by James Pem-berton, would not relent in their pacifism, causing Paine to grow so angry that his words practically shouted off the page. They all should stick to worrying about religion and forget about politics. "O! ye fallen, cringing, priest-and-Pemberton-ridden people! What more can we say of ye than that a religious Quaker is a valuable character, and a political Quaker a real Jesuit."[22] He could hardly have found a more abusive epithet in christening them Jesuits: it was akin to his accusation that monarchy was the "popery of government." Soon, to his delighted surprise, younger Quakers gladly joined the battle, and a new generation of re-publican Quakers was born.

Still, Paine's central theme in *Common Sense* remained that monarchy, hereditary succession, aristocratic rank and privilege everywhere had to be eradicated. It was his own peculiar duty, as he felt it, to make that happen. He served in the Continental Army as an aide-de-camp, though there is no evidence that he wore a uniform or fired a shot, serving first with General Daniel

Roberdeau and then General Nathanael Greene. His main duty was to write propaganda pieces that appeared in various newspapers designed to inspire the American troops in what initially appeared to be a losing battle against indisputably the most powerful military force in the world. If the war could be won and if the Americans could establish a "new world order"—and these are not his words—the first step to global revolution would have been taken. Convinced that God was on the Americans' side, Paine could write with ease in the very first number of the *Crisis* that "the times that try men's souls" would end in a victorious America.

If God indeed sided with the Americans, He therefore must be an interventionist deity. Paine suggested this was the case and used the idea to appeal to the deepest religious beliefs of his audience. He was very careful to personalize his words in the *Crisis* series. They did not amount to a political treatise. Like the Bible's old and new testaments, they encompassed *his* political testament to bear witness in his Jeremiads to the tyrannies of the past and to what the Americans, himself included, must do to annihilate them. He demonized George III and his minions, including all of the ministry and most of Parliament, as godless and fiendish. Their downfall, thanks to God's help, was inevitable.

> I have as little superstition in me as any man living, but my secret opinion has ever been, and still is, that God Almighty will not give up a people to military destruction, or leave them unsupportedly to perish, who have so earnestly and so repeatedly sought to avoid the calamities of war, by every decent method which wisdom could invent. Neither have I so much of the infidel in me, as to suppose that He has relinquished the government of the world, and given us up to the care of devils; and as I do not, I cannot see on what grounds the king of Britain can look up to heaven for help against us; a common murderer, a highwayman, or a house-breaker, has as good a pretence as he.

Even as the war initially went very poorly for the Americans, British forces made divinely guided errors in judgment and strategy. "If we believe the power of hell to be limited, we must likewise believe that their agents are under some providential control." Americans had no choice now that the battle was joined, but even if they were queasy about joining the fight, they must understand the cosmic nature of the struggle. "I should suffer the misery of devils, were I to make a whore of my soul by swearing allegiance to one whose character is that of a sottish, stupid, stubborn, worthless, brutish man. I conceive likewise a horrid idea in receiving mercy from a being, who at the last day shall be shrieking to the rocks and mountains to cover him, and fleeing with terror from the orphan, the widow, and the slain of America."[23]

The imagery in these sentences is profoundly meaningful. We see here an allusion, if just slightly colored, to the last days of the universe, when a just God would oversee the Final Judgment. Screaming for the rocks and mountains to cover and protect him at the end days, George III would have nowhere to hide from the wrath of Paine's God, who viewed the king as did Paine, the Brute of Britain. The demonization of the king and the struggle against him was complete, just as Paine placed all peoples in a world-historical context as the forces of dark battled the forces of light in a final struggle of good against evil—as evil as the serpent in Eden. George III and everyone who waged war on America were ugly and reptilian. "'Tis an incendiary war upon society, which nothing can excuse or palliate,—an improvement upon beggarly villainy—and shows an inbred wretchedness of heart made up between the venomous malignity of a serpent and the spiteful imbecility of an inferior reptile."[24] If not reptilian, they were savage beasts: "Her idea of national honor seems to consist in national insult, and that to be a great people, is to be neither a Christian, a philosopher, or a gentleman, but to threaten with the rudeness of a bear, and to devour with the ferocity of a lion. This perhaps may sound harsh and uncourtly, but it is too true, and the more is the pity."[25]

The Americans were embarked then upon a cosmic struggle. "We have a perfect idea of a natural enemy when we think of the devil, because the enmity is perpetual, unalterable and unabateable. It admits, neither of peace, truce [n]or treaty; consequently the warfare is eternal, and therefore it is natural."[26] The absolutist terms he used to write these sentences made their point as clear as day. He harbored not one *soupçon* of doubt that he was *perpetually* and *unalterably* (his words) correct. The end time would come, and God would judge the Americans for what they did when faced with "the full extent of the evil, which threatens them." With God on the side of right, justice, and freedom, "we have the prospect of a glorious issue" because "Providence has some nobler end to accomplish than the gratification of the petty elector of Hanover, or the ignorant and insignificant king of Britain."[27] In light of his words, it is a wonder that British authorities did not try Paine for treason immediately on his return to England in the summer of 1787 rather than waiting for the publication of part 2 of the *Rights of Man,* with its open attack on George III, which soon led to charges against him of seditious libel (he was later tried and convicted in absentia).

After 1778, the year the United States entered into a military alliance with France, Paine moderated his antimonarchical views as the Americans began dealing with the French king. He did not let go of these views, but he minimized their importance, as he remained focused on the main goal of achieving American independence with French military and financial support. This position became even more essential after 1781, when Paine accompanied the young American commissioner, twenty-six-year-old John Laurens, the son of Paine's friend Henry Laurens, to Paris to join Franklin, who was negotiating with the French about additional gifts of money and loans.[28] The resulting outcome was a major boon to the new nation, and Paine knew it. In all, they secured a 10 million livres loan and gifts and cash of another 6 million, plus clothes, arms, and ammunition.[29] He could not very well publicly condemn the French monarchy when it so lustily showered lavish generosity on the Americans.

But did Paine believe that the French monarchy was different from that of the British just because of its munificent largesse? Or was French support based solely on France's own selfish reasons? France was certainly acting on the basis of its national interest because Britain was its long historic enemy, and America made a good, if convenient, ally to help defeat or seriously wound the British. Or could it be that France actually did possess a monarchy qualitatively different from England's, a kind and beneficent monarchy as opposed to the bellicose and evil British monarchy? Paine did not know the answer to these questions. Despite his one visit to France in 1781, he had little knowledge of what life was like there. He did, however, resolve to return to find out, writing as early as the end of 1781 that he contemplated another visit, but wanted to "postpone my second journey to France a little longer."[30] He also told Washington that it was his "design to get to Europe, either to France or Holland."[31] In the spring of 1783, he wrote to Elias Boudinot, the president of the Congress, that "it is now very probable that circumstances, of which I am, at present, the best, and, perhaps, the only judge, may occasion my departure from America. I found her in adversity and I leave her in prosperity."[32]

REVOLUTION AND THE ABBÉ RAYNAL

Ten years later, at the trial of Louis XVI, Paine had his answers to his own questions about the French monarchy, but he did not have them in 1781. For the present moment, he perhaps contemplated carrying out a revolution in England from the shores of France in light of French support of the American cause. Or perhaps the origins of Paine's initial answer lay in his response to the Abbé Guillaume-Thomas-François Raynal's analysis of the American Revolution. Raynal's *Révolution d'Amérique* enraged Paine when he learned that the French historian had distorted the American cause. Raynal had written that all revolutions were designed only to restore lost liberties and rights, a renewal of or a return to first principles, the *ridurre ai principii,* and that the Americans in particular were fighting only over whether they could still retain their rights as Englishmen to decide on issues of tea and tariffs.[33] Paine thought this analysis was completely misinformed because the American cause and its successful outcome offered people everywhere a model of how and when to take up arms and engage in global revolution.

When, in 1781, Paine first read a London translation of the Abbé's work, illegally reprinted in Philadelphia, he immediately answered it. Although he was a monarchist, Raynal was sympathetic to the American cause. Still, Paine thought he had it all wrong, even though he greatly respected the man personally as a supporter of human freedom. He possessed "a loveliness of sentiment in favour of Liberty," he later recalled in the *Rights of Man* (94). He wanted to respond to Raynal's history because, as he told Washington, "in several places he is mistaken, and in others injudicious and sometimes cynical. I believe I shall publish it in America, but my principal view is to republish it in Europe both in French and English."[34] Once he finished the *Letter to the Abbé Raynal,* he sent Robert Morris fifty copies to forward "to any part of Europe or the West Indies," hoping that it would have "the chance of an European publication, which I suppose it will obtain in France and England."[35] He also sent fifty copies to Washington, "for the use of the army."[36] Paine wanted both a national and an international audience to read his response, as his subtitle suggested: "in which the mistakes in the Abbé's account of the revolution in America are corrected and cleared up." Shortly after the *Letter*'s American publication, editions appeared in London and Dublin, followed by two French translations and soon thereafter by three more.

Paine here was at his subversive best. He wanted his work read by an international audience to provoke revolutions throughout Europe, especially in England, France, and Spain. He hoped revolutions would begin the process of the universal establishment of republican government. To accomplish this, he set out three goals in his argument: first, he declared the newness of the American Revolution, distinguishing it from all other revolutions; second, he argued that the Revolution was based on republican principles, not merely tea and taxes; and third, he was determined to convince his readers that these principles were exportable.[37] Thanks to the events in America, revolution in the modern sense should no longer be associated with the Good Old Cause of 1647–48, which had led to the trial and execution of Charles I in 1649 and the restoration of the ancient rights of Englishmen embodied in the so-called Happy English Constitution. Nor did modern revolution fit the paradigm of the 1688 English Revolution, whose advocates repeated the very same arguments of their fathers from forty years earlier.[38] With some variations and modifications, Burke later expressed these older arguments to extol the results of 1688 in his robust attack on the revolution in France. The new model revolution, for Paine, was different, thanks to the Americans, who had gone beyond first principles, and it certainly was no rebellion, as the British king and ministry had claimed in the summer of 1775. Instead, the American Revolution had vastly transformed how government operated, and even more importantly it had revolutionized the principles by which government's power and authority were exercised.

The Revolution was, therefore, unlike anything that had previously happened in world history. It was not a "usual" revolution designed to restore rights, but one designed to form an entirely new set of political principles and constitutional structures. It was caused not because of anything the Americans did, but because Parliament and the ministry had established tyranny over America in a new way. Until now, tyranny had existed either *without* law or by simply going *against* the law. This time it was created *by* law, and Paine cited as evidence the Declaratory Act, as well as all the other legislative deeds and executive and military actions that preceded and followed it. The Abbé was aware of these laws, but his conclusions were wrong. Raynal thought that political principle was the least part of the revolution and that the Americans were upset mainly because they had been forced to pay taxes decreed by Parliament to which they had not consented. Why else would the Americans have sought an alliance with the French monarchy? Raynal asked. They could hardly be asserting their desire for liberty as a principle while allied to another kingdom.

No, the Americans allied themselves with the French to achieve something more than merely having to pay British taxes. "Our style and manner of thinking have undergone a revolution more extraordinary than the political revolution of the country," he claimed. "We see with other eyes; we hear with other ears; and think with other thoughts, than those we formerly used. We can look back on our own prejudices, as if they had been the prejudices of other people. We now see and know they were prejudices and nothing else; and, relieved from their shackles, enjoy a freedom of mind, we felt not before." The alliance with France was crucial to this changed view of the world because the next step was for the republican ideas underlying the American cause to spread throughout the world, including Britain and maybe eventually France as well. Paine would make sure that America would be first of these by means of the 1778 alliance between America and France, for "every corner of the mind is swept of its cobwebs, poison and dust, and made fit for the reception of generous happiness." The minds of the Americans were opened to the entire world when the alliance was concluded with France, "an alliance not formed for the mere purpose of a day, but on just and generous grounds, and with equal and mutual advantages."[39] Surely, French economic and military support was critical to the Americans. Equally important was the wider vision that America gained by the French association so that now Americans saw themselves as part of a larger world, and with that, global revolution seemed possible.

Now, Dissenters like Richard Price and Joseph Priestley agreed that American resistance to British tyranny was different. Like Paine, they too concluded that God superintended all the affairs of the world. Two years after the publication of Paine's letter to Raynal, Price echoed Paine's views in his *Observations on the Importance of the American Revolution*. Declaring that he was convinced that the magnitude of the events in America outweighed everything the world had yet seen, with but one exception, Price noted, "Perhaps, I do not go too far when I say that, next to the introduction to Christianity among mankind, the American Revolution may prove the most important step in the progressive cause of human improvement," adding quickly that God had imposed his hand on the course of events. "It is a conviction I cannot resist, that the independence of the *English* colonies in America is one step ordained by Providence to introduce these times."[40] Priestley, too, was convinced of the cosmic effects of American resistance to Britain. "It is only by justice, equity, and generosity that nations, as well as individuals, can expect to flourish; and by the violation of them, both single persons and states, in the course of the righteous providence of God, involve themselves in disgrace and ruin."[41]

For all three men—Price, Priestley, and Paine—the old prejudices and narrow-minded thinking that had previously infected the Americans had come to an end. "We are now really another people," Paine told Raynal, "and cannot again go back to ignorance and prejudice. The mind once enlightened cannot again become dark. There is no possibility, neither is there any term to express the supposition by, of the mind *un*knowing anything it already knows."[42] There was indeed no going back, and the imagery he used was as instructive as it was amusing. To reintegrate the Americans into the British empire in the old ways would be tantamount to persuading a seeing man to become blind or a brilliant one to turn into an idiot. This truly new people, this new breed in creation that only God Himself might have foreseen, is suggestive of Crèvecoeur's famous question (and answer): "What is an American?"

> What, then, is the American, this new man? He is neither an European nor the descendant of an European; hence that strange mixture of blood, which you will find in no other country. . . . He is an American, who, leaving behind him all his ancient prejudices and manners, receives new ones from the new mode of life he has embraced, the new government he obeys, and the new rank he holds. He becomes an American by being received in the broad lap of our Alma Mater. Here individuals of all nations are melted into a new race of men, whose labours and posterity will one day cause great changes in the world. Americans are the western pilgrims who are carrying along with them that great mass of arts, sciences, vigor, and industry which began long since in the East; they will finish the great circle. . . . The American is a new man, who acts upon new principles; he must therefore entertain new ideas and form new opinions. From involuntary idleness, service dependence, penury, and useless labour, he has passed to toils of a very different nature, rewarded by ample subsistence. This is an American.[43]

Crèvecoeur's words echoed Paine's sentiments so closely that it would seem impossible to believe that either Paine or Crèvecoeur, who were born within two years of one another, did not know each other's work. But Paine never mentioned the "American farmer" and probably had never even heard of this French-born Tory. Even so, Paine's *Letter* and Crèvecoeur's *Letters* appeared the same year (1782), and the similarity and the parallels in their language is remarkably striking, even if they might not have agreed on political principles beyond the idea of a new American man. To press the resemblance (and tantalizing speculation) further, both publications appeared in the form of "letters," and Crèvecoeur dedicated his work to the Abbé Raynal.

In any event, Paine's purpose was not merely to persuade his readers of the novelty of the American experiment but also to universalize it. America's successful war against the British and the rise of the new government of the United States, despite its renovation as a result of the new 1787 constitution just five years later, heralded a new turn in world politics. It reflected his developing thoughts about the changed nature of revolution itself.

> What were formerly called Revolutions, were little more than a change of persons or an alteration of local circumstances. They rose and fell like things of course, and had nothing in their existence of their fate that could influence beyond the spot that produced them. But what we now see in the world, from the Revolutions of America and France, are *a renovation of the natural order of things*, a system of principles as universal as truth and the existence of man, and combining moral with political happiness and national prosperity. . . . Monarchical sovereignty, the enemy of mankind, and the source of misery, is abolished; and sovereignty itself is restored to its natural and original place, the Nation. Were this the case throughout Europe the cause of wars would be taken away (*RM*, 144, italics added).

Paine's remarks about the universal nature of the American Revolution are an early instance of globalization and internationalism. Absolutely convinced that the events begun on the shores of America would inevitably spread throughout the world, he argued that revolution was exportable, a movable act amenable to every geographical location. It portended the creation of the new man beyond Crèvecoeur's American "new man" to all men in all places.

If Paine could return to France, then, he would work on behalf of these principles, leading revolutions from there. As a product of the Enlightenment, as a philosophe whose purpose was activism to achieve liberty and justice, he believed that contemporary progress in commerce, literature, and the sciences all confirmed that the world was improving. With vast political alterations in the wind, as witnessed by the first step taken in the American Revolution, global revolutionary action would soon wipe out tyranny. Even before the end of hostilities between the Americans and British troops, he told General Nathanael Greene that, when he secretly returned to London, he would "get out a publication" to "open the eyes of the country with respect to the madness and stupidity of its government" (*RM*, 221n). Greene persuaded him that he would likely be hanged as soon as he set foot on English soil.[44] When Paine finally did return to France in 1787, he continued to believe that he possessed a God-given role as a specially appointed divine agent to reform the world. He was willing to perform this service, but his attempt to actually instigate world revolution led to events that nearly killed him.

CHAPTER 4

PERMANENT REVOLUTION AND

CONSTITUTION MAKING

PAINE'S STRONG advocacy of and active participation in revolutionary action and constitution making as global phenomena drove his views in *Common Sense,* but they are most evident in his French revolutionary writings, beginning with the *Rights of Man* and his attack on Burke and Burke's famous *Reflections.*[1] His inspiration for universal transformation lay at the root of his famous statement that we live in "an age of Revolution, in which *everything* may be looked for." Paine hoped that a European Congress, one that paralleled the Americans' First Continental Congress, would challenge the iron grip that monarchy and aristocracy possessed over each country's subject citizenry. If this congress were in fact to take place, it would advance "the progress of free Government" and "the civilization of Nations with each other." It was an event "nearer in probability, than once were the Revolutions and Alliance of France and America" (*RM,* 147).

Paine was thus gradually developing the idea that the twentieth century would know as "the permanent revolution," a global condition of constant upheaval until the rise of a universal civilization of reason, science, and democracy.[2] The very idea of revolution became like wine to his head. Once this new state of affairs came into being in all nations, the world would see the end of warfare, because war reflected aristocratic domination, while democracy did not: "War is the system of Government on the old construction," but "man is not the enemy of man" (*RM,* 146). Universal peace would result only after global revolution had succeeded, when monarchy and aristocracy had been abolished forever. So optimistic was he that he boldly and, as it turned out, naively predicted that no "monarchy and aristocracy will continue seven years longer in any of the enlightened countries in Europe" (156). Universal reformation would be ignited with "a small spark, kindled in America," from which an entire "flame has arisen, not to be extinguished" (210). Representative democracy, the only form of government to adequately protect the rights of man, would replace the English system.

> Government on the old system, is an assumption of power, for the aggrandisement of itself; on the new, a delegation of power, for the common benefit of society. The former supports itself by keeping up a system of war; the latter promotes a system of peace, as the true means of enriching a nation. The one encourages national prejudices; the other promotes universal society, as the means of universal commerce. The one measures its prosperity, by the quantity of revenue it extorts, the other proves its excellence by the small quantity of taxes it requires" (171).

By 1792, because in one single generation, the world witnessed two major revolutions, one in America, the other in process in France, Paine claimed, "the objects that now press on the public attention, are the French Revolution, and the prospect of a general revolution in all governments" (266).

Was all this rhetoric simply nonsense? Paine was a phenomenal rhetorician, whose words were always cultivated with a consistent self-certainty. So, naturally, in the *Rights of Man*, monarchy, rank, and privilege shared a fate even worse than they had in *Common Sense*.[3] We would be hard pressed to find a more blistering critique of these three evils than in his response to Burke's *Reflections*. Echoing Jefferson's famous phrase that "the earth belongs in usufruct to the living," Paine argued that "man has no authority over posterity in matters of personal right; and therefore, no man, or body of men, had, or can have, a right to set up hereditary government" (172).[4] He soundly reemphasized this notion when he contended that "every age and generation is, and must be as a matter of right, as free to act for itself in all cases, as the age and generation that preceded it. The vanity and presumption of governing beyond the grave is the most ridiculous and insolent of all tyrannies. Man has no property in man, neither has one generation a property in the generations that are to follow."[5] Most states, after declaring independence in 1776, had written new constitutions, but Connecticut and Rhode Island simply transformed their colonial charters into their constitutions. All others elected deputies to constitutional conventions to draft their first state constitutions. Franklin, as we have seen, headed the committee in Philadelphia that created the new Pennsylvania constitution. Paine himself later served as a deputy to the French National Convention and worked on a committee, chaired by the Marquis de Condorcet, that developed France's new republican constitution after the fall of the monarchy and the imprisonment of Louis XVI in August 1792. This document included a provision requiring a revision every seven years.[6]

Above all, a good constitution abjures heredity service in elected assemblies, and this principle did not stop at elected lawmakers. The problem was deeper because it also necessarily involved landownership when property-less people were excluded from voting in the elections of the legislature. In his last great work, *Agrarian Justice,* Paine repeated a point Locke had made in the *Second Treatise of Government,* namely, that God had given to men and women a gift of "the earth for their inheritance."[7] Locke's position was that God had given the earth to man to hold in common, so that he could mix his labor with it and then hold it collectively for perpetuity.[8] Burke directly collided with this position with his claim that titled nobility and crowned monarchs held their offices as the result of time, custom, and prescription. While they all owned property, and lots of it, they held onto their offices because of both landownership and tradition. They could not be displaced simply because small-thinking men like Thomas Paine argued that these prescriptive institutions should be abandoned once and for all.

Paine of course thought he had already stated his belief that he was God's chosen instrument to lead global revolutions. He now had to persuade everyone to agree with his political principles. For a while before 1790, he thought Burke did, too. Never one to ignore a self-aggrandizing moment, he wrote that he had advanced above aristocracy by succeeding as a political writer. "Not only" had he "contributed to raise a new empire in the world," the new United States, but he had also "arrived at an eminence in political literature . . . which aristocracy, with all its aids, has not been able to reach or to rival" (*RM*, 219). At the end of 1789 and the beginning of 1790, just before Burke's *Reflections* was published, Paine and Burke, who were fairly close friends, traveled together throughout the Midlands to search the ironworks for proper materials for Paine's experimental bridge design. This traveling, as innocent as it might have seemed to Paine, indirectly contributed to the great political rift between the two men. Burke and Paine had been traveling companions from the time they first met in 1787 and remained so until their clamorous disagreement over the French Revolution. Paine knew Burke primarily as a strong supporter of American independence, and Burke never mentioned to Paine his rapidly growing uneasiness about the revolutionary upheavals in France.

When he was in Paris, Paine kept Burke up-to-date on French events and thus became an unwitting supplier of ideological gunpowder for Burke's coming antirevolutionary cannon. In September 1789, as he was preparing to leave Paris as the American minister, Jefferson wrote to Paine how enthralled he was by the progress of French politics. "These are the materials of a superb edifice," he said in commenting on the new Declaration of Rights of Man that the Constituent Assembly had drafted with Jefferson's covert assistance. "The hands which have prepared them are perfectly capable of putting them together, and of filling up the work of which these are only the outlines. While there are some men among them of very superior abilities, the mass possess such a degree of good sense as enables them to decide well."[9] Paine blindly passed the contents of this letter onto Burke, inadvertently contributing to Burke's rapidly mounting skepticism. A few months later, Paine sent Burke information from Paris about the new 1791 constitution, the government's improving finances, and the "tranquil" attitude of the king concerning the new political arrangements, which that soon resulted in a constitutional monarchy. He even told Burke that the events in France, like those in America thirteen years earlier, so profoundly heralded a new day that Britain had better be wary: "The Revolution in France is certainly a forerunner to other revolutions in Europe." To Burke's increasing horror, he continued:

Politically considered it is a new Mode of forming Alliances affirmatively with Countries and negatively with Courts. There is no foreign Court, not even Prussia, that could now be fond of attacking France; they are afraid of their Armies and their Subjects catching the Contagion. Here are reports of Matters beginning to work in Bohemia and in Rome. In Spain the Inquisition has condemned thirty-nine French Works among which is the French declaration of Rights. But the condemnation by reciting the heads of each Work appear to me to have the effect of spreading the doctrines, at last it makes it known that there are such Works and such doctrines in places where otherways it would not be known, and even *that* knowledge will have some effect.[10]

Paine soon heard rumors that Burke was working on a bitter critique of the French Revolution as early as March 1790. In anticipation of its appearance, he began to think of ways to respond. After Burke's *Reflections* appeared on November 1, 1790, Paine's reply, the *Rights of Man,* part 1, appeared almost immediately, on February 22, 1791, and part 2, almost exactly one year later, on February 16, 1792.

PRESCRIPTIVE VERSUS HUMAN RIGHTS

Richard Price's sermon before the Revolution Society meeting at the Old Jewry in November 1789 provided Burke with his final provocation to attack all that was wrong with France's revolution.[11] Price claimed that the 1688 Revolution had opened the way for Englishmen to achieve three major civil rights: the right of the citizens to choose their governors, to turn out those whom they thought misgoverned them, and to form a government of their choice. Paine agreed with these principles and also agreed that the Revolution in 1688 and the Declaration of Right merely marked the *beginning* of English political progress, and not, as Burke contended, a *final* settlement. At the end of his peroration, Price, who was known to be a particularly poor speaker with a weak voice, nonetheless must have intoned these words in a voice rising with all the force he could muster. He exclaimed:

> What an eventful period is this! I am thankful that I have lived to see it; and I could almost say, Lord now lettest thou servant depart

in peace for mine eyes have seen thy salvation. . . . I have lived to see Thirty Millions of People, indignant and resolute, spurning at slavery and demanding liberty with an irresistible voice. Their king led in triumph and an arbitrary monarch surrendering himself to his subjects. . . . *Tremble* all ye oppressors of the world! Take warning all ye supporters of slavish governments and slavish hierarchies!

His warning was clear, at least to Burke when he read the sermon, that the next revolutionary target was England itself. George III and the Lords were for Price, in words that Paine could have written, the greatest "supporters of slavish governments and slavish hierarchies."[12]

Such principles were abhorrent to Burke, who was appalled that the Paris revolutionaries so quickly and casually obliterated centuries of French historical development. In addressing Price and "the gentlemen of the old Jewry," Burke was so enraged at the historical "confusion" that Price had gleaned from the events of 1688–89 that he set out to teach him and all the "literary caballers and intriguing philosophers . . . political theologians and theological politicians" a severe historical lesson. Beginning with the successes of 1688–89, a wealth of differences distinguished the Glorious Revolution and the Declaration of Right (1688–89), on the one hand, and the French Revolution (1789), on the other. Price and his fellow "caballers" had mixed them up. "It is necessary that we should separate what they confound," he said and went on in his *Reflections* to further distinguish between them and the rashness of Price and company:

> We must recall their erring fancies to the *acts* of the Revolution which we revere, for the discovery of its true *principles.* If the *principles* of the Revolution of 1688 are anywhere to be found, it is in the statute called the *Declaration of Right.* In that most wise, sober, and considerate declaration, drawn up by great lawyers and great statesmen, and not by warm and inexperienced enthusiasts, not one word is said, nor one suggestion made, of a general right "to choose our own *governors,* to cashier them for misconduct, and to *form* a government for *ourselves.* This Declaration of Right . . . is the cornerstone of our constitution, as reinforced, explained, improved, and in its fundamental principles for ever *settled.*[13]

The Settlement of 1688–89 marked permanent features of the political and religious landscape, and these features were designed to last for a very long time. Indeed, they had already lasted for more than a century. Only now, philosophical theologians and theological philosophers like Price wanted to demolish these fine institutions. In fact, the events of those years had established parliamentary supremacy as well as the Protestant Succession. They had firmly set the British monarchy in its proper context and appropriate place, perhaps forever. Burke was appalled to hear that the French Revolution was based on the citizens' rational contemplation of the rights of man. Such abstractions as reason, principles, and rights had no place in his prescriptive understanding of human history. The revolution in France had wiped out, in an instant, hundreds of years of French history and tradition.

Paine, like Price, rejected this construction. The difference between 1649 and 1688–89, on the one hand, and 1789, on the other, wrote Paine, was that "in the case of Charles I and James II of England, the revolt was against the personal despotism of the men; whereas in France, it was against the hereditary despotism of the established government." Because the revolutions in both 1649 and 1688 were directed against particular kings, their successors were free to do whatever they wanted. All that had been destroyed were the effects of monarchy, not its ungodly causes. The only response was the destruction of the evil, which had nothing to do with those who happened to occupy the throne: the institution itself must be torn down. This was why the 1789 events in France, building on the earlier events in America, comprised a new-model revolution based on human rights. Accordingly, "it was not against Louis XVIth, but against the despotic principles of the government, that the nation revolted" (*RM*, 47). For Burke, those very principles, though he certainly would not have called them "despotic," served as the historic foundation of British and French stability.

Four years later Paine reiterated his contempt for Burke's glorification of the 1688 Settlement.

> The English Parliament of 1688, imported a man and his wife from Holland, *William* and *Mary,* and made them King and Queen of England. Having done this, the said Parliament made a law to convey the government of the country to the heirs of William and Mary, in the following words: "we, the Lords Spiritual and Temporal, and Commons, do, in the name of the people of England,

most humbly and faithfully submit *ourselves, our heirs and posterities,* to William and Mary, *their heirs and posterities,* forever." And in a subsequent law, as quoted by Edmund Burke, the said Parliament, in the name of the people of England then living, *binds the said people, their heirs and posterities, to William and Mary, their heirs and posterities, to the end of time.* It is not sufficient that we laugh at the ignorance of such law-makers; it is necessary that we reprobate their want of principle.[14]

First, monarchy, whether under the Stuarts or the Prince of Orange and his English wife, was still monarchy, and second, for one generation to bind another was absurd and inhuman. After all, "it requires but a very small glance of thought to perceive, that although laws made in one generation often continue in force through succeeding generations, yet that they continue to derive their force from the consent of the living" (*RM,* 44).

Paine again reiterated Jefferson's principle that the earth belonged to the living. The dead might have supposedly made binding agreements and laws for all future generations, but any attempt by one generation to bind the next was the moral and political equivalent of despotism. "A single reflection will teach us, that our ancestors, like ourselves, were but tenants for life in the great freehold of rights. The fee-absolute was not in them, it is not in us, it belongs to the whole family of man through all ages."[15] Members of Parliament had no authority to bind anyone except themselves. The king and the Lords had already corrupted the Commons by proving once and for all that England never had a constitution, as Paine had earlier stated in his *Four Letters on Interesting Subjects*: "If you ask an Englishman what he means when he speaks of the English constitution, he is unable to give you any answer. The truth is, the English have no fixed constitution." The English government possessed arbitrary, practically unlimited, power to the extent that "an act of parliament . . . can do any thing but make a man a woman."[16]

Now, more than fifteen years later, he reiterated the same argument. "The continual use of the word *Constitution* in the English Parliament, shows there is none, and that whole is merely a form of government without a constitution, and constituting itself with what powers it pleases" (*RM,* 131). There was merely an appearance of constitutional government, even if everyone

talked about a so-called constitution. While England ha
history of the three estates, of the king, the Lords, and th
mons, no one had actually seen the document that emp
them in government. Paine thus once again denied the N
myth by challenging Burke to show it to him: "Can th
Burke produce the English constitution? If he cannot, v
fairly conclude, that though it has been so much talked abc
such thing as a constitution exists, or ever did exist, and
quently that the people have yet a constitution to form" (71–

Constitutional-less England was a nation of "the gr
Cowards on Earth as all Bullies are," he told William Shor
American chargé d'affaires in Paris. It was time for the ap
ance of an English revolution, stimulated by the French ex
ence.[18] The British monarchy would fall either because of i
creasing indebtedness or because people like Thomas Paine
the people would violently end it. In 1792, Paine publicly
pealed to the English people to rise in revolution to form a
republic: "Two revolutions have taken place, those of Ame
and France; and both of them have rejected the unnatural cc
pounded system of the English Government," and the only
course the people there have is to declare that they, and th
alone, "do constitute and appoint [a republic] to be our syste
and form of government." It was, after all, God's will, as i
quoted St. Paul's letter to Ananias to prove that God Himse
the highest authority of all, had approved of revolution: "Th
Lord will smite thee, thou whitened wall." Even supposed en
lightened Englishmen like Charles James Fox and the member
of the Society of the Friends of the People, who claim that mod
est reforms would transform England, were mistaken. "Moderation in principle," he declared, "is a species of vice."[19]

Once democracy was achieved in America, France, and England, these three nations would become allies to take revolution to the rest of the world: the United States in its hemisphere,
England and France, soon joined by Holland, in theirs. The
Americans would promote "the independence of South America, and the opening of those countries of immense extent and
wealth to the general commerce of the world, as North America
is" (*RM*, 267). The French, along with the British and Dutch,
would make it clear that "the iron is becoming hot all over Eu-

rope. The insulted German and the enslaved Spaniard, the Russ and the Pole, are beginning to think" (268). Again, revolution would become a *permanent* feature of politics until the world has been totally transformed. In this utopian vision of the near future, reason, rights, peace, liberty, and prosperity would reign everywhere. Underlying these principles was the law of God as He had established it. His creation from the beginning was based on principles that encouraged the best in human beings. Those who enslaved others rather than inspiring freedom, those who made war rather than furthering peace, and those who denied the reality of human rights deserved to be driven out. Paine here offered his readers what has become perhaps one of the best-known images in the last pages of the *Rights of Man*. "It is now towards the middle of February," he mused at the end of the second part.

> Were I to take a turn into the country, the trees would present a leafless winterly appearance. As people are apt to pluck the twigs as they walk along, I perhaps might do the same, and by chance might observe, that *a single bud* on that twig had begun to swell. I should reason never unnaturally, or rather not reason at all, to suppose *this* was the *only* bud in England which had this appearance. Instead of deciding thus, I should instantly conclude, that the same appearance was beginning, or about to begin, everywhere; and though the vegetable sleep will continue longer on some trees and plants than on others, and though some of them may not *blossom* for two or three years, all will be in leaf in the summer, except those which are *rotten*. What pace the political summer may keep with the natural, no human foresight can determine. It is, however, not difficult to perceive that the spring is begun. (272–73)

Paine was determined that the time had arrived for action. He was certain of his own role in the coming cosmic events, even as he developed a highly sophisticated theory of rights.

RIGHTS TALK

After the people craft a written constitution based on republican principles, they then must ratify it. Paine preferred the American

style of ratification, in which the people elect ratifying conventions, thus allowing for the participation of the greatest number of people possible. Once this has occurred, they will be assured that their rights and liberties are secure. For Paine, there is no use debating the origins of these rights because they are part of God's creation at the beginning of time. Government, however, does have to guarantee them, lest a monarch eradicate them. This is why his attack on Burke's doctrine of historical prescription was so severe. Burke had a limited historical sense of how and when the first organizers of governmental institutions operated, but Paine identified them as Norman invaders, the "banditti of ruffians" or "an armed banditti (*RM*, 169, *CS*, 78, 95). They immediately stole everything from the people and ruled over them as monarchs and aristocrats. Rights are "original" and "inherent"; they are "neither divisible, nor transferable, nor annihilable, but are descendable only" (171, 124). Rights are, in short, "permanent things," a gift of God, and not something that kings or lords have the power to grant.[20]

Burke strongly opposed this reasoning, arguing that it was unwise for the French or any people to tear down political institutions that had lasted for generations. Revolution was reckless because it wreaked havoc on the nation, destroying any bit of progress made over several centuries. Paine responded that "we live to improve, or we live in vain; and therefore we admit of no maxims of government or policy on the mere score of antiquity," as Burke would have it. Nor do we admit "of other men's authority, the *old* Whigs or the *new*," taking a shot directly at Burke's barrage against those who, like Paine, had acclaimed Price's sermon.[21]

Paine thought that Burke's problem was that he refused to go far enough back in time to analyze the origins of the political institutions he so deeply revered. First, Paine defended Price's three essential principles, which, to reiterate, were that the people have the natural right to choose their own governors, to be rid of them when they are oppressive, and afterward to form the government they prefer. History proved, Burke claimed, that monarchy and aristocracy provide the best mechanism for the best among men to rule the least capable. Price had set forth a wrongheaded set of principles, one that amounted to a "new and hitherto unheard-of bill of rights," which, "though made in the name of the whole people, belongs to those gentlemen and their faction only. The body of the people of England have no share in it. They utterly disclaim it. They will resist the practical assertion of it with their lives and fortunes."[22] But Paine linked these "rights" to all the people of the nation as a whole by holding that they possess their rights simply because they are human. "Wrongs cannot have a legal descent," he said ironically, because rights are derived from God (*RM*, 124). When God fashioned the universe, He created rights and instilled them simultaneously in His human creations. Burke erred when he linked the so-called rights of Englishmen only to the Settlement of 1688, when the Prince of Orange William and his wife Mary, the daughter of James II, were offered the throne after James had escaped from England.

Just as Paine had asked Burke to produce, if he could, the English constitution, he also demanded that he identify the exact origins of human rights. Unwilling to wait for Burke to respond, he answered that "the error of those who reason by precedents drawn from antiquity, respecting the rights of man, is, that they do not go far enough into antiquity. They do not go the whole way" (*RM*, 65). To understand the origins of human rights, we must necessarily return to the beginning of time, to the moment of creation. Paine's deeply held faith in God as the sole creator of the universe included his belief that God had created human rights when he created human beings. Rights emerged at precisely the same moment that "man came from the hand of his Maker." The creation of man and the creation of rights were simultaneous effects of a providential God who deliberately saw to "the divine origin of the rights of man at the creation" (65, 66). Natural man, in short, possesses natural rights. Price's triad of how men might properly exercise these rights was integral to God's plan. Here again, Paine presumed the existence of the power of a First Cause, namely, God or Providence, who declined to abandon human beings after He had given to them the gifts of life and rights. The man—in this case, Burke himself—who denied that human beings naturally possess rights unequivocally "establish[ed] his kinship to the fool who said in his heart there is no God."[23] Burke was the atheist, not Paine.

Paine thus tried to turn the tables on Burke, who, when looking for the historical origins of Englishmen's rights, had located them as recently as 1688. Paine asked Burke to think with greater breadth. When we search for "the origin of man, and . . . the origin of his rights," we will find they are one and the same. The true authority for human rights was not a man-made agreement leading to a "settlement" but God Himself, a point that Paine did not mind repeating. It is "the illuminating and divine principle of the equal rights of man (for it has its origin from the Maker of man)" that "relates, not only to the living individuals, but to generations of men succeeding to the generations which preceded it, by the same rule of every individual is born equal in rights with his contemporary" (*RM*, 65, 66).[24] Paine's faith in natural human equality may be found as early as *Common Sense,* when he declared that human beings were naturally and originally "equals in the order of creation" (*CS*, 71, 76). We now find him clearly holding strongly to the same point in the *Rights of Man* fifteen years later, debunking Burke's attempted verbal artistry to limit English rights to 1688. Determining the origins of human rights was after all "a doctrine," which is "the oldest upon record" (*RM*, 67, 125). Paine's logic told him that no man possesses more authority or more power over another man. As Locke had written, human beings are naturally in "a *state of perfect freedom* to order their actions" and at the same time in "a *state* also *of equality*, wherein all the power and jurisdiction is reciprocal, no one having more than another."[25] Inequality is an artifice, brought into society by the exercise of pure muscular strength or political or military power. It is so unnatural that the rise of heads of states and their kings and minions, their aristocrats, reflect this unnatural development away from God's creation.

Paine's point was as powerful as it must have been shocking to Burke and anyone else who read the *Rights of Man* or who followed Burke's logic: "Every child born into the world must be considered as deriving its existence from God. The world is as new to him as it was to the first man that existed, and his natural right in it is of the same kind." It is not God's fault that scheming, satanic, monstrous men have thrown up "a succession of barriers, or sort of turnpike gates," through which man was forced to pass (*RM*, 66, 67). Paine's "barriers" and "turnpike gates" were curious euphemisms in that they sound relatively benign. A barrier or a gate, even with a toll to pay, might be an ir- ritant, but any human being could easily overcome a barrier or gate. It was as if he declared that men needed only to tear them down to be free. This was hardly his point, which he unmasked in the very next paragraph, when he argued that it was not merely "a wilderness of turnpike gates" that held men back. They must also realize that they had all originally been equal, so now equality must translate into equal rights. Once they knew this, they would know that their "duty was only to God" and their fellow human beings (67).

Paine explained, again in accordance with Lockean conven- tion, the differences between natural and civil rights.[26] Natural rights are those that human beings possess simply by virtue of their being human, whereas civil rights comprise those more lim- ited rights that result from the decision to enter civil society from a natural condition of life. Once in civil society, men relinquish some of their natural rights in exchange for greater security. The passage from natural to civil rights involves an exchange—a deal, as if it were an economic agreement into which men entered with the hope of improving their safety while preserving their basic rights. This transformation of natural to civil rights be- comes the basis for the origins of the social contract, something that Paine considered in 1788, when he wrote to Jefferson, then the American minister to the Paris Court. Certainly, men in a natural state have only themselves to answer to because nothing restrains them. They suffer only when they encounter other men more powerful than they. He told Jefferson that in a natural state a man's "will would be his Law, but his power, in many cases, in- adequate to [secure] his rights."[27]

Now Locke, too, saw that man in the state of nature possessed the freedom to go wherever and do whatever he wished but that he also had certain responsibilities. He enjoyed the irrevocable right of self-preservation, and he owed his fellow human beings that same right. He must therefore never kill anyone except as a matter of self-defense and then only when his own life was truly threatened. He must also live by the law of nature, which pre- sumed that he would be forced to kill if he witnessed one man murder another man. Natural law required that every man "put in every man's hands . . . a right [even a duty] to punish the transgressors of that law," thus forcing every man to become the police, prosecutor, judge, jury, and executioner of the law.[28] Because this was the major inconvenience of living in a natural state, given that some men choose not to obey natural law but rather to dominate others by their greater power, they soon found that they would be better off living in civil society. In choosing to do so, they would have to surrender some of their natural rights, especially the right to bring to justice those who disobeyed the law of nature, in exchange for collective security. Paine asked Jefferson to imagine twenty people who, wishing no longer to have these inconveniencies, joined together. If they decided collectively to pool their strength, they learned that they would have to surrender some of their individual sovereignty to live cooperatively in society. As early as 1777, he noted that it was literally impossible to carry into civil society all the natural rights that an individual enjoyed before there was government. It "would be a Bill of Rights fitted to man in a state of nature without any government at all. It would be an Indian Bill of Rights."[29]

The key was that the people themselves must choose to form a government. They were not forced into it by some higher authority, such as a king or a nobleman. Once they had chosen their rulers, they would find that they continued to possess certain rights of "personal competency," which Paine identified as "intellectual rights." These included those rights that in 1791 would find their way into the First Amendment of the U.S. Constitution, for example, free expression and religious liberty (*RM*, 68). These rights pertain to them as individuals, not members of collective society. The only paramount, nonintellectual right that he included was the right to vote, a personal political right that men actually own as part of their political property. As he later put it in arguing a losing battle for universal manhood suffrage in the 1795 constitution of France, "personal rights, of which the right of voting for representatives is one, are a species of property of the most sacred kind." To eliminate equal voting rights is to enslave one party of the citizenry, "for slavery consists in being subject to the will of another, and he that has not a vote in the election of representatives is in this case [a slave]."[30]

But individuals should never have to compromise their intellectual rights, which always remain with them. After all, it is irrefutable that no man would enter into society "to become *worse* than he was before, nor to have fewer [intellectual] rights than he had before, but to have those rights better secured," practically echoing Locke's statement concerning rights (*RM,* 68). On the basis of this observation, Paine developed his theory of just how government was erected, that "necessary evil" he had identified in *Common Sense.* Government arose from one of three major sources. First, its earliest form was the rule by priests, who asserted that they possessed superior understanding of and faith in a god of their own making. Priestly government resulted from human beings' tendency to believe in superstitions and fairy-tales. Second, monarchy, which usually came about as a result of conquest and often appeared in its absolute form, developed because of the sheer military and political power of tyrants. Only an appreciation and understanding of human rights, which we can know immediately through human reason and common sense, offered men the best, most practicable form of government, namely, the democratic republic.

When he argued that government either developed "out of" or "over" the people, Paine meant that these were the only ways in which government possibly arose. Government either usurped the power that lay innately in the people to govern themselves or it allowed the people to work together to achieve the common good—or in Rousseau's terms, the general will, something with which Paine, in France after 1787, accepted. As early as 1786, when he wrote that "the public good is not a term opposed to the good of individuals; on the contrary, it is the good of every individual collected,"[31] Paine understood that the general will operates in political decision-making in the republic. Six years later, he approvingly quoted from Rousseau's *Social Contract* that monarchs and their ministers could never embody the general will because monarchs and their ministers never achieve the public good.[32]

The first two forms of government, the rule by priests or monarchs, arose when nations had no written constitution. This included the so-called republic-with-hereditary-king in England, allegedly based on its unwritten ancient constitution. Only the third source truly worked to man's advantage: a democratic republican constitution guaranteed the people's civil rights. "A constitution, therefore, is to a government, what the law made afterwards by that government are to a court of judicature. The court or judicature does not make the laws, neither can it alter them; it only acts in conformity to the laws made: and the government is in like manner governed by the constitution" (*RM*, 71). Only written constitutions, therefore, guarantee that intellectual rights like free expression will be protected, because "speech is . . . one of the natural rights of man always retained" (90). But even a free press could be corrupted by becoming licentious and scurrilous, although the government must never shut it down: a free press meant "free from prior restraint," which became the legal standard in U.S. First Amendment constitutional law.[33] After a publication appears, it is up to "the public at large" to be "judges of the matter."[34] Other key intellectual rights follow on the heels of free expression, among them the right of religious liberty, for "religion is one of those rights" (68).

RELIGIOUS LIBERTY

As a man of deep religious convictions, Paine advocated religious freedom. He noted in *Common Sense,* for example, that once the Americans achieved separation between the colonies and England, they could then form a constitution that preserved "above all things the free exercise of religion, according to the dictates of conscience" (*CS*, 97). Indeed, Paine never attended church services or Quaker meetings, and he detested all organized religions with their emphasis on pomp, hierarchy, and lies. He condemned the books that claimed to contain the revealed word of God, Christ, or Allah, such as the Hebrew Bible, the Christian Bible, and the Islamic Koran. Still, despite his distrust of organized religion, he consistently made a powerful distinction between religious freedom and religious tolerance: "Toleration is not the *opposite* of Intolerance, but is the *counterfeit* of it. Religious requirements and religious tolerance were both despotisms," because tolerance and intolerance presume that government either had the power to grant or withhold religious liberty, or what he preferred to call, in very modern terms, "freedom of conscience" (*RM,* 85). Like Madison and Jefferson, he vigorously opposed religious establishments in which the government mandated religious beliefs and then denied political freedoms to those who refused to adhere to those beliefs.[35] When England "*granted* liberty of conscience to every man, every religion," it was not out of English generosity of spirit: it was, he thundered, "a species of tyrannic arrogance."[36] The Anglican Church, with its liturgy bound to the strict Thirty-nine Articles of Faith, in part controlled the definition of British citizenship (lack of sufficient property was also included in the designation). The English government refused to confer full-fledged citizenship on anyone who denied even one of those articles. Under the seventeenth-century Test and Incorporation Acts, the government deprived Dissenters of their political rights, especially the right to vote and to hold public office.[37]

Paine greatly admired the French Declaration of the Rights of Man and of Citizen, which the Marquis de Lafayette presented to the National Assembly in 1789. A remarkable document, it incorporated the political philosophies of Locke, Montesquieu, Voltaire, and Rousseau to set forth many Jeffersonian ideas: inviolable human rights like a free press, the vote, equality before the law, and civilian control of the armed forces. Although Paine quoted the Declaration in the *Rights of Man,* he did not, however, directly comment on the feebleness of Article X, which only indirectly addressed religious liberty: "No man ought to be molested on account of his opinions, not even on account of his *religious* opinions, provided his avowal of them does not disturb the public order established by the law" (*RM,* 111). The provision did not guarantee religious liberty; it merely suggested that the government had the authority to *decline* to persecute the faithful as long as they refrained from causing public disturbances. The provision hardly duplicated the expansive language of the U.S. Constitution's First Amendment, that "Congress shall make *no* law . . . prohibiting the free exercise [of religion]" (emphasis added).[38] The imperative voice with the inclusion of the mandatory "shall" (not "may" or "will") along with the words "no law" gives the provision an absolutist ring, compelling the United States government to maintain what Jefferson later called the wall of separation of church and state.[39]

Paine seemed aware of this weakness when he noted that some

had questioned "whether the 10th article sufficiently guarantees the right it is intended to accord with." One interpretation gave the government authority to control religion by law, but he disagreed. He preferred instead to envision a moment well in the past, when human beings individually entered into a covenant with God, "before any human institution of government was known in the world." This was a moment when they developed a direct relationship with God. No civil authority could ever break this bond. It was, he went on,

> a compact between God and Man, from the beginning of time; and that as the relation and condition which man in his *individual person* stands in towards his Maker, cannot be changed, or anyways altered by any human laws or human authority, that religious devotion, which is part of this compact, cannot so much as be made a subject of human laws; and that all laws must conform themselves to this prior existing compact, and not assume to make the compact conform to the law, which, besides being human, are subsequent thereto. The first act of man, when he looked around and saw himself a creature which he did not make, and a world furnished for his reception, must have been devotion, and devotion must ever continue sacred to every individual man, *as it appears right to him;* and government do mischief by interfering (*RM*, 113).[40]

Far too often overlooked by modern scholarship, this passage clearly points to the centrality of religious liberty in Paine's scheme of individual or intellectual rights: there could be no intermediary between a man and God. This sentiment should have softened his later unrestrained attack on organized religion in *The Age of Reason,* but it did not.

The obverse of this sentiment was, as we have already suggested, Paine's consistent opposition to church establishments like the Church of England. In *Common Sense,* he had argued that government's duty was to allow all religious denominations to flourish and not control any one of them at the expense of the rest. "For myself I fully and conscientiously believe, that it is the will of the Almighty, that there should be diversity of religious opinions among us: It affords a larger field for our Christian kindness. Were we all of one way of thinking, our religious dispositions would want matter for probation; and on this liberal principle, I look on the various denominations among us, to be like children of the same family, differing only, in what is called their Christian names" (109). The root of the problem was in part government control of religion, but the problem was exacerbated when the clergy marched in lockstep with secular authorities. When they were bound together with public officials, "the *adulterous* connection of church and state, wherever it has taken place, whether Jewish, Christian or Turkish, has so effectually prohibited by pains and penalties every discussion upon established creeds, and upon first principles of religion, that until the system of government should be changed, those subjects could not be brought fairly and openly before the world" (*AR*, 1:465). Accompanying the revolution to reform government was a simultaneous revolution in religion, which would lead to true religious liberty. When this revolution finally arrives, we will find just "the two beings," the believer or "the *mortal* who renders the worship, and the IMMORTAL BEING who is worshipped" (*RM*, 85).

This moment when genuine religious liberty flourishes is also part of the permanent revolution. It will last as long as it takes until all men are politically and religiously free: "The revolutions of America and France have thrown a beam of light over the world, which reached into man." That "beam" went directly to "the right of the Nation" to write a constitution guaranteeing all their rights and liberties (*RM*, 118, 120).

CONSTITUTION MAKING

In France, Paine had the opportunity to engage actively in constitution making. The destruction of tyranny required not only revolution, that is, the powerful negative aspects of eliminating the monarchic and aristocratic chokehold on society, but also the positive steps necessary to create a constitutional state. The problem in England, aside from not having a written document, was the overly complex tripartite division of the king, the Lords, and the Commons. It reflected the classical republic only in appearance, not in reality. This artificial division of power was nothing more than the domination by the first two orders (the king and the Lords) over the third (the Commons). The king in particular had rendered the Commons weak and ineffective. In 1776, Paine had argued that a constitution must possess two primary components. First, it sets forth the *form* of the government, and second, it limits its power, "and the last of these two was far more material than the first."[41]

Paine urged his readers to force their governments to create constitutional conventions to prepare written documents clearly spelling out in simple language and form how government is to be organized so as not to intrude on the people's rights and liberties.[42] The constitution will then belong to the people as a whole, or as he was more apt to say in the 1790s, the *nation*. He was quite clear that "a constitution is the property of a nation, and not of those who exercise the government." England lacked this important element, despite Burke's language about an English constitution that was variously "gay with flowers" or "gay and flowery." Such gaudy words simply proved to Paine Burke's adoration of monarchy and heredity. In contrast, this language directly conflicts with Paine's own "manly thinking" or "gigantic manliness." Manly thinking occurs when men work hard to form a limited government with laws that ensured the safety and security of society, including the security of those vaunted rights and liberties that Paine revered. This principle provided the foundation for his idea of the virtuous, civically engaged citizen. He here set up his famous geometric proposition concerning the American state constitutions, which arose after the Declaration of Independence in 1776; they "were to liberty, what a grammar is to language: they define its parts of speech, and practically construct them into syntax." The citizen's duty was to avoid corruption and to defeat kings and aristocrats, that class of "No-ability" (*RM*, 191, 45, 49, 46, 140, 95, 106).

In other words, in good Lockean terms, the people were citizens, not subjects. They gave their consent to those who governed them only when they had a hand in creating the government: "The first thing is, that a nation has a right to establish a constitution." The English people had gotten this backward by allowing their kings and aristocrats to dominate everything at the expense of the people and their interests. Meanwhile, the French people reversed the English mode of governance by demolishing the chains in which kings and nobles had bound them. First, they created a new national assembly, which was "strictly speaking the personal social compact—The members of it are the delegates of the nation in its *original* character." This assembly represented the collective nature of the people in a social contract for the first time since they had risen from their state of nature to begin the process of achieving the general will. They gathered in assembly to begin the process of constitution making. The next step was to create the form of their first elected government, with "delegates of the nation in its *organized* character" (*RM,* 191, 72). Once the constitution and the form of government were set, the people would then be ready to make laws according to the principles set forth in the written document.

Paine next addressed the question of how to limit government, and here he drew directly on Rousseau's notion of popular sovereignty. For Rousseau, the people were the natural rulers of their own selves, but they could join together in a social compact to form a society in which they would build a government based on a common set of goals. "Sovereignty is indivisible, for the same reason that it is inalienable," said Rousseau, "for either the will is general, or it is not. It is the will of either the people as a whole or of only a part. In the first case, this declared will is an act of sovereignty and constituted law. In the second case, it is merely a private will, or an act of magistracy."[43] For Paine as for Rousseau, nature grants to the people the right to reign over their own affairs, and there that right shall stay because the people "are the fountain of power."[44]

The key to limiting government is the representative system. Allow the people to invest themselves in government decision-making through elections, ensuring that the best people emerge victorious, and do not encroach on the people's rights and liberties. Moreover, the offices and departments of government that the constitution created will not become subject to the will of the other branches of government in a system of checks and balances and separation of powers. For Paine, "the representative system takes society and civilization for its basis; nature, reason, and experience, for its guide" (*RM,* 175). Representation, the idea that a well-informed citizen can choose, through elections, someone to *re-present* himself in an assembly to make laws on his behalf, is a position that Paine strongly favored throughout his political career. He worked hard as an elected deputy to the French National Convention, especially as a member of the committee charged with drafting the constitution for new republican France, to achieve this goal.[45] Although, as we have seen, his preference was for a unicameral legislature, the precise form of the republic, which he described in its classical expression as the *res publica*—meaning the political configurations that could best achieve the good of all or the common good—should be left to the people to decide (178).[46]

While the House of Lords was clearly hereditary, even the Commons took on this characteristic because the English government from 1716 on had mandated seven-year intervals between elections. Thus, frequent elections were the only way in which legislators could with certainty pass "the wisest laws, by collecting wisdom from where it can be found. I smile to myself when I contemplate the ridiculous insignificance into which literature and all the sciences would sin, were they made hereditary; and I carry the same idea into government," because "when we are planning for posterity, we ought to remember that virtue is not hereditary. . . . neither is it perpetual" (*RM*, 176, *CS*, 110, 120). Paine's faith in the common man's ability to make political decisions was not shared by all of his contemporary Americans. It is no surprise that many Americans argued for restrictive property qualifications, including James Madison, who told Jefferson in 1786 that he saw "no reason why the rights of property which chiefly bears the burden of Government & is so much an object of Legislation should not be respected as well as personal rights in the choice of Rulers."[47]

But Paine would have none of it, and he surveyed the world in 1791 to determine just where the best republican governments were located. He concluded that at that time only the Americans had successfully created a good republic, based "wholly on the system of representation. . . . Its government has no other object than the public business [the common good] of the nation, and therefore it is properly a republic." The Americans understood what a democracy was as the foundation of the republic, but they feared using the word, which was regarded as a synonym for mob rule. They achieved a democratic order by "ingrafting representation upon democracy" to "arrive at a system of government capable of embracing and confederating all the various interests and every extent of territory and population" (*RM*, 178–79, 180). It was not simple democracy, therefore, which he, like Rousseau, argued was only applicable to a very small state, but rather a representative democracy constituted within the large American republic.[48] But even as he argued that no republic would ever have a king, for after all "kings will go out of fashion as conjurors did," when the question arose as to what fate Louis XVI should face in revolutionary France, Paine developed a theory that distinguished the man from the king.[49]

A KING AND A MAN

Reason, revolution, and the rights of man were all handmaidens in the struggle to achieve global political and social progress. With the fall of the French monarchy and the rise of a democratic republic, Paine had to confront the problem he had long avoided, namely, to make an interesting, though perhaps spurious, distinction between Louis XVI and George III, even while he continued to attack monarchy as a noxious political institution. Both Louis and George were kings, yes, but Louis was never the "Brute of France" as George was the "Brute of Britain." During Louis's trial in January 1793, Paine found one "palliative" measure that should have caused the National Convention, which served as Louis's trial venue, to spare the king's life. Louis's support of the new United States in 1778 "enabled [the Americans] to shake off the unjust and tyrannical yoke of Britain." Although France herself was ruled by "a monarchical organ," it was led by a man who "certainly performed a good, a great action."[50] Besides, Louis Capet, as Paine now preferred to call him, had agreed to sweeping changes brought on by the events of July 14, 1789, though Paine knew that Louis had no choice. In Paine's mind, George III would never have agreed to these changes. Louis Capet should, therefore, definitely face trial for having committed conspiracy with the "crowned brigands" of Europe when, in June 1791, he and Marie Antoinette fled Paris to join French royalist forces and Austrian troops in an effort to re-establish his absolute rule. "There was formed among the crowned brigands of Europe a conspiracy which threatened not only French liberty, but likewise that of all nations. Everything tends to the belief that Louis XVI was the partner of this horde of conspirators."[51]

Paine claimed that the fault lay not with Louis Capet but with the institution of monarchy itself. While Louis Capet was personally in the dock, monarchy as an institution was itself on trial. "I voted that Louis should be tried," he told the Convention, "because it was necessary to afford proofs to the world of the perfidy, corruption and abomination of the monarchical system. The infinity of evidence that has been produced exposes them in the most glaring and hideous colors; thence it results that monarchy, whatever form it may assume, arbitrary or otherwise, becomes necessarily a center round which are united every species of corruption, and the kingly trade is no less destructive of all morality in the human breast, than the trade of an executioner is destructive of its sensibility."[52] He went on to say that "the natural moderation of Louis XVI," unlike the fevered responses of George III concerning American intransigence, "contributed nothing to alter the hereditary despotism of the monarchy" (*RM*, 47). A world of difference distinguished the man from his office: "I am inclined to believe that if Louis Capet had been born in obscure condition, had he lived within the circle of an amiable and respectable neighborhood, at liberty to practise the duties of domestic life, had he been thus situated, I cannot believe that he would have shown himself destitute of social virtues." The question was not simply what should be done with the *king*, whom he considered to have abdicated his throne when he attempted to flee Paris to join royalist forces and who was captured in Varennes in 1791 and returned to Paris. The question was, "What is to be done with this *man?*"[53]

Paine concluded that Louis Capet the man was innocent because the Constituent Assembly in 1791 was more at fault than the king: it had essentially committed the "crime" of restoring him to the throne one month after the king and queen's forced return to the capital. The assembly should have instead proclaimed a republic at that moment, as Paine himself had argued at the time in his essay "A Republican Manifesto," which he had plastered all over the walls of Paris.[54] Rather than face execution, therefore, Louis Capet should be banished to America, a highly innovative proposal. There, he would be "far removed from the miseries and crimes of loyalty. . . . I submit this also as a man, who, although the enemy of kings, cannot forget that they are subject to human frailties. I support my proposition as a citizen of the French Republic because it appears to me the best, the most politic measure that can be adopted."[55] Paine's advice was ignored. The ballot favoring clemency was defeated by one vote, and the king faced the guillotine. Paine rose to plead: "I beg you to delay the execution. Do not, I beseech you, bestow upon the English tyrant the satisfaction of learning that the man who helped America, the land of my love, to burst her fetters, has died on the scaffold."[56]

Paine here lost both the battle and the war. He had devised a theory that distinguished George III, who had no rights and who was a despicable brute, from Louis Capet, who did the right thing by the Americans and who was a mere man. In consequence of the developing events of the French Revolution, Paine formulated a sophisticated theory of rights just as he began to see the potentially ominous consequences of the power of the permanent revolution. His principles were thus as powerful as they were universal. "A Nation has at all times an inherent indefeasible right to abolish any form of Government it finds inconvenient, and establish such as accords with its interest, disposition, and happiness"—where, as he famously wrote, "*everything* may be looked for" in this, our age of revolutions (*RM*, 143, 145, emphasis added). And this revolution included not only radical political reformation but economic, social, and financial transformations as well.

CHAPTER 5

FROM A "HAMILTONIAN" SPIRIT
TO PUBLIC WELFARE

A STRONG ECONOMY based on a vigorous and vibrant commerce was, for Paine, the financial handmaiden of the democratic republic. Once revolution successfully transformed politics by destroying monarchical government and replacing the autocratic state with democratic institutions guaranteeing individual rights and liberty, the nation could then develop new social and economic policies to ensure the financial security of its citizens. Underlying Paine's vision of a muscular commercial republic rested a spirit that might best be termed *Hamiltonian,* though I make this claim with several caveats.[1]

First, we have no evidence that Paine and Hamilton ever met, and Paine seems never to have mentioned Hamilton by name. On the other hand, they might well have encountered each other at Washington's headquarters during the Revolution, when Hamilton served as the general's wartime adjutant and when Paine spent so much time in the general's camp. But those encounters, if indeed they ever took place, would have been long before Hamilton published his major writings on politics, the judiciary, and economics. Paine left America in 1787 and was gone for the next fifteen years, while Hamilton flourished in the Washington administration, serving as the first secretary of the treasury of the United States at the age of thirty-two. If they did not meet at Washington's camp, they could have been introduced sometime between the end of the hostilities in 1781, after Paine returned from his mission to France with John Laurens, and the spring of 1787, when he left America. No extant document suggests, however, that they ever met.

Admittedly, substantial risk accompanies the search for parallels in the financial and economic thought of Paine and Hamilton. The two men had acute disagreements over basic political and social policy, though both were ardent opponents of slavery. "Who talk most about liberty and equality?" asked Hamilton. "Is it not those who hold the bill of rights in one hand and a whip for affrighted slaves in the other?"[2] He could hardly have better echoed Dr. Johnson's famous wry remark on learning that the Americans desired to separate from so-called British tyranny. "If slavery be thus fatally contagious, how is it we hear the loudest yelps for liberty among the drivers of negroes?"[3] Surprisingly, given his love of human freedom and human rights and his known opposition to slavery, Paine did not write very much about African slavery or the slave trade, with the exception of his 1775 essays in the *Pennsylvania Journal* and a few later asides in essays and pamphlets. Still, the slave market, which he witnessed daily outside his Philadelphia residence, must have appalled him. He called slaveholders and slave traders "men stealers," "so the slave, who is the proper owner of his freedom, has a right to reclaim it," if he could.[4]

Beyond their agreement about a powerful commercial republic without slavery, the gap in the ideological persuasions of Hamilton and Paine is as cavernous as the gulf that opens between two warring nations. As a staunch advocate of executive authority, Hamilton advocated the theory of the unitary executive, which holds that the president of the United States is an independent policymaker whose decisions are unrestrained by Congress or the courts.[5] An annoyed Jefferson wrote, clearly out of pique, that Hamilton's fascination with executive power, especially along the lines of the British model, was so great that he "was not only a monarchist, but for a monarchy bottomed on corruption," favoring "a hereditary king with a house of lords & commons, corrupted to his will, and standing between him and the people."[6] Paine's view is quite different, given his support, as we have seen, of a powerful single-house legislature and a very weak executive, whose only task was to enforce laws passed by the assembly. Or, as the Constitution has it in Article II, the president's main power shall be to "take care that the laws be faithfully executed." Hamilton, like Adams, did in fact greatly admire the English government and its financial system. He thought the framers of the American constitution had successfully modeled their new republic on Britain, with its three-part division of power. Paine, as we have seen, detested the English government, its system of finance, and its division of power into two lawmaking bodies. It was a wretched despotism, and its financial system was a recipe for continuous war and inevitable bankruptcy. He hailed the new French government(s)—both of them, given that two constitutions were drafted in 1791 and 1793, each with a single-house legislature.[7]

Other matters separated Paine from Hamilton ideologically. Hamilton believed in a large standing army, whereas Paine believed in the classical model of the citizen-soldier militia accompanied by a strong navy. Militias were sufficient if accompanied by a navy made up of swift gunboats to defend against attacks from across the ocean. Hamilton thought a large army was necessary to fend off potential attacks by the British in Canada, the Spanish in the south, Indians in the west, and possibly the French in the East. Because of his advocacy of a standing professional army—including his active leadership of one raised by President Adams in the quasi-war against France in 1798—Jefferson called Hamilton "our Buonaparte," and even Abigail Adams referred to him as "a second Buonaparty."[8]

In addition, Hamilton believed, contrary to Jefferson, in the importance of an independent judicial system, which, at its supreme level, had the authority to overturn laws it deemed violated the Constitution. In contrast, Paine never developed a mature theory of the judiciary, though he never criticized the independent judiciary created in Article III of the U.S. Constitution. Then again, Article III is so vague that it seems almost to have been an afterthought of the delegates, who devoted most of their time and energy in the summer of 1787 to considering how best to form the Congress. The result was, of course, the so-called Great Compromise, with a popularly elected, democratic House of Representatives based on population and an undemocratic Senate, with two members from each state, no matter its geographical or demographic size.[9]

While Hamilton saw himself as a defender of wealth and capital as the foundation for the ruling class, Paine believed his calling was to help those who were voiceless and poor. Even so, their economic policies were remarkably similar inasmuch as they both hailed republican government as the best guardian of the social class they principally supported. In other words, their economic and financial policies look curiously analogous, even though they used them to achieve entirely different social goals.

Both Hamilton and Paine were city men, despite Hamilton's early life as a boy on his native island of Nevis in the Caribbean and Paine's in the small English village of Thetford. As an adult, Paine is associated with the great cities of Philadelphia, London, and Paris, where he resided for long periods of time, and Hamilton mainly with New York, though also with Philadelphia between 1790 and 1795, when the U.S. capital was temporarily located there. So influential were both men as statesmen and writers in urban areas that their shared perspective of the world underlay the many parallels in their economic theory. For the democratic republic to flourish in a competitive world, they therefore agreed that it had to possess the following:

- A national commercial system based on a strong financial foundation
- A strong, yet fair, system of taxation to ensure the stability of the republic
- A strong military force, though Hamilton favored the army, Paine the navy
- A powerful banking system as the financial mainstay of the commercial republic

One major difference between the two men is that Paine's writings on economics and finance are fairly scattered, whereas Hamilton wrote four major reports as secretary of the treasury in the very short period between 1790 and 1791: one each on the public debt, the bank, the mint, and manufactures. In any event, the sections of Paine's essays and pamphlets that he devoted to the economy demonstrate his sophisticated thinking about economic and financial matters.

PAINE'S HAMILTONIAN SPIRIT

Each of the above-named essential principles may be briefly sum-marized. First, both Paine and Hamilton hailed the benefits of a strong commercial republic. Literally and figuratively, Hamilton was the quintessential Wall Street lawyer with a commercial law practice located in Manhattan. As secretary of the treasury, he fa-vored an integrated economy that supported the manufacturing and the mercantile classes. His 1791 report on manufacturing dis-tinguished his economic plan from the rural, agricultural econ-omy that Jefferson promoted, with its emphasis on yeomen farm-ers as the most virtuous citizens in the republic.[10] Paine agreed with Hamilton that America's future lay in commerce and man-ufacturing, not just agriculture. Banks, factories, stock exchanges, trade, and industry, all of which were anti-Jeffersonian and looked upon with suspicion by classical republicans, made Ham-ilton the most articulate capitalist theorist of his time. England was, he believed, America's natural trading partner, with up to half its exports and three-quarters of its imports.[11] Unlike Ham-ilton, Paine based his desire for a financially powerful republic on his egalitarian principles. Because he believed that a wealthy commonwealth helped the poor escape poverty, he "combined a political outlook of intense egalitarianism with a devotion to free enterprise, commercial expansion and national economic devel-opment."[12] He departed, in short, from Hamilton's adulation of the powerful and the wealthy. He was also more skeptical of the role England would play in the years following the American Revolution, but he certainly applauded the idea of America de-veloping powerful commercial relations with the nations of Eu-rope, commenting that commerce, "well attended to, will secure us the peace and friendship of all of Europe" (*CS*, 86). He even held that a solid world commercial exchange might well bring everlasting peace to the globe: "If commerce were permitted to act to the universal extent it is capable, it would extirpate the system of war, and produce a revolution in the uncivilized state of governments" (*RM*, 212). He envisioned America launching itself onto the world stage as "one imperial Commonwealth," using for the word *commonwealth* the original Latin: the *res publica,* or the common good.[13]

Second, Hamilton, like Paine, thought that a fair tax system best promoted the general welfare. Hamilton proposed a method designed to pay down the debt that accrued during the Revolution over a long time in a controlled way. He advocated permanent and numerous taxes, which he hoped would be increased as the government needed. In this way, the citizens' ties to the new nation would be most successfully cemented. Hamilton's excise tax on wine and spirits is a good example of his policies designed to place government on a stable financial footing and at the same time eventually eliminate the debt. Unfortunately, it led to the upheaval in 1794 in Western Pennsylvania he later called the Whiskey Rebellion, when distillers rose up against the levy.[14] The rebels claimed that they had fought against British-imposed taxes without their consent in the Revolution and that now their own new federal government was emulating their former British overlords. America's first "sin" tax may well have been this tax on wine and spirits. Paine, too, advocated taxes, especially import duties. These, as it turned out, were the sole source of revenue for the new nation until the Constitution was ratified in 1788. Until then, the new government had to rely on the states' financial largess to fund its programs. To take one example, in 1783, Paine wrote a series of letters to persuade the leaders of Rhode Island to support a bill in Congress that levied a 5 percent duty on imported goods.[15] To Paine's anger, Rhode Island refused.[16]

Third, Hamilton, like Paine and indeed Washington, was appalled at the poor performance of the state militias during the Revolution.[17] Paine and Jefferson favored small, swift gunboats as the foundation of American security, thinking that America's distance from England and Europe accounted for the best protection of its America's commercial interests. Hamilton's solution was by far more ambitious, namely, the creation of a peacetime standing army, an institution that directly opposed the classical republican theory of citizen armies or militias: standing armies were dangerous engines of oppression in that they could easily be turned by their leaders on the citizenry. Hamilton was actually willing to use the army on at least two occasions: the Whiskey Rebellion and the Quasi-War with France. To put down the rebellion, Hamilton persuaded Washington to raise an army of some 13,000 men, which he hoped to keep in place afterward. He even persuaded Washington to lead it. Washington thus became the first and only president in American history to lead an army into battle. Hamilton prevailed upon him, however, to return to Philadelphia when they arrived in Harrisburg. Hamilton then led the troops from there into the west.[18]

Three years later, just after the XYZ Affair, in 1797, when American ambassadors failed to negotiate a settlement with France over French attacks on American shipping, Hamilton advocated the creation of a 50,000-man standing army to attack France. President Adams agreed, and he appointed the aging Washington as its commander, and Washington, to John Adams's dismay, chose Hamilton as his major general and second in command.[19] This spectacle caused Adams to remark that Hamilton was "the most restless, impatient, indefatigable and unprincipled intriguer in the United States, if not the world to be second in command under himself."[20] Hamilton later went further, suggesting that the United States should send a standing army to seize Florida, Louisiana, and parts of South America: "We ought certainly to look to the possession of the Floridas and Louisiana [then owned by Spain, an ally of France] and we ought to squint at South America." At one point, he even began to help General Francisco del Miranda, a friend whom Paine inspired to liberate his native Venezuela from Spain. Hamilton planned an army of 12,000 troops, with himself at the head to supplement Miranda's forces. "The command in this case would very naturally fall upon me and I hope I should disappoint no favourable anticipation."[21]

Fourth, both Paine and Hamilton favored the creation of a central bank. For Hamilton, a bank rationalized American finances. He first considered it during the Revolution, when inflation was rampant, driving the new United States toward bankruptcy.[22] He later helped create the Bank of New York, which exists today, and in 1791 the Bank of the United States, which triggered one of the first great speculation scandals in the country when his cronies controlled a majority of seats on the board. Hamilton's goal was to link the most powerful and wealthiest to the government so that they would develop a personal stake in its success. His plan went awry when speculators drove up the price and then unloaded the stock for a profit, leaving smaller shareholders holding the bag. The result was one of the first depressions in the new nation, the Panic of 1792. Hamilton failed to see it coming and was appalled when it arrived, although he saw no relationship between the panic and his financial policies. In support of his actions, he wrote twenty essays, using nine pseudonyms, which appeared in various publications. In the meantime, the states set up local banks on their own, in competition with the federal bank. Instead of short-term loans going to the moneyed interests, they lent long term to farmers, artisans, and craftsmen, creating a source of capitalist investment that Hamilton also supported. Paine also supported a national bank when he strongly supported the Bank of North America during the Revolution.

Finally, both Paine and Hamilton advocated a funded national debt, which, they believed, promoted economic growth. As early as *Common Sense,* Paine supported a reasonable national debt, financially suitable to the new nation and the exact opposite of England's debt, which was so big it was bankrupting that nation. As for Hamilton, the first great debate over the debt occurred at the end of the American Revolution, when the discussion focused on the underpaid and unpaid American soldiers: Hamilton supported speculators, known by his enemies as Hamilton's "paper aristocrats," who had purchased IOUs from veterans at ten cents on the dollar. Opposing him were Madison and Jefferson, who supported the soldiers' interests, arguing that the debt should be split between veterans and speculators. Although the debt did decline, the revenues that funded it had little to do with Hamilton's policies. The nation's income grew because of the huge English demand for American grain and cotton once war had broken out in Europe in 1793, after the execution of Louis XVI.[23]

Paine's very first experience in writing about economic issues did not focus on America but rather on the salaries of his fellow excise tax collectors. His 1772 address to Parliament advocating increased compensation for them stimulated his ongoing support for the financial needs of the less fortunate. He commented, for example, in the *Rights of Man,* that in nations governed by hereditary princes, "when we see age going to the workhouse and youth to the gallows, something must be wrong in the system of government." He then asked, "Why is it that scarcely any are executed but the poor?" He knew that the answer proved "the wretchedness of their condition," a condition that only the entire nation working together, not a corrupt government, could overcome (218). These governments, like that of England, would fail to act every time. After all, he had himself had firsthand experience with English negligence when he requested a small increase in wages on behalf of his fellow excise men.

A Polite, Radical Request

Despite its polite tone, Paine's 1772 address to Parliament was unusually radical for its time: men organizing to demand wage increases by the established political order on its own turf, in Parliament itself. The tract took him to London for the third time in his life, only now with a mission far more critical than his earlier two experiences, when he had been seeking work, attending scientific lectures, or meeting Franklin. Paine's colleagues in the service had specifically urged him to represent them with the hope that his powerful words and personality would persuade the Commons to increase their wages. As we have seen from his Lewes experience, Paine was respected as a highly informed and well-known political debater and orator. He was their logical choice. From their annual salary of £50, the men of the excise service could ill afford to pay for the basic necessities of life, everything from grooming, feeding, and housing their horses to lodging and feeding their families, and paying the expenses of clothing and charitable contributions as well as the costs of moving when they received orders to relocate. Aside from collecting taxes, the job itself was inherently dangerous because the duties of the excise men required them to identify and confront smugglers. Armed only with their writing instruments and paper, they rode alone throughout the countryside on lonely roads for miles at a stretch in all kinds of weather and sometimes late into the night. Smugglers knew that if they were caught, the penalty was hanging, so they were certain to be armed and were fearless when they came upon excise men, who demanded either the tax or the goods.

Even the collectors in urban areas who had no need of a horse (the "footwalks" vs. the "outrides") could not meet their living expenses because the cost of living in the cities was higher than in rural areas. Paine figured that the actual wage was really £32 a year after the men paid their basic expenses, or, as he put it, "one shilling and ninepence farthing a day." It is no wonder that corruption, collusion, and neglect resulted; some taxmen accepted tips or bribes, others let batches of goods like tea, tobacco, or brandy slip through without payment or perhaps only a partial one. Fraud was ironically part of the men's empowerment, a result of "the temptations of downright poverty." Because they were so poor, it was as if they were slaves of the government. It was hardly surprising that cheating was rampant. Outriders relied on friends and family to "keep their children from nakedness, supply them occasionally with perhaps half a hog, a load of wood, a chaldron *[sic]* of coals, or something or other which abates the severity of their distress."[24] Meantime, the English excise collected £5 million a year for the Crown, surely enough to allow for a modest salary increase for men who deserved a living wage. The current rate was outrageous to those who believed that the differences between rich and poor were as natural as the sunrise and sunset. Paine's appeal amounted to an amazing demand, given that this was long before organized labor insisted on collective bargaining.[25]

While Paine's address was radical insofar as it anticipated labor movement demands one hundred years later, ironically, it was not revolutionary. Paine challenged neither British authority nor its structure nor its hierarchy, but he rooted his language in soft pleadings and polite terms. William Lee, Paine's printer friend in Lewes, might well have helped him draft the appeal. In any event, Lee printed four thousand copies of the pamphlet, which Paine and others distributed to members of Parliament, the electors, the excise men themselves, and their supporters. All expenses of printing and Paine's trip were paid for by subscription: almost every excise man in England, some three thousand of them, each chipped in three shillings, but it was to no avail. When Parliament refused to acknowledge the problems and dismissed the appeal, Paine returned home to find he had been discharged from the service for having left his position without permission.

Still, in terms of the origins of collective bargaining, the address is a remarkable piece of work for its time and, perhaps more importantly, for Paine, who after 1792 remained fully engaged in economic issues and social causes, not solely political and religious issues. These include his Hamiltonian-like support of a national bank and a national debt as the foundation for a strong commercial democratic republic.

THE NATIONAL DEBT AND THE BANK OF NORTH AMERICA

While *Common Sense* advocated America's separation from England, it also contained an underlying economic and commercial doctrine, noteworthy for its modern approach to how the national debt might enhance the Americans' future financial growth and stability. In a section entitled "Of the Present Ability of America, with Some Miscellaneous Reflexions," Paine set forth his theory, surprising to some in his own time and in ours, that a national debt had a positive economic impact on America. Like Hamilton's later support for a funded debt, Paine wrote that "debts we have none; and whatever we may contract on this account will serve as *a glorious memento of our virtue*" (*CS*, 101, emphasis added). In raising the issue in terms of virtue, Paine placed himself squarely in the midst of the debate over the emerging science of political economy, which sought to determine how politics and even culture affected the economic and financial arrangements of society. The ideas underlying political economy had their roots in the economic theories of several Scots, especially Scottish philosophers Adam Smith and David Hume, and also of Edmund Burke, who outlined many of his ideas of economics and finance in his *Reflections*.[26]

Paine understood, as did they, that the economy at the end of the century was undergoing vast changes.[27] He had witnessed these changes himself while in England during his various wanderings around the country and in his visits to London. Now residing in America, he accepted the new doctrine that there was an unalterable link between political progress and economic growth as the new nation had to rely increasingly on a commercial, manufacturing economy, rather than an agrarian one, to support itself. In Britain, this view was highly politicized. The Whig governments in control of the ministry throughout the last half of the century promoted the exchange of paper money over hard species, the expansion of public credit over agrarian development, a large national debt and a powerful national bank to oversee it as a budding middle-class developed its values about the virtue of savings and frugality, industriousness and thrift. Paine agreed with the development of most of these ideas, with the exception of the expansion of public credit and the printing of paper currency, which he vigorously opposed because, like society, which is natural, and government, which is an artifice, "gold and silver are the emissions of nature; paper is the emission of art."[28] He once said that any legislator advocating the production of paper money should be executed.[29] Still, given his support of a commercially powerful nation based on banks and a debt, Paine placed himself directly at odds with his intellectual brethren like Jefferson in America and Priestley in England. In contrast to Paine and Hamilton, they railed against these measures as useful only to those who advocated large professional standing military establishments, which promoted imperial designs at the expense of the people.[30]

The new political economy served as a key, if not *the* key, to the increasing power of monarchy and aristocracy. Burke, for example, was a major theorist of the new political economic thought. While Hume in 1776, the year of his death, became skeptical about large national debts, writing that it might well bankrupt England if the nation kept up its expensive military policies, Burke did not question the rise of the new imperial financial structure.[31] As J. G. A. Pocock tells us, Burke was "a defender of Whig aristocratic government. . . . Whig government was identified with the growth of commercial society . . . [and] Burke saw the Revolution as a challenge to the Whig order, arising within the conditions that order made possible; and . . . he employed the language and categories of political economy in order to analyse the revolutionary threat and respond to it."[32] Unlike Burke, Paine declined to employ his economic ideas to support the old regime of titles, rank, and privilege, but for precisely opposite reasons. He advocated a sound economy that promoted his political agenda, a government based on human rights and liberties. The republic's firmest foundation, he believed, rested not only on the rights of man but also on practical considerations of how a strong financial foundation allowed everyone to flourish. In this way, internal strife, or what Marx later called class war, would be avoided.

Paine's argument was simple, but not simplistic. He favored the growth of the national debt and a national bank, the two elements that seemingly placed him in the Burkean camp and at the same time pitted him against the classical republican opposition to Crown and Court.[33] When Paine advocated a system of economic growth, the development of a national debt, the rise of banks, and a muscular commercial republic, he became an economic innovator. He thus rewrote the text on classical-republican virtue in his section on economics in *Common Sense*. Historically, the virtuous citizen in classical-republican thought was the independent yeoman, the debt-free farmer, not the man of commerce, banks, or manufacturing, who believed the nation prospered best as wealth accumulated via trade and industry along with the growth of a large national debt. In his great pamphlet, he said that "no nation should be without a national debt. A national debt is a national bond." But this was not to be a debt for debt's sake, like that of Britain, which came into being through costly and unjustified wars. Such a debt was unworthy of the legacy America would leave to posterity, its written constitution and independent legislators, whom the people trusted. A national debt advanced republican ideals of freedom and justice to help place the new republic on a firm financial footing. To do otherwise was to use "posterity with the utmost cruelty" because future generations would be saddled with huge debt and left without liberty or rights. "Such a thought is unworthy of a man of honor," he said, "and is the true characteristic of a narrow heart and a pedling *[sic]* politician."

Commerce, like the debt, provided the foundation for the economic and financial health of America.[34] A commercial nation worked especially well in combination with a navy that would be "worth more than it cost: And is that nice point in national policy, in which commerce and protection are united" (*CS*, 103). That nation would be financially robust when it was based on commercial achievements that provided protection to the republic in a dangerous world. Even if defeated in the American war, Britain would remain a powerful enemy, and for that reason future British policy toward America would never be trustworthy. Unlike Hamilton, who thought England was America's natural trading partner, Paine thought the Americans should look elsewhere. "Some, perhaps, will say, that after we have made it up with Britain, she will protect us. Can we be so unwise as to mean, that she shall keep a navy in our harbours for that purpose? Common sense will tell us, that the power which hath endeavored to subdue us, is of all others the most improper to defend us. Conquest may be effected under the pretence of friendship; and ourselves, after a long and brave resistance, be at last cheated into slavery" (105).

This was not necessarily commerce in a bourgeois key, as Isaac Kramnick tells us, but commerce designed to foster national and economic security and a public spirit in the new nation.[35] "To unite the sinews of commerce and defence is sound policy," but only in a young country that must unite first to fight Britain and then remain united once the war ended: "Our concord hath withstood our troubles, and fixes a memorable æra for posterity to glory in" (108). Economic strength meant that America could overcome the ravages of the hereditary system and establish "the noblest, purest constitution on the face of the earth" (120). "No country on the globe is so happily situated, so internally capable of raising a fleet as America. Tar, timber, iron, and cordage are her natural produce. We need go abroad for nothing. . . . It is the best money we can lay out . . . for when our strength and our riches, play into each other's hand, we need fear no external enemy." The Americans now had the opportunity "*to begin government at the right end*," a comment Paine printed with emphasis (101–09).

This was why the Bank of North America was so important to him during the Revolutionary War, just as Hamilton later heralded the Bank of the United States in 1791. In light of Paine's advocacy of American independence, Alfred Owen Aldridge, one of the most prolific scholars of the life and thought of Thomas Paine, six decades ago posed the intriguing question, "Why did Thomas Paine write on the Bank?"[36] It seemed ironic to Aldridge that Paine endorsed a decidedly conservative, even Hamiltonian, mercantile institution and even went so far as to deposit his own money in it. Aldridge was concerned that some scholars had concluded that as the American Revolution was drawing to a close, Paine became increasingly conservative or, alternatively, so impoverished that he became the hired pen of financier Robert Morris, the bank's founder, and that he would write whatever Morris demanded of him, including support of a national bank. While he never did have much money of his own and often lived off the largess of his friends, Paine indeed wrote for Morris, but he made it crystal clear from the beginning that he would never write anything with which he disagreed, no matter the fee. To him, he told Morris, it is "a pleasure when men having the same public good in view, and capable, according to their several talents, to promote it, come to understand and place confidence in each other."[37] He had no problem promoting the bank for America's strong commercial future stability because he truly believed that it was a much-needed financial institution.

Paine's views on the bank, like those on the debt, were based on his political, not his economic, views. After all, the controversy over the bank, with Paine siding with Morris and other wealthy men, pitted his normal constituency of backcounty farmers and urban artisans against city financiers and manufacturers: the Pennsylvania Assembly, controlled by the former, was in the process of repealing the bank's charter, though the bank continued to exist under congressional authority, while at the same moment the Assembly voted a stipend of £500 for Paine as compensation for his blistering war commentary. When Paine found himself caught between his assemblymen benefactors and their opposition to an institution that he thought was crucial, he feared the dispute over the bank's future was a sign of class squabbles that threatened to undermine the infant republic.[38] In vigorously supporting the bank, he tried to deflect this problem by showing his lower- and middle-class allies that the bank was not an institution they should fear; it was one that would help create a strong, secure financial foundation for their own and the republic's future commercial stability.

The national bank and a debt achieved three goals: they stabilized America's emerging economy; they helped energize the financial foundation of the constitutional government that would arise from the ruins of Britain's American colonial holdings; and they brought a sense of national unity to the people, who until now had inhabited a hopelessly divided nation. Paine rearticulated these same themes twenty years later, when he argued that America's experience applied to all of Europe. As he had written in the *Rights of Man* that the age of revolution was upon us, he argued in 1796, in *The Decline and Fall of the English System of Finance*, that with the emergence of the new French republic, England would be the next nation to experiment with republican government and, along with it, the renovation of its economic system. Unlike the American debt, which had its roots in the commercial growth and political unity of the nation, the English debt had ballooned because the Crown and its ministry had insisted on going to war throughout the century against other major European nations to increase its imperial power. Citing Adam Smith as his source, Paine noted that from 1697 to 1793 the debt had risen from £2.5 million to £400 million sterling, that is, by a phenomenal 16,000 percent. The only conceivable reason for this growth was that England had been engaged in six major wars since 1689: the War of the Grand Alliance (or Nine Years War), which ended in 1697; the 1702 War of the Spanish Succession; the 1739 War of the Austrian Succession; the 1756 Seven Years War; the American Revolutionary War, which he said actually began in 1775; and the French Revolutionary Wars, which had been ongoing since 1793.[39]

Paine's conclusion was pithy: "Is there a man so mad, so stupid, as to suppose this system can continue?" He predicted the collapse of the system, claiming it was "on the verge, nay even the gulf of bankruptcy" because the Bank of England was unable to service the debt.[40] Paine was almost on target when he argued that the government could pay nothing on the debt's interest, much less the principal: the interest alone, he accurately figured, was £128 million per year.[41] He fervently hoped that a bankrupt system would fuel change in England. It was not merely a matter of moving money around to reduce the debt or its high interest; the crushing debt also fed inflation, which hurt the common people. As the government issued more paper currency, the price of goods and services and interest rates on loans increased.

Those in the lower and middle classes discovered that they had to pay more to acquire fewer goods, and financiers and manufacturers, who held bank notes, soon found that they received no return on them.

As it was, Paine's prediction of economic collapse was unfulfilled, although the Bank of England momentarily stopped converting bank notes into hard specie in 1797.[42] Paine had underestimated the strength and resiliency of imperial Britain both on the sea and in its foreign intrigues, and he continued to predict that "the government of England is in a state of bankruptcy and her total downfall is probable."[43] Unlike his advocacy of the Bank of North America, an institution that remained a private entity throughout its short existence, the Bank of England, founded in 1694, was a public corporation that the English government completely controlled, thus creating an unholy alliance that forced the Bank to do whatever the government wanted it to do. "This is the connection that threatens to ruin every public bank. It is through this connection that the credit of a bank is forced far beyond what it ought to be, and still further beyond its ability to pay. It is through this connection that such an immense redundant quantity of bank notes have gotten into circulation; and which, instead of being issued because there was property in the bank, have been issued because there was none."[44] This attack on public credit and paper currency was among the most devastating of the century: while America and France now had the opportunity to create a new system of finance and commerce benefiting their people, England soon would as well. Paine was, of course, again wrong. But he was undeterred, forcefully arguing that his audience—in England and throughout Europe—could still achieve social and economic transformations, as well as political change, through revolutionary social reform. It is here that he parted company with Hamilton and the Hamiltonian spirit.

SOCIAL RIGHTS AND PRIVILEGES, ECONOMIC DEVELOPMENT

The primary target of Paine's first part of the *Rights of Man* was Edmund Burke and his unsympathetic examination of the revolution in France. Burke's presence in part 2 is hardly discernible. This time Paine merely let loose sharp barbs about why Burke never bothered to respond directly to his first installment. Burke had moaned about the demise of the age of chivalry and rise of the economists, and he should know, because he had displayed his rudeness by remaining silent. Paine preferred "to take the public for my guide (and the world knows I am not a flatterer) that what they do not think worthwhile to read, is not worth mine to answer" (*RM*, 155). So as Burke had done to Paine, Paine now ignored Burke and turned to the social and economic spheres, devising new social services to provide financial help to the less fortunate in society. Although he continued to promote global revolution in the second part of the *Rights of Man*, he also broadened his focus to demand action centered on the financial difficulties and social struggles faced by individuals subjected to the economic control of an autocratic minority. Because the common man never worked to help himself and his family, but only for the enrichment of those who controlled his life, now was the time to reform society by creating a social welfare system—one that was not, in fact, developed until the twentieth century. Here, Paine focused on how best to ameliorate the miserable condition of those at the bottom ranks of society: the poor, the elderly, the young, and the newly married. Paine no longer concentrated solely on individual rights and liberties, which from *Common Sense* to the first part of the *Rights of Man* account for the main themes of his political thought. Now he determined what responsibilities each individual owes to the larger community, to the nation, embodying the "general will" of the people, again echoing Rousseau's *Social Contract*. It is clear he had this work in mind when writing part 2.[45] Although the democratic republic is the form of government most open to his proposals, he thought that even monarchies could implement his ideas. Still, he remained skeptical about whether any monarch would do so. In any event, the statistics he used were from an English context, suggesting that even there, if Parliament were properly motivated and situated, his proposals would work.

Whether Paine actually read Rousseau's work on the general will and communitarian ideas is unclear and problematic, as it is with Locke and other writers. Paine never indicated what he read; instead, he mentioned the great writers only in passing. Just as he often cited Adam Smith's *Wealth of Nations* throughout his writings, so he cited Rousseau, not only in the *Rights of Man,* but in other essays as well, such as his "Essay for the Use of New Republicans in Their Opposition to Monarchy," published the same year as part 2 (1792): "What," he asked, "of those rulers who have no claim to ability, and who substitute for it the vices that seem inherent in Royalty?" His answer, he claimed, might be found in Rousseau. "We have the following description of them in the *Contrat Social* of J. J. Rousseau: 'the men who take the foremost place in monarchies are often simply base marplots, ordinary rogues, mean intriguers. The trivial intellectual qualities that have raised these people to high positions in courts but serve to make more apparent to the public their real insignificance.' In a word, the story of all monarchies supplies proof that, while monarchs do nothing, their ministers do nothing but evil."[46] Even if Paine never revealed a deep exposure to Rousseau's ideas, we might here accept Alfred Cobban's observation that "in a sense, it is true, the whole generation of 1789 was Rousseauist."[47]

Rousseau discussed communitarian concerns crucial to a social philosophy. Like Paine, Rousseau was concerned with the limits of political authority, asking whom to obey and to what extent. Certainly Locke had argued that human beings possess certain inalienable natural rights and liberties that require them to act when government infringes upon them. He articulated this principle in chapter 19 of *The Second Treatise of Government,* where he explained his notion of the right to revolution when tyranny threatened. But unlike Locke, who argued that the people's duty is to resist tyranny when their inalienable natural rights and individual liberties are threatened, Rousseau declined to define human beings as being isolated and atomized individuals. Once the people attach their individual will to the general will, they will understand and act on the needs of society. The people possess communal ties and national obligations.[48] Social action, mutual care, and collective nurturance are part of everyone's life. The general will forms the basis of the social contract, which binds society without destroying one's individual will. As Rousseau put it, the social contract is a form of association which defends and protects with all common forces the person and goods of each associate, and by means of which each one, while uniting with all, nevertheless obeys only himself and remains as free as before. . . . Each of us places his person and all his power in common under the supreme direction of the general will; and as one we receive each member as an indivisible part of the whole. At once, in place of the individual person of each contracting party, this act of association produces a moral and collective body composed of as many members as there are voices in the assembly, which receives from this same act its unity, its common *self,* its life and its will.[49]

As human beings entered the social contract, they understood that their individual, competitive selves were part of a greater, organic whole, like "cells in the human body," as Carol Blum has put it.[50] The people became good citizens when their particular interests merged with the interests of the nation, so the general will, for Rousseau, was essentially an ethical concept that promoted human virtue. Kant later referred to this as the categorical imperative, the ground of true freedom: men would in short be forced to be free, as Rousseau had it.[51]

In the second part of the *Rights of Man,* Paine viewed the general will almost in these precise terms, but he always looked first for the political foundation supporting his ideas.

The greatest forces that can be brought into the field of revolutions are reason and common interest. Where these can have the opportunity of acting, opposition dies with fear, or crumbles away by conviction. It is a great standing which they have now universally obtained; and we may hereafter hope to see revolutions, or changes in governments, produced with the same quiet operation by which any measure, determinable by reason and discussion, is accomplished. When a nation changes its opinion and habits of thinking, it is no longer to be governed as before; but it would not only be wrong, but bad policy, to attempt by force what ought to be accomplished by reason. Rebellion consists in forcibly opposing the general will of a nation, whether by a party or by a government. There ought, therefore, to be in every nation a method of occasionally ascertaining the state of public opinion with respect to government (265).

The general will, Paine thought, could be gauged by ascertaining the public's opinion, something Rousseau dismissed because public opinion and the general will are not one and the same. Attaching one's individual will to the general will is not coequal to what the public claims to think about a particular subject. Paine's approach was therefore far simpler than Rousseau's, although now, like Rousseau, Paine adopted a communitarian and national ideal. While he continued to believe in individual rights and liberties, as well as in Lockean categories of consent and political transformation, he now incorporated these Rousseauist ideals directly into the second part of the *Rights of Man* and *Agrarian Justice*.

First, a government that truly reflects the general will reduces or eliminates taxes on the poor, especially the working poor, and second, it develops a set of social services designed to ameliorate their impoverished condition. Public money "was not the product of riches only, but of the hard earnings of labor and poverty. It is drawn even from the bitterness of want and misery. Not a beggar passes, or perishes in the streets, whose mite is not in that mass" (*RM*, 237). Reducing the size of government is critical, but not at the expense of denying public assistance to those who feel poverty's sting. Paine now laid out, in rudimentary form, the basis for social welfare to alleviate the conditions of the poor and those unable to help themselves, such as young children and the elderly. He also emphasized at least twice that a government's duty to take care of its less fortunate citizens was not charity; it was not "a matter of grace and favour, but of right" (243), and then repeated those same words two paragraphs later.

Paine recommended that the government eliminate all taxes on poor people and increase them on the wealthy, clearly unlikely in a monarchy, where aristocrats paid no taxes at all. Then government must take the amount taxed, double it, and return it to the poor: "The first step . . . of practical relief, would be to abolish the poor rates entirely, and in lieu thereof, to make a remission of taxes to the poor of double the amount of the present poor rates, viz. four millions annually out of the surplus taxes" (*RM*, 240). Now, just who were these poor people Paine addressed? He had two classes in mind: large families with children and the elderly. He estimated that together they amounted to approximately 252,000 families in England. He recommended that for the first fourteen years of a child's life the family receive an annual allocation of £4 from the government, which would enable their parents to send their children to school. After all, he claimed, "it is from the expense [that families have] of bringing up children that their poverty arises." His goal was both to abolish poverty and to instill education at the same time: "Not only the poverty of the parents will be relieved, but ignorance will be banished from the rising generation, and the number of poor will hereafter become less, because their abilities, by the aid of education, will be greater" (241). In other words, his public assistance proposals included a public education system readily available to the entire population. While it was not free public education, it did allow parents to cover their costs by government financial support. As he put it, "education to be useful to the poor, should be on the spot; and the best method, I believe, to accomplish this, is to enable the parents to pay the expense themselves" (245n).

The national government would provide subsidies to local communities for the instruction of children, and each poor family would receive an annual amount of ten shillings per child to cover the costs of school and an additional half a crown each year for paper and spelling books. "A nation under a well-regulated government," Paine said, "should permit none to remain uninstructed" (*RM*, 245). Nor was this all; he knew, perhaps from his own personal experience of having two failed marriages, each lapsing into poverty, that newly married poor couples needed government assistance as well. These couples were to receive twenty shillings when they married and an additional twenty shillings for each child born to them, somewhat akin to today's income tax credit for dependent children. For the working poor who had to find employment far from home, he imagined a death benefit of £20,000 to cover the costs of their funerals. (Perhaps he had his former fellow taxmen in mind when he wrote this.)

An array of public employment jobs rounded out his proposals for the casual poor, that is, those temporarily out of work. He envisioned the English government constructing in its cities, especially in London, at least two "employment buildings" to ensure the temporary employment of every willing and able-bodied person in need of employment. Wages and benefits, including food and housing, would be based on one's work, as Marx envisioned fifty years later. "The only condition to be, that for so much, or so many hours work, each person shall receive so many meals of wholesome food, and a warm lodging, at least as good as a barrack. That a certain portion of what each person's work shall be worth shall be reserved, and given to him, or her, on their going away; and that each person shall stay as long, or as short time, to come as often as he choose, on these conditions" (*RM,* 247). Paine did not see these employment factories, which he said could handle 6,000 workers each, as permanent locations for people to live or work but as places to help them over their initial impoverishment. In a year, if most workers stayed only three months, each building could annually help 24,000 people. "By establishing an asylum of this kind, persons to whom temporary distresses occur, would have an opportunity to recruit themselves, and be enabled to look out for better employment" (247).

As for the elderly, Paine presented two alternatives. First, he devised a plan for those who reached the age of fifty: if they were still working, they would receive an annual payment of £6 pounds per year. These people consisted of "husbandmen, common labourers, journeymen of every trade and their wives, sailors, and disbanded soldiers, worn out servants of both sexes, and poor widows" (*RM,* 242). For the second, when the elderly retired, most likely at age sixty, they would receive an annual social security payment of £10. The number of people in this category he estimated ranged up to 420,000. The cost for "the comfortable provision" of "aged persons" would be approximately £140,000 per year (247).

All these proposals anticipated the twentieth-century social welfare state, an extraordinary vision shared by few other imaginative thinkers of his time.[52] Paine foresaw only positive results deriving from this plan, which was to be funded by excise taxes, no doubt collected by his former colleagues in the service. After all, he said, the collection is "made eight times a year in every market town in England," so there would be enough money to pay for the requirements of this program (*RM,* 248). But if excise taxes did not cover these costs, he proposed other ways and means, such as the dissolution of most of the armed forces and the reorganization of the tax code, an idea he reiterated in a piece he collaborated on with the Marquis de Condorcet. Entitled "Answer to Four Questions on the Legislative and Executive Powers," the essay did not appear in print until 1792. Among Paine and Condorcet's most radical ideas was that the nations of the world, led by France and its National Assembly, should call an international conference for the purposes of spreading republican ideas, "a convention of the representatives of the various nations of Europe, which would adopt measures for the general welfare. The felicity which liberty insures us is transformed into virtues when we communicate its enjoyment to others."[53] When this happened, he naively argued that a large British army and navy would, "in great measure, become useless" (249). As a result, Britain would end its hostility toward France.

Second, the retooling of the armed forces meant that the government could restructure the tax system by ending the levies that especially harmed the poor: the taxes on hops, soap, candles, windows, and houses. Once these direct taxes ended, "relief will be instantly felt." The house and window tax, in particular, "falls heavy on the middling class of people." For this reason, he also advocated ending the commutation tax, which was a duty on consumption; it was, he said, "most heavily felt" (*RM*, 250). One of the highest of the commutation taxes was on beer. It hurt the poor, not aristocrats, because the latter "do not purchase beer brewed for sale, but brew their own beer free of the duty" (254). In place of such commutation taxes, he suggested the imposition of a luxury tax, thus placing the heaviest burden on those who had successfully in the past avoided taxes but who were also those most capable of paying them. "If they, or their champion Mr Burke, who, I fear, is growing out of date like the man in armour, can prove that an estate of twenty, thirty or forty thousand pounds a year is not a luxury, I will give up the argument"(251).

To determine what exactly a "luxury" is Paine argued that any income that remained after the expenses of supporting a family was a luxury. If a family spent £1,000 per annum, all income beyond that amount must be taxed as luxury. This scheme amounted to a progressive income tax, an extraordinary proposal for the end of the eighteenth century. It constituted "the justice of rendering taxes more equal than they are" (*RM*, 254). It ensured that the wealthiest were taxed at the highest rate, leading to the end of "the aristocratical law of primogeniture" (251). This long-held English practice, an example of social injustice and inequity, had the deleterious consequence of causing corruption in elections and undue political influence when the younger sons were forced to beg for "useless posts, places, and offices" in government because they owned no estates (255). As property taxes rose on individual property, families of the nobility would grasp that it was pointless to pass entire estates only to their eldest sons. These families, he proved mathematically, would save hundred of thousands of pounds once they divided their property. An estate worth £23,000, if split into four estates of £4,000 each and one at £3,000, would each pay £1,129 in taxes at a 5 percent rate, whereas if one person held the original estate, the cost to him alone would be £10,630 pounds, which was above a 46 percent rate (256). The rate was obviously higher because it was a progressive tax.

The dismemberment of estates was the natural consequence of Paine's radical proposal to restructure English society and economy. To assist in convincing estate owners that this outcome was inevitable, Paine briefly mentioned the imposition of a heavy inheritance tax on landed property or, as he put it, the placement of "a limit to property, or the accumulation of it, by bequest" (*RM*, 251). While he did not provide details about inheritance taxes here, he soon devoted his last great work, *Agrarian Justice* (1796), to an extended analysis of this progressive proposal as a means to overcome social and economic inequality.

Private Property in the Progressive State

Despite his radical ideas about social and economic reform, Paine cannot justly be defined as a proto-socialist. He consistently adhered to the right of individuals to own private property and to do with it whatever they wished. He also consistently favored a strong democratic commercial republic based on free trade and individual rights. Meantime, he also understood the limits to the accumulation of property that went beyond the needs of the individual. When human beings resided in a natural condition of life, a condition that Hobbes, Locke, and Rousseau had termed the state of nature, the miserable impact of property ownership was insignificant because human beings derived their subsistence from the earth. Imagining that the North American Indians still resided in a state of nature, Paine remarked that "the life of an Indian is a continual holiday, compared with the poor of Europe" (*AJ,* 1:610). Locke had explained, in laying out his labor theory of value, that man's capacity to work amounted to a commodity that he alone owned. In working the land, a man joined his labor to the land and "made it his own," thus removing it from the state of nature and placing ownership, his ownership, over it. But there were limits to how much land any one person might accumulate; when asked whether a man might "ingross as much as he will," Locke answered, "not so," but only "as much land as a man tills, plants, improves, cultivates, and can use the product of, so much is his property."[54]

Paine agreed with Locke that labor was the personal property of an individual, who could use it as he wished. He noted that "the faculty [as he called it] of performing any kind of work or services by which he acquires a livelihood, or maintaining his family, is of the nature of property. It is property to him; he has acquired it; and it is as much the object of his protection as exterior property, possessed without that faculty, can be the object of protection in another person."[55] But Paine differed from Locke in denying that someone in the state of nature actually owned property simply by mixing his labor with it. When a person combined his labor with the land, he did not really own it; he only enjoyed the opportunity to use it. His ability to work was intrinsic to a man's very being. Those who claimed to own land had actually stolen it from those who had once owned it in common, as a gift from God. To resolve the problem of the poor, Paine rejected any proposal to redistribute property by forcing the wealthy to surrender their land. Such a concept had to wait for the utopian socialists of the next century and for Karl Marx, his 1844 manuscripts, and *Das Kapital.* Nor was Paine an eighteenth-century version of the Levellers of the previous century, those who followed the egalitarian concepts of John Lilburne, although Paine's contemporary enemies often confused his views with those of his leveling predecessors. On the other hand, his focus on private property as part of the fabric of society has, again, led commentators like Isaac Kramnick to associate him with bourgeois, or middle-class, radicalism.[56]

In *Agrarian Justice,* Paine displayed innovations that take him beyond one-dimensional attempts to associate him with either proto-socialism or bourgeois radicalism. He extended the ideas he had first set forth in the *Rights of Man,* freely using Lockean notions of property ownership and revolution, as he interpreted them through his own lens and Rousseau's ideal of social solidarity, to develop a theory of how to improve the lives of the poor. He first distinguished natural from artificial property. "Firstly, natural property, or that which comes to us from the Creator of the universe—such as the earth, air, water. Secondly, artificial or acquired property—the invention of man" (*AJ,* 1: 606). Artificial property is, therefore, not the result of God's actions; no doubt with a sly glint in his eye, Paine commented that "man did not make the earth, and, though he had a natural right to *occupy* it, he had no right to *locate his property* in perpetuity any part of it; neither did the Creator of the earth open a land office, from whence the first title-deeds should issue" (611).

Here Paine was close to Rousseau's view of private property, an unsurprising turn, given the length of time he had resided in Paris by the time he crafted *Agrarian Justice.* Rousseau, in his *Essay on Inequality,* had noted that the development of private property had created false distinctions between people. "The first person who, having enclosed a plot of land, took it into his head to say *this is mine* and found people simple enough to believe him was the true founder of civil society. What crimes, wars, murders, what miseries and horrors would the human race have been spared, had someone pulled up the stakes or filled the ditch and cried out to his fellow men: 'Do not listen to this imposter. You are lost if you forget that the fruits of the earth belong to all and the earth to no one!'"[57] Though chagrined by these developments, Rousseau knew that civilization could not turn back the clock to a simpler time. Because human beings could never annihilate civil society to return to a state of nature, they were duty bound by the social contract to improve the lives of the less fortunate. A person residing in civil society was different from one who resided in a state of nature. As Rousseau noted in *The Social Contract*, "his faculties are exercised and developed, his ideas are broadened, his feelings are ennobled, his entire soul is elevated to such a height that, if the abuse did not often lower his status to beneath the level he left, he ought constantly to bless the happy moment that pulled him away from it forever and which transformed him from a stupid, limited animal into an intelligent being and a man."[58] If men are unable to return to their natural state when they hold property in common, the government's policy must solve the problem of poverty without forcing the redistribution of wealth.

Paine built on these ideas by creating a legal fiction. The powerful and the wealthy had seized property; they do not truly own it; their families held it through inheritance to the detriment of those who enjoyed none. Based on these premises, those who claimed to own private property actually owed a debt to those who were property-less, that is, the poor. This argument was based on the precept that "the condition of every person born into the world, after a state of civilization commences, ought not be worse than if he had been born before that period" (*AJ*, 1:610). God had given men and women "the earth for their inheritance" (620).[59] It did not matter whether anyone happened to reside on a piece of real estate; it always belonged to everyone. Those who claimed ownership owed a subvention in the form of a ground rent to the landless; the occupiers of the land merely rented it, and the owners found a way to transform the inhabitant into lessees. "Every proprietor, therefore, of cultivated lands, owed to the community a *ground-rent* (for I know of no better term to express the idea) for the land he holds." New owners, the beneficiaries of the land passed down on the death of the former owner, would have to pay "rent" in the form of an inheritance tax, the very concept he had briefly set forth at the end of the *Rights of Man*. This "just imposition" on a beneficiary was a tax of one-tenth the value of the land at the moment it was transferred from decedent to beneficiary. The resulting funds were deposited into a common treasury, which were later allocated to cover the costs of social welfare and social services required by the poor. "It is from this ground-rent that the fund

proposed in this plan is to issue" (611). The families of landowners remained on their property for perpetuity. The only difference was that they now had to pay for the right to do so. So
while the right to own land was inviolable, so was the right to a
decent standard of living that the "dispossessed" also deserved.
From Paine's perspective, "it is a right, not a charity that I am
pleading for," a notion echoing his long list of proposals for public assistance he outlined in the *Rights of Man* (612, 618).

Paine's plan was truly visionary. The government could create
a program that combined public welfare payments with social security outlays. At the age of twenty-one, all persons, no matter
whether they were rich or poor and regardless of whether they
were male or female, were to receive payments of £15 to compensate them for the loss of their "natural inheritance, by the introduction of private property." They also received social security payments when they reached age fifty, an idea Paine also
drew on from the *Rights of Man*. At that time, whether they
worked or not, the landless received payments of £10 every year
for life. This program was free to the poor, so only the wealthy
landowners had to pay for it through the ground rent as an inheritance tax. Paine was careful to avoid what he called "invidi-
ous distinctions" between people, which was why he included
rich and poor, men and women. He did not want to cause more
divisions than those that already arisen between social classes. He
hoped, however naively, that those who were sufficiently comfortable would not collect their allocations at twenty-one or
their social security payments at fifty. Instead, they would volun-
tarily forego them by transferring them to the common fund. To
show how serious he was, he announced toward the end of
Agrarian Justice that he was willing to begin the program himself by contributing £100 as a gift (1:621).

Rousseau's pervasive influence on Paine's economic and social
thought clearly runs through this late work. Paine was certain
that if revolutionary France implemented his social welfare programs, the social fabric of French culture and civilization would
be radically transformed. It would become a model for the
world. "The plan here proposed will . . . immediately relieve and
take out of view three classes of wretchedness—the blind, the
lame, the aged poor; and it will furnish the rising generation with

means to prevent their becoming poor; and it do this without deranging or interfering with any national measures" (*AJ*, 1:618). This was not an agrarian law, as the even more radical Thomas Spence advocated, empowering the government to seize and redistribute the land equally to the people. This is why Paine carefully titled his pamphlet "agrarian *justice*," not "agrarian law," which would have made it far more radical than his taste or his ideological persuasion allowed.[60] Of course, his ideas at the end of the eighteenth century were destined to go nowhere, especially in monarchical England, but for Paine economic justice coincided with political freedom and human rights: "I care not how affluent some may be, provided that none be miserable in consequence of it" (617).

Paine's proposal appealed to his lower- and lower-middle-class readers, but his middle-class audience might well have considered it to be yet another tax burden on the small amount of landed property they owned. Perhaps in an attempt to allay their fears, Paine stressed that social equality was possible, something that most of those in the middling classes—artisans, small shop owners, craftsmen, and maybe even small manufacturers—likely believed to be impossible. Note that he strung together all the middle-class values he could think of in a single paragraph in an attempt to attract their support.

> That property will ever be unequal is certain. Industry, superiority of talents, dexterity of management, extreme frugality, fortunate opportunities, or the opposite, or the means of those things, will ever produce that effect, without having recourse to the hard, ill-sounding names of avarice and oppression; and besides this there are some men who, though they do not despise wealth, will not stoop to the drudgery or the means of acquiring it, nor will be troubled with it beyond their wants or their independence; while in others there is an avidity to obtain it by every means not punishable; it makes the sole business of their lives, and they follow it as a religion. All that is required with respect to property is to obtain it honestly, and not employ it criminally.

The radical undertone of his concession that a man had a right to own private property was no barrier to keeping those who owned none from being dispossessed of his civic and political rights: the right to vote or hold office, the right to believe and practice whatever religion one preferred, the right to write freely and to speak one's mind openly. To mix property with rights in a negative way—a way that kept the landless and the poor out of the political realm and public sphere—was "a total departure from every moral principle of liberty, because it is attaching rights to mere matter, and making man the agent of that matter."[61]

Paine's ideal for social reformation was complex. People might acquire as much property as they wished, but they must be prepared to compensate those who owned none. Landowners must be prepared, having been given notice well in advance, to undertake their civic duty, pay their ground rents as inheritance taxes, and thus avoid future upheaval and even revolution. It was a tax based on the moral duty of each citizen to ameliorate the problem of the poor and near poor. Had France, once its revolution had settled down and constitution writing begun, developed a constitution that included his idea of an inheritance tax, "the violences" the nation suffered through the Terror would "have been prevented. . . . But, instead of this, a revolutionary government," by which he meant the tyranny of Robespierre and the Committee of Public Safety and their Reign of Terror, "a thing without either principle or authority, was substituted in its place; virtue and crime depended upon accident; and that which was patriotism one day became treason the next."[62] Property ownership was a function of the growth of civil society over the centuries. But property owners had their responsibilities, including their huge financial debt to the rest of society. They must be willing to pay it, even in a politically unreformed England. The right to a decent standard of living thus became part of the essential core of Thomas Paine's constellation of human rights.

CHAPTER 6

PUBLIC SPIRIT, CIVIC ENGAGEMENT,

AND EVOLUTIONARY CHANGE

ARRESTED IN DECEMBER of 1793 by French authorities and charged, ironically, with being an English spy, Paine spent ten months in the Luxembourg prison. On his release in November of 1794, he explicitly disavowed revolution. This was not a very difficult decision. Living every day under the fear of the guillotine—he saw the death warrant Robespierre had prepared for him, and he escaped the scaffold by pure coincidence—he left the Luxembourg in broken health. Suffering from a dreadful lung ailment and prison fever, he also had a large abscess in his side.[1] Whether his physical ailments affected his political, moral, and religious thought is something we will never know for certain, but we do know that his views clearly matured. He no longer acknowledged that he enjoyed a special divine role to perform good deeds, nor did he continue to assert that his was an age of revolution. He was more modest in his claims, though he continued to promote political and social reform. He devoted his efforts to constitution making for post-Terror France until his 1802 return to America, developing a new system of checks and balances that he thought far more workable than the American system of the separation of powers. In his last active years, he became a more sophisticated thinker and writer, while never once losing touch with his literary flair for ridicule, humor, and prickliness.[2]

During these last years, Paine continued to argue that human rights were deeply rooted in the divine creation, a belief embedded in his deist faith. He also continued to attack organized religion, asserting that it blinded human beings to the laws of God's impeccable universe. As he had claimed in *The Age of Reason*, religions with hierarchies and seats of power turned people from God's truth by setting forth a series of myths and superstitions. These were the result, not of God's will, but of men who had misappropriated God's message, which could only be determined from the perfection of the universal laws of his creation. The liberation of the mind, body, and soul are intrinsically linked because freedom and rights could never be compromised by fables that depoliticized the people and led to their physical enslavement by monarchs and aristocrats and their spiritual enslavement by priests, despite the famous creedal statement by his nemesis Burke: "We are resolved to keep an established church, and established monarchy, an established aristocracy."[3]

In one of his first publications after his release from prison, Paine again attacked the Bible and organized religion, especially when the church was united with the government. "Religion is a private affair between man and his Maker," he insisted, as he always had, "and no tribunal or third party has a right to interfere between them. It is not properly a thing of this world; it is only practiced in this world; but its object is in a future world; and it is not otherwise an object of just laws than for the purpose of protecting the equal rights of all, however various their beliefs may be." His was, he said, "a pure religious belief, founded on the idea of the perfection of the Creator." God was careful with his creation, though He knew some men would try to destroy His work: "We see that God takes good care of the creation He has made. He suffers no part of it to be extinguished: and He will take the same care of His word, if he ever gave *one*."[4] To improve the world now meant that the people must cultivate a public spirit, eschew revolution, and advocate and work for social and political reform. The Terror proved that violence had too many dangerous consequences. Paine's mature deism and his new emphasis on political processes underscored his political and moral philosophy in his final years.[5]

True religion stimulates a public spirit in the people by instilling in them the desire to help the poor and less fortunate. It requires them to improve the people's political and social standing by maintaining the republic and its social welfare programs as he envisioned them in the *Rights of Man* and *Agrarian Justice*. "It is a want of feeling to talk of priests and bells while so many infants are perishing in the hospitals, and aged and infirm poor in the streets."[6] Paine learned from his revolutionary experiences in America and France that a truly moral and religious man looks with skepticism on revolution, because "the moral principle of revolutions is to instruct, not to destroy."[7] A man's duty is to transform political evil into political good, to perform, in other words, the good deeds that God demands. If people were to read only the first part of the *Rights of Man*, they would wrongly conclude that Paine believed in the absolute necessity of revolutionary action as the sole means to rid the world of evil monocrats, as Jefferson called them, and corrupt noblemen. At the end of the Terror, as he grew skeptical of his earlier radical ideals of revolution, he was determined that political change would best take place incrementally—indeed, surprisingly, in more Burkean ways. Before men undertake the drastic step of revolution, they must carefully anticipate its consequences. Paine's approach to politics, political transformation, and constitution writing was now grounded in his appreciation of God's gift to men of self-government, an approach that was tempered by the experiences France had undergone in the Terror. These results, which he had never foreseen, he regretted the rest of his life.

RETREAT FROM REVOLUTION

Paine never formally admitted that Burke had been right, namely, that the French Revolution was doomed to end in horrific consequences for its citizens and ultimately in dictatorship, although, at the end of the 1790s, Napoleon Bonaparte's coronation as emperor was still a few years off (that occurred on December 2, 1804). Yet, the shift in his thinking may be seen in the following terms. *Common Sense* had opened with the memorable distinction between society, which was "a blessing," and government, which "even in its best state" was "a necessary evil" (65). Nearly twenty years later, Paine argued that "there is no subject more interesting to every man than the subject of government. His security, be he rich or poor, and in a great measure his prosperity, are connected therewith; it is therefore his interest as well as his duty to make himself acquainted with its principles, and what the practise ought to be."[8] Hereditary governments, by which he meant those that claimed power by usurpation, never had the right to exist. But after the Terror, dictatorship was always a potential, even an inevitable, outcome of revolution. The tyranny that Robespierre established was no different from the worst hereditary monarchy in history. "The right which any man or any family had to set itself up at first to govern a nation, and to establish itself as hereditarily, was no other than the right which Robespierre had to do the same thing in France."[9] If revolution was a choice of action, it had to be undertaken with hesitation and skepticism.

Here Paine again reflected Locke's view concerning revolutionary action as a last resort. Locke had surmised that "revolutions happen not upon every little mismanagement in public affairs," "but only after a long train of abuses, prevarications, and artifices, all tending the same way."[10] Only now, Paine concluded that revolution's promise was quite different from his initial beliefs as he set them forth in his writings from 1776 to 1792, from *Common Sense* to the *Rights of Man*. Hopefully, people would never have to undertake a revolution, but if revolution became necessary because other choices were unavailable, revolutionaries must immediately stop killing one another and begin the project of tackling the difficult business of constitution making.

Political *evolution*, not *revolution*, must therefore be the goal of the polity. Here history vindicated Paine's changed mind. England never experienced the revolution that Paine had advocated for it in *Common Sense* and the *Rights of Man*. The 1688–89 Glorious Revolution and Settlement was all England had needed. Instead of later violent revolution, the nation's focus moved toward the expansion of the franchise, culminating in the Reform Act of 1832, which doubled the size of the nation's electorate, and a subsequent larger extension of the vote in 1867.[11] Historian Martin Malia has argued that after early-modern revolutionary activity originated in seventeenth-century England, it then moved progressively over the course of the eighteenth century to America, in 1776, and then France, in 1789. The Americans undertook a revolution to restore lost rights, he says, but "when they got through, they had created a new nation and a re-public, an outcome that was obviously 'revolutionary' in the modern sense of post-Old Regime." In France, we see the full development of what we call revolution "in the modern sense." The "first to occur in a secular culture," it consequently sought to tear down "the whole of Europe's thousand-year-old *ancien régime*: monarchy, aristocracy, and church." It took longer in France than in America and England to develop a democratic order because there revolution degenerated first into Terror in 1794 and then, ten years later, into empire. Revolutionary activity in Europe thereafter moved along a West-East cultural "gradient," rather than two separate cultural zones of west and east, composed of "a spectrum of zones graded in level of development from the former to the latter."[12] After the seventeenth-century English Revolution, radical violence moved to France in the eighteenth, and from there into Central Europe in the nineteenth, and finally to Russia and China in the twentieth century. Each time revolution erupted, it became increasingly violent and more radical, culminating with the Bolshevik Revolution of 1917.[13]

England in the nineteenth century meanwhile settled into a mode of political reform based on negotiation and compromise, which led to the removal of property and other voting qualifications faced by working-class men. Paine would have undoubtedly approved of this development now that he agreed that oppression through hereditary rule alone was an insufficient cause of revolution. The goal of progressive-thinking and reform-minded men ought not to be the forceful removal of particular tyrants and aristocrats, but the termination of the hereditary principle itself. He began to believe, naively perhaps, that given sufficient time, that principle might well come to an end on its own. "As to what are called monarchy, royalty, and aristocracy, they do not, either as things or as terms, sufficiently describe the hereditary system; they are but secondary things or signs of the hereditary system, and which *fall of themselves* if that system has not a right to exist."[14] The illegitimacy of hereditary rule was as provable as a mathematical theorem, and once enough people were convinced of this proof, hereditary rule would collapse. All a person needed to do was to see how absurd it was when "the government of a nation fall[s], as it frequently does, into the hands of a lad necessarily destitute of experience, and often little better than a fool. It is an insult to every man of years, of character, and of talents, in a country." The logical question was to determine whether a thing had a right to exist, or, as he put it, whether it had "a right to begin" in the first place.

Paine thus asked by what right did "the Capets, the Guelphs, the Robespierres, the Marats" govern (note his inclusion here of monarchs, tyrants, and bloodthirsty killers of all stripes in his catalogue of evildoers). They had no right to rule other than that they had seized control of government, but this did not give them the *right* to rule. "This would be supposing an absurdity, for either it is putting time in the place of principle, or making it superior to principle; whereas time has no more connection with, or influence upon principle, than principle has upon time." Wrongs begun thousands of years ago were as wrong today as they were at the beginning, just as those things that were right remain steadfastly so over time. It was not time that mattered, but the principle that was crucial. "Time with respect to principles is an eternal NOW," and the sooner the people understood these circumstances the better off they would be.[15]

One measure of how well a government supported rights and liberties was to gauge the rights of minors. In most contemporary European nations, including Britain, minors—those not yet twenty-one years old—represented a majority of the people because "in general the minority in years are the majority in numbers." Minors possessed rights commensurate to those over twenty-one insofar as all natural rights were immutable. A person always possessed them, independent of chronological age. Minors might be unable to exercise their rights, but they always possessed them. These young people were as human as their elders, whose duty was to secure and safeguard the rights of the adolescents, which were "under the sacred guardianship of the aged." Those who occupied political office did so therefore only temporarily, or as Paine put it, "for the *time being*." They knew they eventually had to surrender their positions to make room for the next generation. They had no authority to establish a hereditary government because that destroyed the proper relationship between elderly protector-lawmakers and those whom they were supposed to protect. Hereditary rule "deprive[d] every minor in the nation, at the time such a law is made, of his inheritance of rights when he shall come of age, and to subjugate him to a system of government to which, during his minority, he could neither consent nor object."[16] A young person who reached the age of his majority must oppose those trying to create a hereditary system. He had a right to object and vote against it, not merely resort to revolutionary action. In short, his time would come to displace those in power who had become dictatorial and complacent about the political positions they thought were permanent.[17]

The people best protected themselves against hereditary succession with good constitutions, which, once drafted, meant that "nothing . . . can justify an insurrection, neither can it ever be necessary where rights are equal and opinions free." Good constitutions, therefore, obviated the need for revolution. Without them, revolution might well be necessary, but insurrection was an alternative only when people faced an extreme tyranny, one that ignored all appeals and all constitutional limitations on their authority. But once revolution had rid the country of its despots and their cohorts, the new rulers, to preserve liberty, must "permit to themselves a *discretionary exercise of power* regulated more by circumstances than by principle, which, were the practice to continue, liberty would never be established."

The people, then, must never take revolutions lightly. Revolutions were unnecessary in democratic republics in which citizens possessed sufficient channels to rectify oppression, should it occur. But even in republics, some dangers arose when revolutions lasted too long. Revolutionaries must avoid becoming like those whom they had overthrown. This was France's problem during the Terror. "The moral principle of revolution is to instruct, not to destroy." France had failed in 1793 to establish a democratic constitution, even though it had one in hand—the one drafted by Paine, Condorcet, and others. If it had been implemented, the Terror and its miserable consequences would have been avoided. "Had a constitution been established two years ago (as ought to have been done), the violences that have since desolated France and injured the character of the Revolution, would, in my opinion, have been prevented." Rather than creating a democratic republic, the Convention allowed France to transform itself into

> a revolutionary government, a thing without either principle or authority. . . . Virtue and crime depended upon accident; and that which was patriotism one day became treason the next. All these things have followed from the want of a constitution; for it is the nature and intention of a constitution to *prevent governing by party*, by establishing a common principle that shall limit and controul the power and impulse of party, and that says to all parties, *thus far shalt thou go and no further*. But in the absence of a constitution, men look entirely to party; and instead of principle governing party, party governs principle.[18]

With the fall of Robespierre's revolutionary government, the reconvened National Convention, with Paine as a deputy back in his seat, completed work on a new constitution in 1795.[19] On reviewing its work after two years, Paine commented that "a better *organized* Constitution has never yet been devised by human wisdom."[20]

Based in part on the American experience, the 1795 document divided power between the executive and legislative branches of government but went further in two ways: first, it included a compound executive council consisting of five men, called the Directory; and second, the legislative was a quasi-bicameral legislature made up of a Council of Five Hundred and a Council of Elders. For the first time, Paine acknowledged the prudence of a legislature with two branches. Seventeen years earlier, he had advocated only unicameral designs.[21] But now he modified his view, suggesting that the United States had the best model. He told Monroe that he "wished to see America the *Mother Church* of government, and I have done my utmost to exalt her character and her condition."[22] Given Paine's consistent animus against churches generally, this was an astounding remark, demonstrating how dramatically his political thought had changed.

Still, the differences between the American Congress and the French legislature were striking. The French model was not a straightforward division along the lines required by the U.S. Constitution. In America, both houses of Congress had to agree to a law before it was sent to the president for signature. In

France, the lower house, the Five Hundred, only proposed laws, which were then passed on to the Elders for passage or rejection. "All the security is given [in America] that can arise from the coolness of reflection acting upon, or correcting the precipitency *[sic]* or enthusiasm of conception and imagination."[23] Laws were well examined and thought through before their enactment. The American Constitution forced both houses to consider all the ramifications a potential law might have. This focus on government structure and organization occupied Paine after his return to the Convention in 1795 as he focused on constitutional developments.

A BROAD FRANCHISE

A virtue of the new 1795 French constitution was that the right to vote, "a species of property of the most sacred kind," replaced revolutionary action, just as the Americans had provided for in their Constitution.[24] The franchise alone could not, however, stave off despotism or hereditary rank and privilege unless it was universal, a position Paine had consistently argued since *Common Sense*. He reiterated that all men—he did not, notably, include women—over the age of twenty-one must be eligible to vote, and not just the propertied few. "Wealth is no proof of moral character; nor poverty of the want of it." Wealth could often be a sign of moral depravity and dishonesty, whereas poverty was a sign of innocence and a pure spirit. Paine's enormous ego would have led him to believe he was addressing himself here. Besides, the consequences of a narrow suffrage would be disastrous if those excluded from voting united against the government when they found that they played no role in decision-making.

A government was not a true republic if some citizens were disenfranchised, if some remained outside the pale of engaging their public spirit. Such a government was no different from one based on the hereditary principle because it transformed the people into slaves when they could not vote. "To take away this right is to reduce a man to slavery, for slavery consists in being subject to the will of another, and he that has not a vote in the election of representatives is in this case. The proposal therefore to disenfranchise any class of men is as criminal as the proposal to take away property."[25] Paine argued for a return to the ancient Anglo-Saxon principle of universal voting rights for all men, originally embodied in the theory of the English ancient constitution, the very same document he once demanded Burke present to him.[26] Without the vote for all men, hereditary succession ruled the day. The earliest aristocrats "were the Robespierres and Jacobins of that day. When they had committed the robbery, they endeavored to lose the disgrace of it by sinking their real names under fictitious ones, which they called titles." The right to vote, like all civil rights, was natural, and it had to be equal, except for women. There could be no distinctions among men about who makes political decisions, no hierarchy of who exercised which rights and who did not. Ultimately, for countries the size of the United States and France, the right to vote meant the right to elect representatives, a prospect that avoided the Terror France had experienced. "All the disorders that have arisen in France during the progress of the Revolution have had their origin, not in the *principle of equal rights,* but in the violation of that principle. The principle of equal rights has been repeatedly violated, and that not by the majority but by the minority, and *that minority has been composed of men possessing property, as well as of men without property; property, therefore, even upon the experience already had, is no more a criterion of character than it is of rights.*"[27] Anyone who denied that right was no better than a thief.

That was why he again emphasized that "it is dangerous and impolitic, sometimes ridiculous, and always unjust to make property the criterion of the right of voting." If even a small amount of property is made a prerequisite to voting, that too exhibits "liberty in disgrace, by putting it in competition with accident and insignificance." Once again, Paine offered a witty analogy to prove his point: "When a broodmare shall fortunately produce a foal or a mule that, by being worth the sum in question, shall convey to its owner the right of voting, or by its death take it from him, in whom does the origin of such a right exist? Is it in the man, or in the mule?" No, the right to vote was the first principle of constitutional democracy.

In the end, property was fungible, but voting was not. Private property resulted from a variety of circumstances, none of which had anything to do with voting or voting rights. Some men were energetic about accumulating riches, whereas others found other opportunities to hold their attention. Still others simply had little or no interest in wealth or property. In the end, in fact, all men owned property, if only in their own person. "The protection of a man's person is more sacred than the protection of property; and besides, this, the faculty of performing any kind of work or services by which he acquires a livelihood, or maintaining his family, is of the nature of property."[28] Paine was deeply disappointed when he failed to inspire the framers of the 1795 constitution to add the one provision he desired the most, namely, universal manhood suffrage. When he addressed the convention on this point, his words were greeted with a stony silence, and he never again returned to the assembly. To deny this fundamental right of citizenship "is an easy matter in theory or on paper; but it is a most dangerous experiment, and rarely practicable in the execution."[29]

And yet, the expansion of the right to vote to all eligible men over twenty-one did not mean that war and violence were suddenly at an end. Some nations would never change on their own, which meant the people might never possess the franchise. This was the situation in England at the end of the eighteenth and beginning of the nineteenth century, before the passage of those reform acts in 1832 and 1867 that Paine had no way of anticipating. If England refused to transform itself from a monarchy to a democratic republic, Paine now called not for revolution, but for France to destroy the British government, root out its tyranny, and establish a new democratic order. So enamored was Paine with this idea that he even sent a plan for a descent on England first to the Directory and then to Napoleon, whom he termed "the most enterprising and fortunate man."[30] He had already announced that if an invasion did occur, the people of England would rise up against their oppressive government, and, he said, "I intend to be among them."[31] He had no doubt that such an act would be the only recourse to an intransigent, entrenched despotism, but he also harbored doubts about the efficacy of revolution.

Paine was clearly disappointed when Napoleon abandoned a planned expedition to invade England and instead attacked

Egypt. Paine had witnessed how the emperor had actually readied the invasion by ordering the construction of several hundred gunboats—another Paine idea—but he used them instead in Egypt. Paine concluded that Napoleon had never intended to invade England but only wanted world leaders to think he was about to move against the island kingdom. His sights were in fact always on Egypt. Once the war between France and England began again, despite the treaty signed at Amiens, Paine was again encouraged that he would at long last see a new government established in the British Isles. "If the invasion succeed, I hope Bonaparte will remember that his war has not been provoked by the people. It is altogether the act of the Government, without their consent or knowledge; and though the last peace appears to have been insidious from the first, on the part of the government, it was received by the people with a sincerity of joy." Once the British monarchy fell, "the excellence of the representative system" would arise in its place. The people of England understand this, so "their own wisdom will direct them what to choose and what to avoid, and in everything which regards their happiness, combined with the common good [the *res publica* or republic] of mankind."[32] Paine even offered his services "to assist in forming a Constitution for England" after the people had been freed from the chains of the hereditary system.[33] As it turned out, a more pressing problem faced the Americans when, in 1803, Napoleon sold the Louisiana territory to the United States; the question then was what to do with the politically unformed people who inhabited the territory. Paine thought he had the answer.

The people, Paine thought, had no experience with any discernible form of government and thus none with erecting a democratic order. They "know little or nothing of election and representation as constituting government."[34] In fact, Paine initially thought that the people in Louisiana resided in a theocracy. He had never been to the territory, but he thought the Roman Catholic Church completely controlled its inhabitants, meaning that the priests controlled the residents' conduct. The priests, in turn, took their orders from Rome. The first step the people must take was to elect their priests rather than having them appointed by the Pope. This would introduce them to representative government. It would also give the United States time to allow them to evolve into adherents of republican principles. They would then elect local government officials and afterward be prepared to elect representative assemblies, which would be needed for the new states that would be carved from the vast territory. Paine envisioned that this evolution from formlessness and theocracy to democracy would take only three to seven years to achieve.

Paine told Jefferson that the promotion of republican ideals in the area might require thousands of English-speaking people, who understood what a democracy was, to immigrate to Louisiana. "There are thousands and tens of thousands in England and Ireland and also in Scotland who are friends of mine by principle, and who would gladly change their present country and condition."[35] As the new inhabitants, well versed in democratic principles and republican practices, moved to the new territory and integrated into the native population of French- and Spanish-speaking Catholics, the transformation would "soon change the first face of things." In this way, "the Idea proper to be held out is, that we have neither conquered them, nor bought them, but formed a Union with them and they become in consequence of that union a part of the national sovereignty."[36] No war, no revolution, only diplomacy and education, and eventually universal suffrage. After all, the Louisiana inhabitants were God-fearing people who could adapt to the new American polity.

WAR ON THE FEDERALISTS

In his final years, Paine became increasingly paranoid about those who he thought were undermining the new American republic.[37] His flood of commentary concerned party and faction, accusing the Federalists of undermining the new nation during the second Washington and the Adams administrations. He did not oppose the rise of political parties in the United States and even thought the Jeffersonian-Republican party was genuine. Its Federalist opponents did not deserve to exist because they almost ruined American democracy. His views were shaped by his myopic fear that shadowy enemies of the democratic order lurked in the dark corners of government before the 1800 presidential election and then afterward in hidden, conspiracy-ridden caverns.[38] His political observations after Jefferson's election to the presidency in 1800 reflected many of his earlier ideas as he had expressed them in both *Common Sense* and the *Rights of Man,* giving his political thought a consistency lasting for more than forty years, from 1776 until his death in 1809. He now noticed the eerie parallels between the Federalists led by John Adams and the Jacobins controlled by Robespierre. Whereas the French republic had been undone by the Reign of Terror, the American Constitution managed to survive because its electoral process had worked to defeat the Federalists peacefully, as power passed to a president and Congress of the opposing party.

The Jeffersonians would remain ascendant until the contested election of John Quincy Adams in 1824. Had he lived to see it, Paine would have found that a vigilant citizenry protected its rights when its written constitution kept party and faction in check, when the citizens were engaged in decision-making, and when the franchise was sufficiently broad to include all men over the age of twenty-one, no matter their economic or social status. Such a constitution made citizens aware of the important issues driving them to develop a public spirit. Only when they were fully acquainted with the issues could they employ their inventive powers collectively to solve their problems. As long as the constitution protected their fundamental civil and political rights, they could make the necessary changes as the conditions of life changed. Revolutions were dubious affairs as long as the citizens' public spirit prevailed over greed and divisiveness.

Paine's late essays and pamphlets promoted Jeffersonian democracy against the encroachments by the Federalists. Paine was convinced that these Federalists planned to establish a new tyranny. The followers of John Adams and Alexander Hamilton, though out of office, constantly claimed that their heroes had taken the right steps to centralize political authority, which was the goal of the Constitution. Between 1802 and 1805, Paine published eight letters addressed to the citizens of the United States, mostly written in the new federal city of Washington. He found on his return to America that "the people were divided into two classes, under the names of *republicans* and *federalists,* and in point of numbers appeared to be nearly balanced."[39] When he attempted to promote his vision of republican ideals and truths over Federalist lies and slander, one wag observed that Paine's letters were so good because they were "calculated to prevent the mischief that might have arisen from a set of disappointed men, endeavoring to propagate the disaffection to the best government in the world."[40] For Paine, if the Federalists had remained in control longer than 1800, their monopoly on power would have fostered a government designed for their selfish advantage.

Now Paine confessed that he favored the greater unity the nation had under the Constitution over the way it had been before 1789, when, under the Articles of Confederation, the "several States were united in name but not in fact." If a "Federalist" was someone who believed in greater unification of the states with a general government that embraced the common good, then he himself would have been "first on the list of Federalists, for the proposition for establishing a general government over the Union, came originally from me in 1783."[41] In that year, the issue of national unity had initially arisen when Congress attempted to tax the states' imports. When the Rhode Island assembly refused to comply, congressional leaders sent Paine to that state to persuade its leaders that the tax meant nothing less than the survival of the new nation. He failed to persuade state leaders, an experience that convinced him that Congress had to have the authority to pass laws binding on the states. In this sense, he anticipated by four years Article VI of the Constitution and its famous supremacy clause: "This Constitution, and the Laws of the United States, which shall be made in Pursuance thereof; and all Treaties made, or which shall be made, under the Authority of the United States, shall be the supreme Law of the Land."

Unfortunately, he said, those who called themselves Federalists were not true "federalists" because they sought more to empower a single individual in the executive office, a one-way ticket to tyranny, than to establish a nation united under divided powers. It was one thing to have a strong federal government, but quite another to centralize authority with the power of war and peace in the hands of one man. While the Federalists claimed to believe in liberty and rights, their actions belied this assertion. They were "imposters and hypocrites" who "correspond to the story told of a man who was become so proud and famous for lying that he disdained speaking truth lest he should lose his character."[42] The chief malefactor was John Adams and his "black cockades," who wanted America to adopt a hereditary British-style system of government supported by a large standing army and a steady flow of revenue from the states.[43] Paine's use of the image of the "cockade" reveals that his purpose was to associate their cockade with the one worn by the revolutionaries in Paris after 1789. Just as the French cockade became a mark of violence and horror in the Reign of Terror, so too would the black cockade.

Americans therefore should now fear a Federalist Reign of Terror. Adams and his cohorts had tried to persuade Americans that because they were in severe danger from a French invasion, they had to sacrifice their hard-won liberty in the name of increased security. This so-called Quasi-War with France, as it is called in history, said the Federalists, required a strong executive to preserve national security by a large professional military establishment and an endless stream of revenue. Adams's "head was full of kings, queens and knaves, as a pack of cards. But John has lost [the] deal."[44] Adams knew that Washington, who was childless, could not establish a hereditary executive but that Adams could: he had "his hopeful son Quincy."[45] Even worse, Adams and his secretary of state Timothy Pickering, who was an ally of Hamilton, along with the Federalist-controlled Congress promoted the infamous Sedition Act, which created "a magic circle of terror," making it a crime, punishable by fine and imprisonment, to criticize the government or any governmental official. "Violent and mysterious in its measures and arrogant in its manners, it affected to disdain information, and insulted the principles that raised it from obscurity."[46]

Finally, the shameful and vile love affair between the Federalists and England especially annoyed Paine because it threatened America's far more important relationship with France. Paine attacked the 1794 Jay Treaty as an example of one of the worst actions undertaken during the second Washington administration; it "had so disgracefully surrendered the right and freedom of the American flag, that all the commerce of the United States on the ocean became exposed to capture, and suffered in consequence of it."[47] America's only hope in dealing with a revanchist England, which might well want to reincorporate America into the empire, was for the Americans to bind themselves diplomatically and financially to France, Britain's historic enemy. As long as the war between revolutionary France and her monarchist enemies continued, America must remain neutral. Accordingly, Paine told his fellow Americans that while he was still in France in 1800, he had written a treatise on maritime neutrality entitled "Proposals for an Association of Nations for the Protection of Rights and Commerce of Nations That shall be Neutral in Time of War."[48]

In his rancorous broadsides, Paine blamed every leader of the Federalist faction. After Adams, his list was topped by Washington, perhaps the greatest iconic figure at the time.[49] Hamilton, too, was continually posturing to become a dictator; no better spectacle was Hamilton's attempt to drive America into a war with France in 1798. And Secretary of State Pickering was so enamored of England that he could never be trusted. Pickering, called by historian William Hogeland a "third-rate" functionary of high federalism," in 1804 fulfilled Paine's criticism of him when he argued for the separation of the northeastern states from the union in anticipation of the Hartford Convention during the War of 1812.[50] But representative government prevailed in 1800, when the "Reign of Terror," raging during the tail end of Washington's administration and the "whole of that of Adams," ended with a Jeffersonian-Republican victory. Power for the first time passed peacefully from one political party to that of its enemies.[51] "What is become of the mighty clamor of French invasion, and the cry that our country is in danger, and taxes and armies must be raised to defend it?" he querulously demanded in 1802. "The danger is fled with the faction that created it."[52] In his attempt to alleviate the passions between the parties, Jefferson famously incorporated the famous phrase "we are all Federalists, we are all Republicans" into his inaugural address.[53] Although he was still in Paris at the time of the inauguration, Paine might well have missed the new president's attempt at reconciliation. In any event, Paine never commented on it. It would have been more than revealing to learn just what he might have made of Jefferson's remark; it would certainly have been out of character for him to have ignored it.

CONCLUSION

THE CONSISTENCY and coherence in Thomas Paine's political philosophy and religious faith become obvious when we study his writings from the moment he stepped onto the world stage in 1776 until his death thirty-three years later. In an 1806 letter, he himself noted the following:

> My motive and object in all my political works, beginning with *Common Sense,* the first work I ever published, have been to rescue man from tyranny and false systems and false principles of government and enable him to be free, and establish government for himself. . . . And my motive and object in all my publications on religious subjects, beginning with the first part of *The Age of Reason,* have been to bring man to a right reason that God has given him; to impress on him the great principles of divine morality, justice, mercy, and a benevolent disposition to all men and to all creatures; and to excite in him a spirit of trust, confidence and consolation in his creator, unshackled by the fable and fiction of books, by whatever invented name they may be called.[1]

Toward the end of his eighth and final letter to the citizens of the United States, which he wrote in 1805, Paine reiterated identical principles to those he had first set forth in *Common Sense.* The creation of the American republic "was the opportunity of *beginning the world anew,*" he now reiterated, echoing almost the very words he had used in that pamphlet and providing his own emphasis for them, "and of bringing forward a *new system* of government in which the rights of *all* men should be preserved that gave *value* to independence."[2] To stress the parallel between his current ideas and those of his pamphlet, he even cited *Common Sense* to provide the source of his basic political principles: the establishment of a just government was merely the beginning of the movement toward preservation of all men's rights and liberties. This too was his purpose when he urged the American solders on to victory under very trying circumstances in his *American Crisis* series. It was his goal when he moved onto the world stage during that Revolution in France, where he wrote his two-volume *Rights of Man*. There, he hoped to persuade people throughout the world that the rights and liberties he had advocated first for America and then for France were universally applicable. The only way to achieve them was perhaps through revolution. Nations everywhere can establish a democratic order based on the people's consent and their natural rights and liberties; then and only then will people understand that they must create governments that best protect them, their rights, and their liberties. This understanding will never occur if leaders constantly frighten their citizens with phantom external enemies, as he claimed Adams, Hamilton, Pickering, and all the Federalists had done, with their steady stoking of Americans' fear of a purported French invasion. National loyalty and true patriotism must come from within each citizen: "Make it the interest of the people to live in a state of government, and they will protect that which protects them. But when they are harassed with alarms which time discovers to be false, and burdened with taxes for which they can see no cause, their confidence in such government withers away, and they laugh at the energy that attempts to restore it."[3]

Consistent themes in Paine's political philosophy included his long-held belief that human beings possess certain natural rights and civil liberties, which a written constitution can best protect. In addition to free expression, they include the right to vote unsecured by any property qualification as well as religious liberty— not tolerance—religion and government being wholly separate. He consistently held that the simplest forms of government were the best, which was why for such a long time he rejected the idea of a bicameral legislature, something he regarded as a recipe for stagnation and failure. Only later, after seeing the renovation of the Pennsylvania constitution after 1790, the workings of the American Congress after 1789, and the collapse of the French

National Convention in 1793 did he realize that the classical republican model of a two-house legislature might well be a more practicable form of lawmaking. Above all, he demanded that his fellow citizens be vigilant and combat any attempt by their government to place them in a state of somnolence; if necessary, as times changed, they might have to undo those things their predecessors had done.

The major change in Paine's political thinking over the years was his view of the efficacy of revolution. In his work from *Common Sense* to the *Rights of Man,* revolution was the best catalyst for political change. But after 1794, he held that an expansive franchise supplanted revolutionary action if all men over twenty-one could vote, a situation proven in America by the successful transition of power after the presidential and congressional elections of 1800. He himself felt the impact of the power of the vote when, in 1806, an elections magistrate denied him the right to vote. The Jeffersonians had governed New York during the first few years after his return, but the new election supervisors in New Rochelle were Federalists—"Tories" all, Paine called them. When he went to his polling station to cast his ballot, he was turned away. "You are not an American; our minister at Paris, Gouverneur Morris, would not reclaim you when you were imprisoned in the Luxembourg prison at Paris, and General Washington refused to do so."[4] Morris had denounced Paine, believing him to be far too radical to be an American, and in any event Morris thought Paine was not truly an American citizen; while in the Luxembourg, Morris said that Paine "thinks that I ought to claim him as an American citizen; but considering his birth, his naturalization in this country [France], and the place he filled [as a deputy from Pas-de-Calais in the National Convention], I doubt much the right." Moreover, Morris was certain Paine was a blasphemer, given *The Age of Reason.* "Lest I should forget it, I must mention that Thomas Paine is in prison, where he amuses himself with publishing a pamphlet against Jesus Christ."[5]

Paine was of course as consistent in his overall religious views as he was in his political thought. In one of his last writings about religion, he reiterated his belief that man's duty was to imitate God by improving the world and ensuring the happiness of all people everywhere. He left himself in his creator's hands, "that

He will dispose of me after this life consistently with His justice and goodness."[6] Even then, Paine showed that he still believed in God's superintending care over him—and over all creatures. Still, in old age, Paine continued to argue that all human beings, individually and collectively, possess a sacred spark of goodness as God's creatures. Not everyone saw this piety in Paine's thought. His longtime friend and compatriot Samuel Adams in 1802 thanked Paine for his service to the American cause, but he complained of Paine's "defense of infidelity."[7] Paine responded that he had composed *The Age of Reason* as an antidote to his perception that the French were "running headlong into atheism" after Robespierre had replaced God with a new Religion of Reason.[8] *The Age of Reason* was designed to "stop them in that career." While Paine expected critics to respond to his work on religion, he was astonished by their vitriol, because he was not an atheist. He merely set forth his belief in an all-benevolent Deity who oversaw His handiwork through the agency of His human creation. He was shocked at the reaction to his work by those who said, for example, "What an infidel, what a wicked man, is Thomas Paine! They might as well add, for he believes in God and is against shedding blood."[9]

Paine told Sam Adams he had seen a letter that Adams had written to his cousin John in which Sam expressed the hope that "divines and philosophers, statesmen and patriots [should] unite their endeavors to *renovate the age* by inculcating in the minds of youth *the fear and love of the Deity and universal philanthropy.*" So, claimed Paine, these sentiments are "exactly *my* religion, and is the whole of it."[10] The entire first part of *The Age of Reason* supported his "fear and love" of God, and in the second part he argued only that doing good works is tantamount to serving God by improving the world because renovation reflects a respect for God's handiwork. "The man, Sir, who puts his trust and confidence in God" will be the one who "leads a just and moral life, and endeavors to do good."[11] Ultimately, God "needs no service from us. We can add nothing to eternity, but it is in our power to render a service *acceptable* to Him, and that is not by praying, but by endeavoring to make his creatures happy." While incarcerated in Luxembourg, he asked for God's protection and believed he received it; he did not face execution, as had so many of his friends and associates. "The key to heaven is not in the keeping of any sect, nor ought the road to it be obstructed by any."[12] Like Sam Adams, he too had worked hard to do God's work on earth.

Politically a republican and theologically a Quaker, then a deist, Thomas Paine drastically transformed himself after the degeneration of the French Revolution. After abandoning his Quaker theology and turning to deism, he was a social democrat, who wrote some of the most penetrating social welfare reform plans until the mature works of John Stuart Mill in the mid-nineteenth century. Perhaps Thomas Paine used religious imagery and quotations from scripture to advance his political and social agenda, and at the same time he consistently believed in his own salvation and that of the people. Through political and social reform— the vote guaranteed by written constitutions, social welfare programs to help the unfortunate, and high taxes to pay for them— he believed that the world could finally be made better, a thirty-year belief that he held until his death on June 8, 1809.[13]

APPENDIX

A NOTE ON PAINE'S AMERICAN
NATIONAL CONSCIOUSNESS

DESPITE HIS English birth in 1737 and his longtime residency in Paris, which included his service in the French National Convention, after his arrival in the colonies in 1774, Thomas Paine considered himself an American citizen and patriot.[1] At the same time, we often find him speaking of "universal civilization" and referring to himself as "a citizen of the world."[2] Can we reconcile these two incongruous thoughts? Because Paine articulated a democratic vision of the world, some commentators are convinced that he possessed only an international consciousness. Thomas Walker argues, for example, that "Paine was the first to offer an integrated, modern, cosmopolitan vision of international relations," an assessment that echoes the position of David Fitzsimons and Mark Philp.[3] Ian Dyck confirms this view when he says that "Paine put little store in these [national] citizenships, preferring to identify himself as a citizen of the world who held national identifications in contempt."[4] The question is then to inquire into how Paine presents his views of national consciousness. First, was Paine concerned with nationality at all, and second, what did it mean to him to be an American? The answer to these two critical questions will help us understand just how and why he saw himself as an American.

When Paine first immigrated to America in 1774, he was most likely uncertain as to his nationality. During his first thirteen years in Philadelphia, from 1774 to 1787, he, like his fellow citizens, was gradually developing an American sensibility. Most Americans, until they realized that reconciliation with England was impossible, believed that they were English, with all the rights and liberties accorded to Englishmen. At the same time, their sense of a national consciousness gave them the distinct sense of what they were *not*. Hence, they typically distinguished between a "new" American world and an "old" European or English one. Their national character had an entirely different emphasis from their patriotism because national consciousness involved more than love of one's country. It included an identity with one's nation, its values, its language, and its future. Patriotism lacked the intensity of identification that citizens felt toward their own people, their mores, their language, and their destiny. Writing from London in 1775 to his friend Joseph Galloway, Benjamin Franklin best summarized this view when he expressed his sense of American self-identity in negative terms by depicting the crisis in terms of the old and new worlds:

> When I consider the extream Corruption prevalent among all Orders of Men in this old rotten State, and the glorious publick Virtue so predominant in our rising Country, I cannot but apprehend more Mischief than Benefit from a closer Union. I fear they will drag us after them in all their plundering Wars, which their desperate Circumstances, Injustice and Rapacity, may prompt them to undertake; and their wide-wasting Prodigality and Profusion is a Gulph that will swallow up every aid we may distress ourselves to afford them. Here Numberless and needless Places, enormous Salaries, Pensions, Perquisites, Bribes, groundless Quarrels, foolish Expeditions, false Accounpts and no Accounpts, Contracts and Jobbs, devour all Revenue, and produce continual Necessity in the Midst of natural Plenty.[5]

Americans like Franklin and Paine perceived the differences between the two worlds, separated by the great gulf of the Atlantic, as serious and deep, perilous and unfathomable.

Franklin's words came at the moment when Paine was searching for his own roots in his newly adopted nation. In *Common Sense,* he emphasized the same differences Franklin had expressed setting Americans apart from their English cousins. In his famous, often quoted statement—"we [Americans] have it in our power to begin the world over again"—he told his new countrymen that America was different because of its newness and that its differences distinguished it from those nations of the old world that Franklin condemned (120). During the Revolution, Paine was unequivocally a patriot, as can be seen throughout his *American Crisis* series, but to be a patriot does not necessarily connote a national consciousness. It would take something more than the willingness of a people to cast aside the feeling that they were no longer English. The Continental Army's retreat from the Hudson stimulated words from Paine's pen about patriotism that are timeless. His ringing words at that bleak moment appealed to Americans' distinctiveness, urging them to distinguish themselves from their English taskmasters. "These are the times that try men's souls. The summer soldier and the sunshine patriot will, in this crisis, shrink from the service of their country; but he that stands it now, deserves the love and thanks of man and woman. Tyranny, like hell, is not easily conquered: yet we have this consolation with us, that the harder the conflict, the more glorious the triumph."[6] Those fighting for the American cause certainly were no "sunshine patriots," unless they were among those who returned home immediately at the end of their tour of duty. They became more than patriots as they grew to share an "American" nationality, a common sense of mission to create a new democratic order—as Paine put it, "to form the noblest, purest constitution on the face of the earth," an effort that many of them knew required heroic sacrifice (*CS*, 120).

Paine's growing sense of his national consciousness paralleled the way in which Americans were beginning to think of themselves. After 1776, Paine understood that a true national consciousness had to move beyond patriotism and even constitution making—in other words, beyond the business of politics. Despite his adulation of the inherent justice of the American cause, his *sense* of being an American still contained some of the baggage of sorting through the differences between those characteristics that made some people American, others English. In *Common Sense,* for example, he wrote that Americans knew that they were different from Englishmen and that they would have to act soon on that knowledge by uniting against the empire. Until that time, they were like "a man who continues putting off some unpleasant business from day to day, yet knows it must be done, hates to set about it, wishes it over, and is continually haunted with the thoughts of its necessity" (112). Americans who agreed with separation already knew that they were united to face a common enemy. "Mutual fear," he wrote in the *Crisis*, "is the principal link in the chain of mutual love."[7] By the end of the war, he was confident in challenging a remark made by Lord Sheffield on just this point. Sheffield had noted that he thought it would "be a long time before the American states [could] be brought to act as a nation." But Paine said that Sheffield was wrong, because "when we view a[n American] flag" and "contemplate its rise and origin," it "inspires a sensation of sublime delight."[8]

The seeds of these formative nationalist ideas developed fully as Paine moved from America to France. There, he began to long to return to his adopted American home. His encounter with Rousseau's ideas especially gave him a new perspective on national consciousness. Rousseau investigated how society achieved collective freedom and responsibility rather than solely anomic individual rights: the rights and freedom of the nation as a whole worked through the operation of the general will, not just the individual will of one person. In 1789, in one of his most succinct definitions of *nation,* Paine reflected this position when he said that "a nation is only a great individual," whereby the collective personality of the people congealed to form a single composite whole.[9] A nation was not society per se, nor was it government. It was prior to both because it comprised the collective organization of human beings acting synchronously in all regards. Paine understood the organic nature of a nation that united its people, an idea he cited in Rousseau's writings.[10]

This Rousseauist element runs throughout the second part of the *Rights of Man,* where Paine mused about the nature of a nation, nationhood, nationality, and nationalism. "A nation is not a body, the figure of which is to be represented by the human body." No Hobbesian body natural was reified as the body politic, as Hobbes's famous frontispiece to his 1751 work depicted Leviathan: the monster displayed the state in all its grandeur, comprising the thousands of heads of its subjects. A nation, for

Paine, "is like a body contained within a circle, having a common center, in which every radius meets." A nation was more than simply a geographic region with a united people. A nation was bound together by the circle's perimeter. It "possesses a perpetual stamina, as well of body as of mind" (181–82). Nations enjoyed basic rights, among which was, as Price had contended from the pulpit of the Old Jewry, the right of the people to form their own constitutions, an echo of Paine's argument as early as *Common Sense*. Only now Paine's emphasis had shifted; because "a nation can have no interest in being wrong" (198), the nation as a whole must collectively form a constitution and not try to create one devised by only a few individuals acting in conventions. No nation must ever do anything that was ruinous to itself or its people. On the other hand, small groups of people might inadvertently destroy the nation even as they claimed to be acting in its best interests. Paine addressed this issue in a 1794 letter to James Monroe, the American minister to France, when he argued that the American people might have called themselves "Americans" before July 4, 1776, but that they were not really Americans until after that date. "The Americans were not called citizens till after the government was established," he said, "and not even then until they had taken the oath of allegiance to the United States of America on two occasions, once in 1776, again in 1777."[11]

Thus, Paine's encounter with Rousseauist ideas, coupled with his experiences first in America and later in France, consciously drove him to believe that he was incontrovertibly and deeply American. In so doing, he resolved the problem of his own personal national identity. Writing from France just after its Revolution, he mentioned how much he missed "my much loved America. It is the country from whence all reformation must originally spring."[12] His years in Philadelphia seemed now to have been more powerfully inspirational than he himself had ever imagined. His newly minted American spirit now became firmly rooted in his consciousness.

So why, despite his newfound sense of Americanness, did he accept French citizenship when the National Assembly awarded it to him in August 1792? Indeed, just one month later, he was elected by no less than four constituencies to serve in the new National Convention. He agreed to serve as a deputy from Pas-de-Calais. And then when the Jacobins, on Robespierre's order, arrested him, he was charged, ironically, with being an *English* spy because of his birth and long early residency in England. And yet, his service on the convention's constitution-drafting committee and subsequent imprisonment did not transform him into a Frenchman, and he vociferously argued that he was no Englishman. He told Monroe that he "had no more idea than [Washington] of vacating any part of my real Citizenship of America for a nominal one in France, especially at a time when she did not know whether she would be a Nation or not." He considered himself a true citizen of America because "France was not yet aware that it was a Nation." But he did, curiously, identify himself as "a [French] national man," given his election to the convention. While he said he might have conducted himself as a French national as a deputy on the convention, he still thought of himself as American. "I certainly then remained, even upon their own tactics, what I was before, a citizen of America."[13] He believed that while he could assist France in adopting a republican constitution, he remained an American. He never felt he fitted into that "circle with a common center" in France, as he had earlier put it. Nor did he think his award of French citizenship was anything but symbolic. "I acted only as a friend *invited* among them as I supposed on honorable terms. I did not come to join myself to a government already formed, but to assist in forming one *de nouveau*, which was afterwards to be submitted to the people whether they would accept it or not, and this any foreigner might do."[14]

When Paine finally returned to America, he wrote that America "is the country of my heart." She was "the place of my political and literary birth. It was the American Revolution that made me an author, and forced into action the mind that had been dormant, and had no wish for public life."[15] His national consciousness had now become a firm, final reality after his fifteen years abroad. Still, we must come to terms with that other side of Paine's conscious, which is dissonant with this analysis, namely, the view taken by Thomas Walker cited above.[16]

As early as 1782, Walker reminds us, Paine had not spoken a language of nationalism but had used the vocabulary of internationalism. In his *Letter to Raynal* that year, he used global language for the first time to refer to international citizenship, an idea that seems contrary to his later expression of national consciousness. There, the whole point of human progress, he said, was to move not merely toward the creation of a nation of virtue like America but also to extend and promote "universal society, whose mind rises above the atmosphere of local thoughts, and considers mankind, of whatever nation or profession they may be, as the work of one Creator." The world needed a system of "extended" civilization, and he considered himself be "a universal citizen."[17] Could Paine have made these assertions only as a literary convenience or an intellectual strategy? This was hardly the case, because five years later, in 1787, he told the Marquis of Lansdowne that he was "a man who considers the world as his home."[18] And a few years afterward, writing in the *Rights of Man,* in direct contradiction to his prison letters to Monroe, he claimed that "my country is the world" (228). One year later, in defending the life of Louis XVI during his January 1793 trial, he told the convention that he was "a citizen of the world."[19]

Perhaps the apparent contradiction between nationalism and internationalism may be resolved by asking whether the issue was a matter of convenience. First, Paine declared himself an American because it was convenient. During and just after the American Revolution, if his new compatriots believed that he was American, they would invite him to play a direct role in the new government. He held only one (fleeting) national position, that of secretary to the committee of foreign affairs, from which he was forced to resign over the Silas Deane affair.[20] Or perhaps Paine wanted to be a member of Washington's first cabinet or a foreign ambassador in 1789. Indeed, he later sought to serve as the American minister to France after Jefferson had returned to America to serve as the first secretary of state in the new federal government. Paine was deeply disappointed when his archenemy, Gouverneur Morris, was appointed instead. Or perhaps he hoped that Jefferson would appoint him to a position in his administration. At one point, while still in France, he even offered his expertise to Jefferson, who he hoped would allow him to become the United States agent for American goods imported into France.[21] Jefferson declined.

A second consideration is that it was convenient for Paine to claim that he was an American when he wanted to be let out of prison. Paine's hope of liberation would be based, not on his past service to France, but "on the government of America, that it would *remember me*."[22] Finally, perhaps it was convenient because Paine knew that he could never return to England as a free man. After an English court had found him guilty of seditious libel in absentia, it declared him an outlaw for publishing the second part of the *Rights of Man*, which included a hefty attack on George III. Should he ever try to return to England, or if he was picked up by an English warship on the high seas, he knew he would be transported to England and jailed or hanged. If he wished to leave France, he had only America to turn to, a request he frequently sent to Thomas Jefferson.

To assert that Paine was an American as a matter of convenience, however, fails to fairly explain his newly formed national consciousness. Throughout his Parisian correspondence, he spoke often of his desire to return to his home, America, something he believed, in the words of Carey McWilliams, was "a redemptive land."[23] "I am always intending to return to America," he wrote in 1797, and he later told Madison that he intended "to have set off for America" on a particular date, but decided against leaving France because he did not like the ship's captain. "My intention is to return to America as soon as I can cross the sea in safety," he said, fearing English men-of-war sailing off the French coast. And he told Jefferson that "if any American frigate should come to France . . . I will be glad if you give me the opportunity of returning."[24]

Now, Paine may well have been conscious of the possible contradiction between his American national consciousness and his internationalism. He testified more than once that he was emotionally an American after 1776, but intellectually an internationalist until his post-French revolutionary encounter with the Jacobins. Writing from France just before the Revolution erupted in 1789, he said, "my heart and myself are 3000 miles apart; and I had rather see my horse Button in his own stable, or eating the grass of Bordentown or Morrisania, than see all the pomp and show of Europe."[25]

In the end, the two positions—his American nationality and his internationalism—are not incompatible. He fused them in a manner that allowed him at once to say that although he was consciously an American, he focused his mind always on the entire world because, as he put it, "I defend the cause of humanity."[26] Paine's American consciousness was, therefore, always purely American, especially after the break with England, thanks to his Philadelphia years. While he himself might not have fully realized that until twenty years later, the awareness remained until his death, giving a renewed impetus to what it meant to be an American with a cause designed to transform the entire world into a liberal democratic order.

NOTES

Introduction

1. Joyce Appleby, *Inheriting the Revolution: The First Generation of Americans* (Cambridge, MA: Harvard University Press, 2000), 65, where she points out that between 1800 and 1820, for example, the population beyond the Appalachians grew from two-thirds of a million to more than two million people.

2. See, for example, Peter S. Onuf, *The Mind of Thomas Jefferson* (Charlottesville: University of Virginia Press, 2007); Joseph J. Ellis, *His Excellency: George Washington* (New York: Alfred A. Knopf, 2004); Ron Chernow, *Alexander Hamilton* (New York: Penguin Press, 2004); Gordon S. Wood, *The Americanization of Benjamin Franklin* (New York: Penguin Press, 2004); Melanie Randolph Miller, *Envoy to the Terror: Gouverneur Morris and the French Revolution* (Washington, DC: Potomac Books, 2004); Walter Isaacson, *Benjamin Franklin: An American Life* (New York: Simon & Schuster, 2003); Nancy Isenberg, *Fallen Founder: The Life of Aaron Burr* (New York: Viking, 2007). The first use of the term *Founders Chic* appears to have been by Evan Thomas, " 'Founders Chic': Live from Philadelphia," *Newsweek*, 9 July 2001, 48. Thomas went on to write a book about John Paul Jones; see Evan Thomas, *John Paul Jones: Sailor, Hero, Father of the American Navy* (New York: Simon & Schuster, 2003).

3. Franklin's image appeared on 7 July 2003 and Jefferson's followed a year later, on 5 July 2004.

4. American history has demonstrated the changing perceptions we have of the founders, sometimes revered for forming what some claim to be the longest lasting republic in world history, sometimes despised for refusing to resolve all the problems of the end of the eighteenth century. See, for example, William Lloyd Garrison's famous remark, as he burned his copy of the American Constitution, that the document was "a covenant with death, an agreement from Hell." Quoted by H. W. Brands, "Founders Chic: Our Reverence for the Founding Fathers Has Gotten Out of Hand," *Atlantic Monthly* 292 (Sept. 2003): 105.

5. For the classic study of Paine as Quaker or deist, see Robert P. Falk,

"Thomas Paine: Deist or Quaker?" *Pennsylvania Magazine of History and Biography* 62 (1938): 52–63.

6. The most recent biographies include Craig Nelson, *Thomas Paine: Enlightenment, Revolution, and the Birth of Modern Nations* (New York: Viking, 2006); Maurice Ezran, *Thomas Paine: Le combattant des deux révolutions, américaine et française* (Paris: L'Harmattan, 2004); John Keane, *Tom Paine: A Political Life* (Boston: Little, Brown, 1995); Jack Fruchtman Jr., *Thomas Paine: Apostle of Freedom* (New York: Four Walls Eight Windows, 1994); Mark Philp, *Paine* (Oxford: Oxford University Press, 1989); A. J. Ayer, *Thomas Paine* (London: Secker & Warburg, 1988); Bernard Vincent, *Thomas Paine, ou la religion de la liberté* (Paris: Aubier, 1987); Jean Lessay, *L'Américain de la convention, professeur de revolutions, député de Pas-de-Calais* (Paris: Librarie Académique Perrin, 1987); David Powell, *Tom Paine: The Greatest Exile* (New York: St. Martin's Press, 1985).

7. For recent studies of his thought and work, see Christopher Hitchens, *Thomas Paine's "Rights of Man": A Biography* (New York: Atlantic Monthly Press, 2007); Paul Collins, *The Trouble with Tom: The Strange Afterlife and Times of Thomas Paine* (New York: Bloomsbury, 2005); Vikki J. Vickers, *"My Pen and My Soul Have Ever Gone Together": Thomas Paine and the American Revolution* (New York: Routledge, 2006); Harvey J. Kaye, *Thomas Paine and the Promise of America* (New York: Hill & Wang, 2005); Edward Larkin, *Thomas Paine and the Literature of Revolution* (Cambridge: Cambridge University Press, 2005); Jack Fruchtman Jr., *Thomas Paine and the Religion of Nature* (Baltimore: Johns Hopkins University Press, 1993); and Gregory Claeys, *Thomas Paine: Social and Political Thought* (Boston: Unwin Hyman, 1989).

8. *Thomas Paine: Collected Writings,* ed. Eric Foner (New York: Library of America, 1995).

9. Fred Inglis refers to writer Christopher Hitchens as "a Tom Paine for our troubled times" in the *Independent* (London), 1 Mar. 2001, and Jon Katz made the comment that Paine was the precursor to the Internet in "The Age of Paine," *Wired Magazine*, May 1995. Hitchens's study is identified above in note 7.

10. Adams to Waterhouse, 29 Oct. 1805, in *Statesman and Friend: Correspondence of John Adams with Benjamin Waterhouse, 1784–1822*, ed. Worthington Chauncey Ford (Boston: Little, Brown, 1927), 31. The "disastrous meteor" quotation is from *The Diary and Autobiography of John Adams*, ed. Lyman H. Butterfield, 4 vols. (Cambridge, MA: Harvard University Press, 1961), 3:330.

11. See David McCullough, *John Adams* (New York: Simon & Schuster, 2001), Joseph J. Ellis, *Founding Brothers: The Revolutionary Genera-*

tion (New York: Alfred A. Knopf, 2000), and Pauline Maier, *American Scripture: Making the Declaration of Independence* (New York: Alfred A. Knopf, 1997), wherein Paine is either dismissed or simply ignored. More balanced are Chernow, *Alexander Hamilton*, and Isaacson, *Benjamin Franklin*.

12. Jack N. Rakove, "Hamilton, Presidents' Friend, Co-Author of the Federalist Papers Defined Executive Powers Perhaps Too Expansively," *San Francisco Chronicle*, 18 July 2004, E-3. See also Joseph J. Ellis, *American Creation: Triumph and Tragedies at the Founding of the Republic* (New York: Alfred A. Knopf, 2007), esp. 177–86, and more recently, Kevin J. Hayes, *The Road to Monticello: The Life and Mind of Thomas Jefferson* (New York: Oxford University Press, 2008).

13. Thomas Paine, *Rights of Man* (1791, 1792), ed. Henry Collins, with an introduction by Eric Foner (Harmondsworth, UK: Penguin, 1984), 219, hereinafter cited in the text as *RM*. See also Paine's letter to Robert Morris, 20 Feb. 1782, in *The Complete Writings of Thomas Paine*, ed. Philip S. Foner, 2 vols. (New York: Citadel Press, 1945), 2:1206–7.

14. Eric Foner, *Tom Paine and Revolutionary America* (1976; New York: Oxford University Press, 2005), xiii-xiv, and Sean Wilentz, *The Rise of American Democracy: Jefferson to Lincoln* (New York: W. W. Norton, 2005), 23.

15. A debate has been ongoing for many years concerning Paine's literary style. For a critique of modern commentary and a levelheaded assessment, see Jane Hodson, *Language and Revolution in Burke, Wollstonecraft, Paine, and Godwin* (Aldershot: Ashgate, 2007), 115–48. The classic study continues to be James T. Boulton, *The Language of Politics in the Age of Wilkes and Burke* (London: Routledge, Kegan & Paul, 1963), and Olivia Smith, *The Politics of Language, 1791–1819* (Oxford: Clarendon Press, 1984). See also Evelyn Hinz, "The 'Reasonable' Style of Tom Paine," *Queen's Quarterly* 79 (Summer 1972): 231–41; John Turner, "Burke, Paine, and the Nature of Language": The French Revolution in English Literature and Art, Special Edition, *Yearbook of English Studies* 19 (1989): 36–53; Tom Furniss, "Rhetoric in Revolution: The Role of Language in Paine's Critique of Burke," in *Revolution and English Romanticism: Politics and Rhetoric*, ed. Keith Hanley and Raman Selden (New York: St. Martin's Press, 1990), 23–48; and Bruce Woodcock, "Writing the Revolution: Aspects of Thomas Paine's Prose," *Prose Studies* 15 (Aug. 1992): 171–86. A recent articulation of Paine's "simple" and "plain" style addressing his countrymen is Ellis, *American Creation*, 47–49.

16. See Vickers, *"My Pen and My Soul Have Ever Gone Together,"* Claeys, *Thomas Paine*, Hitchens, *Thomas Paine's "Rights of Man,"* and Ed-

ward H. Davidson and William J. Scheick, *Paine, Scripture, and Authority: "The Age of Reason" as Religious and Political Idea* (Bethlehem, PA: Lehigh University Press, 1994).

17. The *Rights of Man*, esp. part 1, was a response to Edmund Burke's *Reflections on the Revolution in France*, and *Agrarian Justice* as a response to Gracchus (François Noël) Babeuf's attempt to overthrow the French Directory in his 1796 Conspiracy of the Equals. Babeuf was guillotined for his labors.

18. Common Sense [Thomas Paine], *American Crisis*, no. 1, 3 Dec. 1776, in *CW*, 1:56–57.

19. A strong echo of Spinozistic theory of revolution echoes throughout his writings at this time, though we have no clear evidence that Paine was familiar with Spinoza's ideas at the time of the American Revolution. Jonathan Israel notes, however, Spinoza's belief in revolution in these terms: "Whenever a state no longer upholds a liberty which safeguards the individual from the irrationality, selfishness, greed, unruliness and passions of others, including the sovereign, its citizens ipso facto have the right as well as the motivation to change it," including if necessary "the right of armed resistance." Israel, "The Intellectual Origins of Modern Democratic Republicanism (1660–1720), *European Journal of Political Theory* 3 (2004): 25, 29.

20. Thomas Paine, "Essay on Cheetham," 22 Aug. 1807, in the *New York Public Advertiser*, quoted in Gilbert Vale, *The Life of Thomas Paine* (New York: Privately printed, 1841), 265, and [Thomas Paine], "The Forester's Letters," letter 3, 24 Apr. 1776, in *CW*, 2:78. Paine's relations with ideas of Locke and Rousseau are well documented. See A. Owen Aldridge, *Thomas Paine's American Ideology* (Newark: University of Delaware Press, 1984), 107–22, 137–46, and for Locke alone, see Isaac Kramnick, *Republicanism and Bourgeois Radicalism: Political Ideology in Late Eighteenth-Century England and America* (Ithaca: Cornell University Press, 1990), 146–48.

21. Etienne Dumont, *Souvenirs sur Mirabeau et sur les deux premières assemblées legislatives* (Paris: C. Gosselin et H. Bossange, 1832), 331–32. Dumont added at the same time that Paine was "mad with vanity" and "vainer than the French."

22. Thomas Paine, "To John Inskeep, Mayor of the City of Philadelphia" (Feb. 1806), in *CW*, 2:1480.

23. Kramnick, *Republicanism and Bourgeois Radicalism*, 158.

24. J. G. A. Pocock, *Virtue, Commerce, and History: Essays on Political Thought and History, Chiefly in the Eighteenth Century* (Cambridge: Cambridge University Press, 1985), 276. See also J. G. A. Pocock, "Political Thought in the English-speaking Atlantic, 1760–1790, pt. 1: The Imper-

ial Crisis," in *The Varieties of British Political Thought, 1500–1800*, ed. J. G. A. Pocock, with the Assistance of Gordon J. Schochet and Lois G. Schwoerer (Cambridge: Cambridge University Press, 1993), 279–80, 282. Normanism refers to the ancient myth of the English constitution, which held that when the Normans invaded from France they brought with them the outlines of a constitutional structure to ensure the balance of the king, the Lords, and the Commons. Anti-Normanism debunks this construction. The "New Model" army was the citizen armed force under Cromwell during the mid-seventeenth-century English Civil War.

25. Harvey J. Kaye, *Thomas Paine: Firebrand of the Revolution* (Oxford: Oxford University Press, 2000); Kramnick, "Tom Paine: Radical Democrat," *Democracy* 1 (Jan. 1981): 127–38; Ezran, *Thomas Paine: Le combattant des deux révolutions*; and Lessay, *L'Américain de la convention*.

26. These observations concerning the centrality of God in Paine's political thought, his "Hamiltonian" spirit in desiring the development of a great commercial republic, and his resolute decision to renounce revolution all distinguish the present study from my own earlier work on Paine, especially *Thomas Paine and the Religion of Nature*.

27. I take the suggestion for this subhead title from Ernst Cassirer, *The Question of Jean-Jacques Rousseau*, trans. and ed. Peter Gay (Bloomington: Indiana University Press, 1963), although Cassirer's original title was *Das Problem Jean-Jacques Rousseau*. The best analysis remains Foner's *Tom Paine and Revolutionary America*, in which Foner too addresses what he prefers to call "the problem of Thomas Paine," the title of chapter 1. See also Claeys, *Thomas Paine*, 1.

28. Thomas Paine, *The Age of Reason* (in two parts, 1794, 1795), in *CW*, 1:498, italics added and hereafter cited in the text as *AR*.

29. Barry Alan Shain, *The Myth of American Individualism: The Protestant Origins of American Political Thought* (Princeton: Princeton University Press, 1994), 321.

30. See, for example, Michael Hill, "Historian of Upheaval," *Baltimore Sun*, 14 Oct. 2007, 3F, where Paine is liberally cited. In addition, Paine's words have long been favorites of presidents, especially Gerald Ford and Ronald Reagan. See Kramnick, "Tom Paine, Radical Democrat," 127–38. For other politicians, such as Jesse Helms, see Foner, *Tom Paine and Revolutionary America*, xv.

31. See Nelson, *Thomas Paine*, 118–21.

32. See, for example, in the *Rights of Man*, 75, 93–94, 104.

33. Foner, *Tom Paine and Revolutionary America*, 103–4.

34. The idea of a single Enlightenment with many philosophes was most ardently articulated by Peter Gay in his magisterial two-volume *The Enlightenment: An Interpretation* (New York: Alfred A. Knopf, 1966,

1969), 1:3, for his one Enlightenment concept. But in Pocock's terms, there were many "Enlightenments": J. G. A. Pocock, *Barbarism and Religion: The Enlightenments of Edward Gibbon, 1727–1764*, 4 vols. to date (Cambridge: Cambridge University Press, 1999–), 1:5. Pocock's configuration has been most vigorously answered by Jonathan Israel, *Enlightenment Contested: Philosophy Modernity, and the Emancipation of Man, 1670–1752* (Oxford: Oxford University Press, 2006), 10–11, 863–67, where Israel argues on behalf of what he calls two Enlightenments, a moderate and a radical version, both of which stimulated a third, the Counter-Enlightenment. The Radical Enlightenment, he argues, became the foundation of modernity, with its emphasis on "democracy, equality, individual freedom, full toleration, liberty of expression, anti-colonialism, and our universalist secular morality based on equity" (871).

35. J. G. A. Pocock made this statement at a conference at the Folger Library, Institute Center for the Study of British Political Thought. For Talmon, see J. L. Talmon, *The Origins of Totalitarian Democracy* (New York: W. W. Norton, 1970), 70. Jonathan Israel makes the same point in a different context. See Israel, *Enlightenment Contested*, 23–26.

36. The classic statement on the philosophes is Henry Steele Commager, *The Empire of Reason: How Europe Imagined and American Realized the Enlightenment* (New York: Anchor, 1978), esp. 256–66. For a more contemporary assessment, see Jonathan Israel, *Radical Enlightenment: Philosophy and the Making of Modernity, 1650–1750* (Oxford: Oxford University Press, 2001), 10–13, and Neal Postman, *Building a Bridge to the 18th Century: How the Past Can Improve Our Future* (New York: Vintage, 1999), esp. 103–11. Gordon Wood refers to Paine as America's first "public intellectual": see Gordon S. Wood, *Revolutionary Characters: What Made the Founders Different* (New York: Penguin Press, 2006), 203–22.

37. Ellis, *American Creation*, 43. Ellis refers to Paine as a "romantic revolutionary" as opposed to a "prudent revolutionary," like John Adams and George Washington (251n60). Ellis, curiously, calls Adams "a conservative revolutionary," using a rather unusual oxymoron (46). See also Gordon S. Wood, *The Radicalism of the American Revolution: How a Revolution Transformed a Monarchical Society into a Democratic One Unlike Any That Had Ever Existed* (New York: Alfred A. Knopf, 1992).

38. On sales, see Trish Loughran, "Disseminating *Common Sense*: Thomas Paine and the Problem of the Early National Bestseller," *American Literature* 78 (2006): 1–28.

39. Stacy Schiff, *A Great Improvisation: Franklin, France, and the Birth of America* (New York: Holt, 2005), and Jonathan R. Dull, *Franklin the*

Diplomat: The French Mission (Philadelphia: American Philosophical Society, 1982).

40. Jay Winik, *The Great Upheaval: America and the Making of the Modern World* (New York: HarperCollins, 2007), 52.

1. Paine's Political Thought in Historical Context

1. I am particularly grateful to James E. Bradley for our 2002 discussions on this point at the Clark Library symposium, noted in the acknowledgments.

2. We see this most starkly when, in 1772, during his work as a tax collector, Paine prepared and delivered to Parliament a plea on behalf of his fellow excise men to increase their wages. Thomas Paine, "The Case of the Officers of Excise, with Remarks on the Qualifications of the Officers, and on the Numerous Evils Arising to the Revenue, from the Insufficiency of the Present Salary: Humbly Addressed to the Members of Both Houses of Parliament" (1772), in *CW,* 2:3–15. The piece, though printed for Parliament, was not published until 1793. See chapter 5 of this volume.

3. John Keane asserts that Paine even contemplated becoming an ordained Anglican minister. Keane, *Tom Paine: A Political Life* (Boston: Little, Brown, 1995), 45–49 and 60–62. Keane hedges only slightly when he quotes Oldys's charge from 1791 that Paine thought about seeking ordination until he realized that his formal education was defective in Latin (547n63). Otherwise, his work is useful in illuminating Paine's early life. For a more recent criticism, see Vikki J. Vickers, *"My Pen and My Soul Have Ever Gone Together": Thomas Paine and the American Revolution* (New York: Routledge, 2006), 91–94, who points out that, at best, Keane's evidence is thrice indirect.

4. Craig Nelson, *Thomas Paine: Enlightenment, Revolution, and the Birth of Modern Nations* (New York: Viking, 2006), 39, makes this observation.

5. Isaac Kramnick, *Republicanism and Bourgeois Radicalism: Political Ideology in Late Eighteenth-Century England and America* (Ithaca: Cornell University Press, 1990), chap. 5.

6. Nelson, *Thomas Paine,* 41–42, and Audrey Williamson, *Thomas Paine: His Life, Work, and Times* (London: George Allen & Unwin, 1973), passim.

7. Thomas Clio Rickman, *The Life of Thomas Paine* (London, 1819), 12. Paine had known Rickman as a boy in Lewes.

8. THE HEADSTRONG BOOK;/or,/THE ORIGINAL BOOK OF OBSTINACY./written by/**** ***, OF LEWES, IN SUSSEX,/and revised and cor-

rected by/THOMAS PAIN. See Nelson, *Thomas Paine*, 40–42, Keane, *Tom Paine*, 68, and Fruchtman, *Thomas Paine: Apostle of Freedom*, 30–32.

9. Quoted in Rickman, *The Life of Thomas Paine*, 39.

10. Keane, *Tom Paine*, 69.

11. The petition is discussed in chapter 5 of this volume.

12. Elizabeth Ollive Pain(e) died in 1808, a year before Paine's death.

13. By 1770, Franklin was also the official agent of New Jersey, Massachusetts, and Georgia.

14. Moncure D. Conway, *The Life of Thomas Paine*, 2 vols. (New York: Putnam, 1892), app. B, 2:468.

15. The letter reads as follows: "The bearer, Mr. Thomas Pain, is very well recommended to me as an ingenious worthy young man. He goes to Pennsylvania with a view of settling there. I request you to give him your best advice and countenance, as he is quite a stranger there. If you can put him in a way of obtaining employment as a clerk, or assistant tutor in a school, or assistant surveyor (of all which I think him very capable) so that he may procure a subsistence at least, till he can make acquaintance and obtain a knowledge of the country, you will do well, and much oblige your affectionate father." Benjamin Franklin to Richard Bache, 30 Sept. 1774, in *The Papers of Benjamin Franklin*, ed. Leonard W. Labaree et al., 39 vols. to date (New Haven: Yale University Press, 1959–), 21:325–26.

16. Paine to Benjamin Franklin, 4 Mar. 1775, in *CW*, 2:1131.

17. Catholics and Jews were not considered Dissenters, but they suffered the same disabilities. Catholic emancipation did not occur until 1791, with the passage of the Catholic Relief Act, and Jews were legally prohibited from living in England (a Jew Bill had passed in 1753 but was repealed the following year). The Test and Corporation Acts, which had disabled Dissenters, were not repealed until 1828.

18. Formally known as Friends of Truth, they were called Quakers because of their visible shudder when they were moved by the Holy Spirit. See the succinct summary by Vincent Carretta, *Equiano the African: Biography of a Self-made Man* (Athens: University of Georgia Press, 2005), 95.

19. Jack Fruchtman Jr., *The Apocalyptic Politics of Richard Price and Joseph Priestley: A Study in Late Eighteenth-Century English Republican Millennialism* (Philadelphia: American Philosophical Society, 1983), and Clark Garrett, *Respectable Folly: Millenarians and the French Revolution in France and England* (Baltimore: Johns Hopkins University Press, 1975).

20. See, for example, Raymond G. Cowherd, *The Politics of English Dissent: The Religious Aspects of Liberal and Humanitarian Reform Movements from 1815 to 1848* (New York: New York University Press, 1956), who

includes the Quakers in his constellation of Dissenters, although Anthony Lincoln does not. He does not include Paine, however. See Anthony Lincoln, *Some Political and Social Ideas of English Dissent, 1763–1800* (1938; New York: Octagon Books, 1971).

21. James E. Bradley, *Religion, Revolution, and English Radicalism: Non-Conformity in Eighteenth-Century Politics and Society* (Cambridge: Cambridge University Press, 1990), and Gerald R. McDermott, *Jonathan Edwards Confronts the Gods: Christian Theology, Enlightenment Religion, and Non-Christian Faiths* (Oxford: Oxford University Press, 2000).

22. David Holmes, *The Faith of Our Fathers* (New York: Oxford University Press, 2006). Washington, Jefferson, Hamilton, Madison, John Hancock, and both Robert and Gouverneur Morris (though unrelated) were deists. See also Brooke Allen, *Moral Minority: Our Skeptical Founding Fathers* (Chicago: Ivan R. Dee, 2006).

23. Jonathan Israel, *Radical Enlightenment: Philosophy and the Making of Modernity, 1650–1750* (Oxford: Oxford University Press, 2001), 98, 471–72, and esp. 599–619, where Israel makes a case that Benedict de Spinoza was the most influential philosopher in the rise of English deism, and indeed in general for the creation of the Radical Enlightenment, with its emphasis on democracy, liberty, free expression, and religious liberty. According to John Redwood, the "first" English deist, Charles Blount, writing at the end of the seventeenth century, was "Spinoza's disciple." See John Redwood, *Reason, Ridicule, and Religion: The Age of Enlightenment, 1660–1750* (London: Thames & Hudson, 1976), 99. For the background, see Peter Harrison, *"Religion" and the Religions of the Enlightenment* (Cambridge: Cambridge University Press, 1990).

24. Thomas Paine, "Of the Religion of Deism Compared with the Christian Religions" (1804), in *CW*, 2:797. For Paine's ideas forming a civil religion, see Wilson Carey McWilliams, "Civil Religion in the Age of Reason: Thomas Paine on Liberalism, Redemption, and Revolution," *Social Research* (Autumn 1987): 447–90, and more generally, Catherine L. Albanese, *Sons of the Fathers: Civil Religion of the American Revolution* (Philadelphia: Temple University Press, 1976).

25. James A. Herrick, *The Radical Rhetoric of the English Deists* (Columbia: University of South Carolina Press, 1997), Steven C. Bullock, *Revolutionary Brotherhood: Freemasonry and the Transformation of the Social Order, 1730–1840* (Chapel Hill: University of North Carolina Press, 1996), and J. A. I. Champion, *The Pillars of Priestcraft Shaken: The Church of England and Its Enemies, 1660–1730* (Cambridge: Cambridge University Press, 1992).

26. David A. Wilson, *Paine and Cobbett: The Transatlantic Connection*

(Kingston: McGill-Queen's University Press, 1988), and Edward H. Davidson and William J. Scheick, *Paine, Scripture, and Authority: "The Age of Reason" as Religious and Political Idea* (Bethlehem, PA: Lehigh University Press, 1994).

27. John Adams, *The Adams Papers: The Diary and Autobiography of John Adams*, ed. L. H. Butterfield, 4 vols. (Cambridge, MA: Harvard University Press, 1961), 3:283, 234.

28. Jack Fruchtman Jr., *Thomas Paine and the Religion of Nature* (Baltimore: Johns Hopkins University Press, 1993).

29. For a different view, see Gregory Claeys, *Thomas Paine: Social and Political Thought* (Boston: Unwin Hyman, 1989), 103–4, 178–79, and esp. Christopher Hitchens, *Thomas Paine's "Rights of Man": A Biography* (New York: Atlantic Monthly Press, 2007), 102–4, when he quotes Paine's reliance on divine guidance, but does not acknowledge it.

2. Faith and Reason, Human Nature and Sociability

1. Edward Larkin, *Thomas Paine and the Literature of Revolution* (Cambridge: Cambridge University Press, 2005), 8–9 and 133–47, and Thomas L. Pangle, *The Spirit of Modern Republicanism: The Moral Vision of the American Founders and the Philosophy of Locke* (Chicago: University of Chicago Press, 1988), 198–229.

2. The clearly important works of this voluminous subject include Harry Hayden Clark, "An Historical Interpretation of Thomas Paine's Religion," *University of California Chronicle* 35 (1933): 56–87; Stephen Newman, "A Note on *Common Sense* and Christian Eschatology," *Political Theory* 6 (Feb. 1978): 101–8; and Edward H. Davison and William J. Scheick, *Paine, Scripture, and Authority: "The Age of Reason" as Religious and Political Idea* (Bethlehem, PA: Lehigh University Press, 1994). Most concentrate on *The Age of Reason*.

3. Theodore Roosevelt, *Gouverneur Morris* (Boston: Houghton, Mifflin, 1888), 288–89. Hitchens seems confused about Paine and atheism: Christopher Hitchens, *God Is Not Great: How Religion Poisons Everything* (New York: Warner Books, 2007), 268, though Hitchens admits that Paine "wrote not to disprove religion but rather to vindicate deism," 107. Regarding Theodore Roosevelt's use of the term *filthy*, stories of Paine's slovenly habits of not bathing and rumors of his irrepressible drunkenness originated in the very first biography about him, which appeared in 1791, shortly after the publication of the first part of the *Rights of Man*, when Paine was just fifty-four. Written by his enemy George Chalmers, who wrote under a pseudonym, it was commissioned by the government for a fee of £500. Despite the original title, the work was filled with damning lies and made-up stories. See [George Chalmers], *Life of*

Thomas Pain, Author of Rights of Men [sic], with a Defence of his Writings, by Francis Oldys, A.M., of the University of Pennsylvania (London, 1791). The work later appeared with a title that reflected its true character: *Life of Thomas Pain, Author of the Seditious Writings, entitled Rights of Man* (London, 1793).

4. Jonathan Israel, *Enlightenment Contested: Philosophy, Modernity, and the Emancipation of Man, 1670–1752* (Oxford: Oxford University Press, 2006), 108; although Israel was addressing the deist critique of priests one hundred years before Paine was writing, the parallels are clear.

5. Paine did not use the term *Islam*, but preferred to refer to the "religion of the Turks."

6. John Adams, *The Adams Papers: The Diary and Autobiography of John Adams*, ed. L. H. Butterfield, 4 vols. (Cambridge, MA: Harvard University Press, 1961), 3:333, 283, and 284.

7. Common Sense [Thomas Paine], "Candid and Critical Remarks on a Letter Signed Ludlow" (1777), in *CW*, 2:276.

8. Thomas Paine, "Prosecution of *The Age of Reason*" (1797), in *CW*, 2:744. Recent assessments have set forth the position that it is important to see how his "religious convictions" coincided with his "political aspirations." See, for example, Vikki J. Vickers, *"My Pen and My Soul Have Ever Gone Together"; Thomas Paine and the American Revolution* (New York: Routledge, 2006), 77 and 77–103.

9. Vickers, *"My Pen and My Soul Have Ever Gone Together,"* 78–94, dates the origins of his beliefs earlier, to his experiences in England before he left for America.

10. Paine repeats this sentiment in "My Private Thoughts on a Future State" (1809), in *CW*, 2:892–93, which is an appendix to his final work, "The Examination of the Prophecies." He later told Sam Adams that one factor that stimulated him to write *The Age of Reason* was that "the people of France were running headlong into atheism, and I had the work translated and published in their own language to stop them in that career, and fix them to the first article (as I have before said) of every man's creed who has any creed at all, *I believe in God.*" Paine to Samuel Adams, Jan. 1, 1803, in *CW*, 2:1437.

11. Paine to Samuel Adams, Jan. 1, 1803, in *CW*, 2:1437. See David Bindman, "'My own mind is my own church': Blake, Paine, and the French Revolution," in *Reflections of Revolution: Images of Romanticism*, ed. Alison Yarrington and Kelvin Everest (London: Routledge, 1993), 112–33.

12. Benjamin Franklin to George Whatley, 23 May 1785, in *Benjamin Franklin: Writings*, ed. J. A. Leo Lemay (New York: Library of America, 1987), 1104. In 1728, Franklin composed his famous epitaph, which incorporated these same sentiments:

The Body of
B. Franklin,
Printer;
Like the Cover of an old Book,
Its Contents torn out,
And stript of its Lettering and Gilding,
Lies here, Food for Worms.
But the Work shall not be wholly lost;
For it will, as he believ'd, appear once more,
In a new & more perfect Edition,
Corrected and amended
By the Author.
He was born Jan. 6, 1706.
Died   17____

See Franklin, "Epitaph," in ibid., 91.

13. For contrasting views, see Louise Smith Pangle, *The Political Philosophy of Benjamin Franklin* (Baltimore: Johns Hopkins University Press, 2007), and Jerry Weinberger, *Benjamin Franklin Unmasked: On the Unity of His Moral, Religious, and Political Thought* (Lawrence: University Press of Kansas, 2005).

14. Thomas Paine, "An Essay for the Use of New Republicans in Their Opposition to Monarchy" (1792), in *CW*, 2:544–45.

15. Paine offered no explanation for his distinction between a female Providence and a male God. I have thought long about this difference and now conclude that at the least he viewed Providence as an immanent divine element, as part of all of nature (or Nature, in deist terms), whereas his vision of God was as creator of the universe, or First Cause.

16. Paine, "Prosecution of *The Age of Reason*, in *CW*, 2:737.

17. An argument can be made in another context that one of the reasons Paine could not countenance being Quaker was because of the Quaker conscientious objection to bearing arms and fighting in wars. See his appendix to *Common Sense*, where he attacks Quakers just on this point (*CS*, 122–28). For his Quaker background, see Vickers, *"My Pen and My Soul Have Ever Gone Together,"* 79–86.

18. Bernard S. Capp, *The Fifth Monarchy Men: A Study in Seventeenth-Century Millenarianism* (London: Faber, 1972), 14, and Margaret Jacob, *The Newtonians and the English Revolution, 1689–1720* (Ithaca: Cornell University Press, 1976), 102–3; alternatively, see Norman Cohn, *The Pursuit of the Millennium: Revolutionary Millenarianism and Mystical Anarchists of the Middle Ages*, rev. and expanded ed. (1957; New York: Oxford University Press, 1970), 80–81, and Christopher Hill, *Antichrist in*

Seventeenth-Century England (London: Oxford University Press, 1971), 6–13.

19. See also *Rights of Man*, 196, where Paine argues that revolution is moving the people toward freedom just as hereditary government tries to hold them back: "This political popery, like the ecclesiastical popery of old, has had its day, and is hastening to its exit."

20. Common Sense [Paine], *American Crisis*, no. 1, 23 Dec. 1776, in *CW*, 1:50–51.

21. Thomas Paine, *Public Good* (1780), in *CW*, 2:305.

22. Paine to Nathanael Greene, 17 Oct. 1780, quoted in A. Owen Aldridge, *Thomas Paine's American Ideology* (Newark: University of Delaware Press, 1984), 104, from an unpublished letter Aldridge discovered in the Richard Gimbel Thomas Paine Collection in the American Philosophical Society.

23. Paine, "My Private Thoughts on a Future State" (1807), in *CW*, 2:893. See chapter 5 in this volume.

24. John Turner, "Burke, Paine, and the Nature of Language," *Yearbook of English Studies* 19 (1989): 50.

25. Paine re-emphasizes these themes in several essays, which, when taken together, amount to the third part of *The Age of Reason*: "Extracts from a Reply to the Bishop of Llandaff" (1810), in *CW*, 2:764–88, and "Examination of the Prophecies" (1807), in *CW*, 2:848–91. See Hitchens, *God Is Not Great*, 107.

26. Thomas Paine, *The Prospect Papers* (1804), in *CW*, 2:790, 798–99, and also the note on 811, in which he repeated this theme.

27. See Jack Fruchtman Jr., *Thomas Paine and the Religion of Nature* (Baltimore: Johns Hopkins University Press, 1933), 58–61, on which these observations are based. Spinoza's biblical criticism is remarkably akin to that of Paine. See Jonathan Israel, *Radical Enlightenment Philosophy and the Making of Modernity, 1650–1750* (Oxford: Oxford University Press, 2001), 447–49.

28. Benedict de Spinoza to Henry Oldenburg, Nov. or Dec. 1675, in *The Correspondence of Spinoza*, ed. A. Wolf (London: Frank Cass, 1966), 343. Jonathan Israel fails to see, however, any trace of theism in Spinoza's philosophy. See Israel, *Enlightenment Contested*, 45–46.

29. Lewis Samuel Feuer, *Spinoza and the Rise of Liberalism* (Boston: Beacon Press, 1958), 101; see also 65–69, 179–82, and 100–107.

30. Jonathan Israel, ed., in Spinoza, *Theological-Political Treatise* (Cambridge: Cambridge University Press, 2007), xxvii. See also Israel, *Radical Enlightenment*, 159–74, 218–41, and Israel, *Enlightenment Contested: Philosophy, Modernity, and the Emancipation of Man, 1670–1752* (Oxford: Oxford University Press, 2006), 240–63. For a summary of this view, see

Israel, "The Intellectual Origins of Modern Democratic Republicanism (1660–1720)," *European Journal of Political Theory* 3 (2004): 7–36.

31. Benedict de Spinoza, "Proposition 36," in *Ethics*, quoted by Israel, *Radical Enlightenment*, 238.

32. Benedict de Spinoza, *Theological-Political Treatise*, ed. Jonathan Israel (Cambridge: Cambridge University Press, 2007), 202.

33. In fact, Israel makes the link between Spinoza and Rousseau, that is, the French-Dutch Enlightenment nexus, in *Radical Enlightenment*, 714–20.

34. Paine, *The Prospect Papers*, in *CW*, 2:816.

35. Note the female character Paine has attributed to Providence.

36. Thomas Paine, "The Existence of God: A Discourse at the Society of Theophilanthropists, Paris" (1797), in *CW*, 2:749.

37. The classic study is by Roy N. Lokken, "The Concept of Democracy in Colonial Political Thought," *William and Mary Quarterly*, 3rd ser., 16 (Oct. 1959): 568–80. See also, among many examples, Sean Wilentz, *The Rise of American Democracy: From Jefferson to Lincoln* (New York: W. W. Norton, 2005), 7–10, Robert A. Dahl, *How Democratic Is the American Constitution?* (New Haven: Yale University Press, 2002), 159–62, and Martin Malia, *The Soviet Tragedy: A History of Socialism in Russia, 1917–1991* (New York: Free Press, 1994), 25, 31–33.

38. Henry St. John, Viscount Bolingbroke, *Political Writings*, ed. David Armitage (Cambridge: Cambridge University Press, 1997), 127.

39. Comments on "democracy" are cited in the revisionist study by Woody Holton, *Unruly Americans and the Origins of the Constitution* (New York: Hill & Wang, 2007), 5, 162–76, and 100–107, for the tax burden on ordinary citizens, and 235 for George Mason's comments on state democracies.

40. John Adams, *Diary and Autobiography of John Adams*, 3:333. On "democracy," see John Dunn, *Democracy: A History* (New York: Atlantic Monthly Press, 2005). Undoubtedly the study that most establishes Paine's "democratic" credentials (and Paine, unlike his fellow republican advocates, never feared using the term *democracy*, despite its association with mob rule) is Harvey J. Kaye, *Thomas Paine and the Promise of America* (New York: Hill & Wang, 2005).

41. Thomas Paine, "To the Abbé Sieyès" (1791), in *CW*, 2:520. But see Robert de Prospero, "Paine and Sieyès," *Thought* 65 (June 1990): 190–202. As a proponent of progress and modernization, see Jack P. Greene, "Paine, America, and the 'Modernization' of Political Consciousness," *Political Science Quarterly* 93 (Spring 1972): 73–92.

42. Thomas Paine, *Letter to George Washington* (1796), in *CW*, 2:691–723.

43. Thomas Paine, *To the Citizens of the United States*, letter 3 (1802), in *CW*, 2:920.

44. James Madison, Federalist 51 (1788), in *The Federalist Papers*, ed. Isaac Kramnick (New York: Penguin Press, 1987), 319.

45. Garrett Ward Sheldon, *The Political Philosophy of James Madison* (Baltimore: Johns Hopkins University Press, 2001), 25, 55–57, and 60–77, esp. 72–74.

46. Madison, Federalist 55 (1788), in Kramnick, *The Federalist Papers*, 336.

47. Madison, Federalist 48 (1788), in ibid., 309.

48. Madison, Federalist 51 (1788), in ibid., 319.

49. Thomas Paine, "A Republican Manifesto" (1791), a placard posted on Paris streets by Paine and Achille Duchâtelet, 1 July 1791, in ibid., 518. The placard was sponsored by the new Republican Society (*la Société républicaine*) Paine, Condorcet, Nicolas de Bonneville, and others organized for the purpose of creating the French Republic.

50. Edmund Burke, *Reflections on the Revolution in France* (1790), ed. J. G. A. Pocock (Indianapolis: Hackett Publishing, 1987), 69, 66.

51. Thomas Paine, *Dissertation on First Principles of Government* (1795), in *CW*, 2:586.

52. Thomas Paine, "An Essay for the Use of New Republicans" (1792), in *CW*, 2:543.

53. Franklin was an exception to this belief. See Pangle, *The Political Philosophy of Franklin*, 128.

54. Thomas Paine, "Answer to Four Questions Concerning the Legislative and Executive Powers" (1792), in *CW*, 2:525 and 527.

55. Note that this is not a question Paine is posing; for him, it is a statement of fact.

56. Ronald Paulson, *Representation of Revolution (1789–1820)* (New Haven: Yale University Press, 1983), 24, 364, 366, and esp. 77–78, who addresses how this imagery was employed in both the American and French contexts during revolutionary times.

57. Note Shakespeare's *Othello*, act 1, scene 3: "Wherein I spake of most disastrous chances, / Or moving accidents by flood and field, . . . / And of he Cannibals that each other eat, / The Anthropophagi."

58. Paine, "An Essay for the Use of New Republicans," in *CW*, 2:542.

59. Quoted in Jay Winik, *The Great Upheaval: America and the Birth of the Modern World, 1788–1800* (New York: HarperCollins, 2007), 366. Vergniaud was guillotined later that year.

60. Paine's design was later endorsed by both the Royal Society of London and the Royal Academy of Sciences in Paris.

61. Jean-Jacques Rousseau, "The Discourse on the Origin of Inequal-

ity," in *On the Social Contract*, ed. Donald A. Cress (Indianapolis: Hackett Publishing, 1987), 53.

62. Quoted in Holton, *Unruly Americans*, 117.

63. [Thomas Paine], *Four Letters on Interesting Subjects*, letter 4 (1776), in *The Origins of the American Constitution: A Documentary History*, ed. Michael Kammen (New York: Penguin Books, 1986), 4–5. These letters were published anonymously in the spring of 1776, but after careful research A. Owen Aldridge, the most dedicated Paine scholar in America, has determined conclusively that Paine wrote them. See Alfred Owen Aldridge, *Thomas Paine's American Ideology* (Newark: University of Delaware Press, 1984), 219–21. Eric Foner, unconvinced that Paine wrote these essays, declined to include them in his Library of America collection.

64. Paine's remark about Franklin appeared in [Thomas Paine], "A Serious Address to the People of Pennsylvania" (1778), in *CW*, 2:280. Paine began to change his mind about the efficacy of unicameral legislatures after the Reign of Terror in France. See chapter 5 of this volume and Thomas Paine, *The Eighteenth Fructidor, To the People of France and the French Armies* (1797), in *CW*, 2:594–613. For Franklin's view, see Pangle, *Political Philosophy of Franklin*, 128, and Alan Houston, *Benjamin Franklin and the Politics of Improvement* (New Haven: Yale University Press, 2008), 189–91.

65. [Paine], "A Serious Address to the People of Pennsylvania," in *CW*, 2:288.

66. Paine, *Dissertation on the First Principles of Government*," in *CW*, 2:577–578. See also Thomas Paine, "The Constitution of 1795," in *CW*, 2:588–94.

67. The most elegant explanation of the tripartite Aristotelian division remains J. G. A. Pocock, *The Machiavellian Moment: Florentine Political Thought and the Atlantic Republican Tradition* (Princeton: Princeton University Press, 1975), 21–24, 66–72. See also Thomas L. Pangle, *The Spirit of Modern Republicanism: The Moral Vision of the American Founders and the Philosophy of Locke* (Chicago: University of Chicago Press, 1988), 53–61, for the "Socratic Dialectic."

68. Paine, "Constitutional Reform" (1805), in *CW*, 2:1006. Franklin also likened a two-house legislature to a two-headed snake that could not decide how to pass by a bush: one head wanted to go to the left, the other to the right, so it went nowhere. Franklin actually found a two-headed snake in Philadelphia during the Constitutional Convention, and he showed it to the delegates there. See Pangle, *Political Philosophy of Franklin*, 172 and 253n104, and Houston, *Franklin and the Politics of Improvement*, 190.

69. This is the assessment of Craig Nelson, *Thomas Paine: Enlightenment, Revolution, and the Birth of Modern Nations* (New York: Viking, 2006), 142. Sean Wilentz is more modest, calling it merely "the most egalitarian constitution produced anywhere in Revolutionary America." See Wilentz, *The Rise of American Democracy*, 14.

70. [Paine], "A Serious Address too the People of Pennsylvania" (1777), in *CW,* 2:271–72. For Paine's denial of participating in the drafting of the constitution, see *CW,* 2:270.

71. On Franklin's role in the drafting of the Articles of Confederation, see Walter Isaacson, *Benjamin Franklin: An American Life* (New York: Simon & Schuster, 2003), 299–300.

72. [Paine], *Four Letters on Interesting Subjects*, in Kammen, *The Origins of the American Constitution*, 4–5, where he raised the possibility of twenty houses.

73. John Adams, "Thoughts on Government," in *The Political Writings of John Adams: Representative Selections*, ed. George A. Peek Jr. (Indianapolis: Bobbs-Merrill, 1954), 87; Joseph J. Ellis, *American Creation: Triumph and Tragedies at the Founding of the Republic* (New York: Alfred A. Knopf, 2007), 46–48; and Aldridge, *Thomas Paine's American Ideology*, 233–34.

74. William Hogeland, *The Whiskey Rebellion: George Washington, Alexander Hamilton, and the Frontier Rebels Who Challenged America's Newfound Sovereignty* (New York: Scribner, 2006), 36.

75. [Paine], "A Serious Address to the People of Pennsylvania," in *CW,* 2:271.

76. Benjamin Franklin, *Autobiography*, in *Benjamin Franklin: Writings*, ed. J. A. Leo Lemay (New York: Library of America: 1987), 1463, and Paine, "Address and Declaration at a Select Meeting of the Friends of Universal Peace and Liberty" (1791), in *CW,* 2:536.

77. [Paine], "A Serious Address to the People of Pennsylvania," in *CW,* 2:281.

78. Madison, Federalist 37, in Kramnick, *The Federalist Papers*, 243.

79. Winik, *The Great Upheaval*, 511.

80. Quoted by David McCullough, *John Adams* (New York: Simon & Schuster, 2001), 375.

81. Israel, *Enlightenment Contested*, 56.

82. Thomas Jefferson, *The Anas*, 4 Feb. 1818, in *Thomas Jefferson: Writings*, ed. Merrill D. Peterson (New York: Library of America, 1984), 671.

83. Winik, *The Great Upheaval*, 368.

84. See Jack Fruchtman Jr., *Atlantic Cousins: Benjamin Franklin and His Visionary Friends* (New York: Thunder's Mouth Press, 2005), 259–62.

85. Thomas Paine, "Constitutional Reform," in *CW,* 2:1001.

86. Thomas Paine, *Dissertations on Government; The Affairs of the Bank; and Paper Money* (1786), in *CW*, 2:409. For more on Paine's views of paper money, see chapter 5 of this volume. See Holton, *Unruly Americans*, 113. For a classic study of Paine's constitutional thought, see John J. Meng, "The Constitutional Theories of Thomas Paine," *Review of Politics* 8 (July 1946): 283–306.

87. Paine to a Committee of the Continental Congress, October, 1783, in *CW*, 2:1227.

88. Paine to Franklin, 16 May 1778, in *CW*, 2:1150–51. For the other times he used the "fire around the ears" imagery, Paine to A Committee of the Continental Congress, in *CW*, 2:1227, and Common Sense [Paine], *American Crisis*, no. 7, 21 Nov. 1778, in *CW*, 1:143–44.

89. Common Sense [Paine], *American Crisis*, no, 7, in *CW*, 1:143.

3. Common Sense, Authority, and Autonomy

1. Thomas Paine, *Dissertation on First Principles of Government* (1795), in *CW*, 2:573–74.

2. Isaac Kramnick, "Tom Paine, Radical Democrat," *Democracy* 1 (Jan. 1981): 127–38.

3. Pocock's words on this subject are debatable here: "*Common Sense* is not a call for an English revolution, but for an American separation." See *The Varieties of British Political Thought: 1500–1800*, ed. J. G. A. Pocock, with the Assistance of Gordon J. Schochet and Lois G. Schwoerer (Cambridge: Cambridge University Press, 1993), 279–80.

4. George W. Corner, ed., *The Autobiography of Benjamin Rush* (Princeton: Princeton University Press, published for the American Philosophical Society, 1948), 114.

5. Rush to Cheetham, 17 July 1809, in *Letters of Benjamin Rush*, ed. L. H. Butterfield, 2 vols. (Princeton: Princeton University Press, published for the American Philosophical Society, 1951), 2:1008. Rush had been asked by Cheetham, then preparing his hostile biography of Paine, to send him some reflections about the man. See also Corner, *The Autobiography of Benjamin Rush*, 114, where Rush recalled that, in suggesting the title to Paine, he referred to Bell as "a thoughtless and fearless Whig, and an open friend to independence."

6. There are exceptions, notably, Harvey J. Kaye, *Thomas Paine and the Promise of America* (New York: Hill & Wang, 2005), most recently, and Isaac Kramnick, "Tommy Paine and the Idea of America," in *The American Revolution and Eighteenth-Century Culture*, ed. Paul Korshin (New York: AMS Press, 1986), 75–91.

7. See also Common Sense [Thomas Paine], *American Crisis*, no. 10, 5 Mar. 1782, in *CW*, 1:192: "Like the Pharaoh on the edge of the Red Sea,

he [George III] sees not the plunge he is making, and precipitately drives across the flood that is closing over his head."

8. Eric Foner, *Tom Paine and Revolutionary America* (New York: Oxford University Press, 2005), 78.

9. For an analysis of the 1772 excise petition to Parliament, see chapter 5 of this volume.

10. Quoted in Robert Middlekauff, *The Glorious Cause: The American Revolution, 1763–1789* (New York: Oxford University Press, 1982), 270.

11. Bucks County [Thomas Paine], "A Dream Interpreted" (May 1775), *Pennsylvania Magazine*, in *CW*, 2:51–52.

12. Joseph J. Ellis, *American Creation: Triumph and Tragedies at the Founding of the Republic* (New York: Alfred A. Knopf, 2007), 74–75.

13. A Lover of Peace [Thomas Paine], "Thoughts on Defensive War" (July 1775), *Pennsylvania Magazine*, in *CW*, 2:53.

14. Humanus [Thomas Paine], "A Serious Thought" (Oct. 1775), *Pennsylvania Journal*, in *CW*, 2:20.

15. The theological and millennial components of *Common Sense* have been discussed in detail by Stephen Newman, "A Note on *Common Sense* and Christian Eschatology," *Political Theory* 6 (Feb. 1978): 101–8; Foner, *Tom Paine and Revolutionary America;* and Fruchtman, *Thomas Paine and the Religion of Nature.* See also Barry Alan Shain, *The Myth of American Individualism: The Protestant Origins of American Political Thought* (Princeton: Princeton University Press, 1994).

16. Winthrop D. Jordan, "Familial Politics: Thomas Paine and the Killing of the King," *Journal of American History* 60 (Sept. 1973): 294–308.

17. Common Sense [Paine], *American Crisis*, no. 2, 13 Jan. 1777, in *CW*, 1:72.

18. Paine quoted this passage himself in *Common Sense*, 126.

19. John Locke, *Second Treatise of Government*, ed. C. B. Macpherson (Indianapolis: Hackett Publishing, 1980), 113.

20. Among other things, Jonathan Israel traces the notion of a right to revolution from Spinoza to Locke, who lived in Spinoza's Holland while in exile just before the Revolution of 1688, and we can see this link then moving into England, ultimately to Paine. For Israel, "according to Spinoza, the purpose of the State is to secure the freedom and common good of all, and if the State becomes malign, or despotic, revolution may well be the consequence." Paine would have wholeheartedly agreed. Jonathan Israel, *Radical Enlightenment: Philosophy and the Making of Modernity, 1650–1750* (Oxford: Oxford University Press, 2001), 76. Israel is quick to point out that Locke remained committed to "mixed govern-

ment, limited monarchy, and institutionalized aristocracy," all three of which Paine unequivocally rejected. See Jonathan Israel, *Enlightenment Contested: Philosophy, Modernity, and the Emancipation of Man, 1670–1752* (Oxford: Oxford University Press, 2006), 546.

21. Common Sense [Paine], *American Crisis*, no. 1, 23 Dec. 1776, in *CW*, 1:53. See also ibid., no. 3, 19 Apr. 1777, in *CW*, 1:73–101, where Paine detailed his definition of a Tory and Toryism, which he unequivocally equated with treason.

22. Ibid., no. 3, 19 Apr. 1777, in *CW*, 1:94, 83. This was published on the two-year anniversary of the battles of Lexington and Concord.

23. Ibid., no. 1, in *CW*, 1:50–51, 52, 56.

24. Ibid., no. 5, 21 Mar. 1778, in *CW*, 1:109.

25. Ibid., no. 7, 21 Nov. 1778, in *CW*, 1:147.

26. Ibid., no. 6, 20 Oct. 1778, in *CW*, 1:136.

27. Ibid., no. 1, in *CW*, 1: 57, and no. 5, in *CW*, 1:121.

28. Paine paid his own way with what little money he had because Congress refused to subsidize his travel. When Laurens returned with Paine to America, he joined Washington at Yorktown. He was killed in South Carolina in a minor skirmish with British troops caught stealing rice. See Sara Bertha Townsend, *An American Soldier: The Life of John Laurens* (Raleigh, NC: Edwards & Broughton, 1958).

29. The total amount of money France gave to the new United States for the war effort was 12 million livres and loans of 18 million. In addition, the French spent two billion livres on sixty-three ships with 3,668 cannon, and 47,000 soldiers and sailors. It is no wonder that French debt bankrupted the government, helping to heap fire on the coming revolution just eight years later. See Craig Nelson, *Thomas Paine: Enlightenment, Revolution, and the Birth of Modern Nations* (New York: Viking, 2006), 155.

30. Paine to Jonathan Williams, 26 Nov. 1781, in *CW*, 2:1200.

31. Paine to George Washington, 30 Nov. 1781, in *CW*, 2:1204.

32. Paine to Elias Boudinot, 7 June 1783, in *CW*, 2:1218.

33. For a full discussion of the concept of revolution, see Martin Malia, *History's Locomotives: Revolutions and the Making of the Modern World* (New Haven: Yale University Press, 2006), 287–301, app. 1, "Revolution: What's in a Name?". For the now-classic study of how this view of revolution as a return to first principles is worked out, see J. G. A. Pocock, *The Machiavellian Moment: Florentine Political Thought and the Atlantic Republican Tradition* (Princeton: Princeton University Press, 1975). For a different view from that of Pocock, see Israel, *Enlightenment Contested*, 3–15.

34. Paine to Washington, in *CW,* 2:1204. He outlined his objections to Morris in his letter of 26 Nov. 1782, in *CW,* 2:1202.

35. Paine to Robert Morris, 6 Sept. 1782, in *CW,* 2:1211.

36. Paine to George Washington, 7 Sept. 1782, in *CW,* 2:1212.

37. While Paine's response is a point-by-point refutation of the Abbé's history, what follows here are the main political themes in his letter to Raynal. For a different assessment, see Vikki J. Vickers, *"My Pen and My Soul Have Ever Gone Together": Thomas Paine and the American Revolution* (New York: Routledge, 1006), 109–15.

38. See Claeys, *Thomas Paine*, 45–51, and Bernard Bailyn, *The Ideological Origins of the American Revolution*, rev. ed. (Cambridge, MA: Harvard University Press, 1992), 285–87.

39. Paine, *Letter to the Abbé Raynal, on the Affairs of North America: in which the Mistakes in the Abbé's Account of the Revolution of America are Corrected and Cleared up* (1782), in *CW,* 2:243–44.

40. Richard Price, *Observations on the Importance of the American Revolution, and the Means of Making It a Benefit to the World* (London, 1784), 7–8.

41. [Joseph Priestley], *An Address to Protestant Dissenters of All Denominations on the Approaching elections of Members to Parliament with Respect to the State of Public Liberty in General, and of American Affairs in Particular* (London, 1774), in *The Theological and Miscellaneous Works of Joseph Priestley*, ed. John Towill Rutt, 25 vols. in 26 (Hackney, 1816–31), 22:493. Although Priestley was writing before the hostilities broke out between American and British forces, his comments are relevant to this point.

42. Paine, *Letter to the Abbé Raynal*, in *CW,* 2:244.

43. J. Hector St. John de Crèvecoeur, *Letters from an American Farmer and Sketches of Eighteenth-Century America* (1782), ed. Albert E. Stone (Harmondsworth, UK: Penguin, 1981), 66, 69–70.

44. Nelson, *Thomas Paine*, 150.

4. Permanent Revolution and Constitution Making

1. *Rights of Man* was published simultaneously in London, Baltimore, and Paris.

2. A principle ascribed to the Russian revolutionary leader, Leon Trotsky, "the permanent revolution" was based on the idea that once a political revolution has been successful, it must continue until the financial and economic forces and institutions of the country fall into the hands of the oppressed working class, that is, the proletariat. This concept differed in degree only from Paine's views, which envisioned permanent revolution throughout the world until all nations became democratic republics, with social welfare institutions along the lines he outlined in the sec-

ond part of the *Rights of Man* and in *Agrarian Justice*. I do not take this comparison much farther, however. See Leon Trotsky, *The Permanent Revolution: Results and Prospects* (New York: Pathfinder Press, 1976).

3. The Burke-Paine controversy is a subject of seemingly unending discussion and fascination. See R. R. Fennessy, *Burke, Paine, and the Rights of Man: A Difference of Political Opinion* (The Hague: Martinus Nijhoff, 1963), for an older study, and Marilyn Morris, *The British Monarchy and the French Revolution* (New Haven: Yale University Press, 1998), esp. 37–55 ("The Burke-Paine Controversy"), and Craig Nelson, *Thomas Paine: Enlightenment, Revolution, and the Birth of Modern Nations* (New York: Viking, 2006), 193–204, for more recent ones.

4. Thomas Jefferson to James Madison, 6 Sept. 1789, in *Thomas Jefferson: Writings,* ed. Merrill D. Peterson (New York: Library of America, 1984), 959, where he made the famous remark, which in context reads as follows: "I set on this ground, which I suppose to be self-evident, *that the earth belongs in usufruct to the living.*" For an authoritative interpretation of that remark, see Joseph J. Ellis, *American Sphinx: The Character of Thomas Jefferson* (New York: Vintage, 1998), 131–32.

5. Thomas Paine, *Dissertation on First Principles of Government* (1795), in *CW,* 2:576.

6. Thomas Paine, "Answer to Four Questions on Legislative and Executive Powers" (1792), in *CW,* 2:533.

7. Thomas Paine, *Agrarian Justice* (1796), in *CW,* 1:611, and hereafter referred to in the text as *AJ.*

8. John Locke, *Second Treatise of Government* (1690), ed. C. B. Macpherson (Indianapolis: Hackett Publishing, 1980), 21, 29. See chapter 5 of this volume.

9. Jefferson to Paine, 15 Sept. 1789, in *The Papers of Thomas Jefferson,* ed. Julian P. Boyd, 35 vols. to date (Princeton: Princeton University Press, 1950–), 15:269.

10. Paine to Edmund Burke, 17 Jan. 1790, in J. T. Boulton, "An Unpublished Letter from Paine to Burke," *Durham University Journal* 43 (Mar. 1951): 52.

11. The Revolution Society met each November to celebrate the anniversary of the 1688 Revolution.

12. Richard Price, *A Discourse on the Love of Our Country, Delivered on November 4, 1789, at the Meeting House in the Old Jewry, to the Society for Commemorating the Revolution in Great Britain* (London, 1790), 40. The Old Jewry was so-called because it was erected on the site of the old Jewish ghetto.

13. Burke, *Reflections on the Revolution in France* (1790), ed. J. G. A. Pocock (Indianapolis: Hackett Publishing, 1987), 15 (emphasis added).

14. Paine, *Dissertation on the First Principles of Government*, in *CW,* 2:577. See also Paine, *Letter Addressed to the Addressers on the Late Proclamations* (1792), in *CW,* 2:495–96. Gregory Claeys rightly points out that much of Paine's criticism of 1688 can also be found in the *Rights of Man.* Claeys, *Thomas Paine*, 86–87.

15. Paine, *Dissertation on the First Principles of Government*, in *CW,* 2:575.

16. [Thomas Paine], *Four Letters on Interesting Subjects*, letter 4, in *The Origins of the American Constitution: A Documentary History,* ed. Michael Kammen (New York: Penguin Books, 1986), 3–4.

17. J. G. A. Pocock, *Virtue, Commerce, and History: Essays on Political Thought and History, Chiefly in the Eighteenth Century* (Cambridge: Cambridge University Press, 1985), 276.

18. Paine to Short, 22 June 1790, in *CW,* 2:1309. See also Paine, *Letter Addressed to the Addressers*, in *CW,* 2:484–85, where he reiterates this point yet again.

19. Thomas Paine, *Letter Addressed to the Addressers,* in *CW,* 2:482, 485, 491, 511. On the Society of the Friends of the People, an organization that Paine attacks in this pamphlet, see Eugene Charlton Black, *The Association: British Extraparliamentary Political Organization, 1769–1793* (Cambridge, MA: Harvard University Press, 1963), 218–23; H. T. Dickinson, *Liberty and Property: Political Ideology in Eighteenth-Century Britain* (New York: Holmes & Meier, 1977), 237–39; and Albert Goodwin, *The Friends of Liberty: The English Democratic Movement in the Age of the French Revolution* (Cambridge, MA: Harvard University Press, 1979), 203–14.

20. [Thomas Paine], "A Serious Address to the People of Pennsylvania on the Present Situation of Their Affairs" (1778), in *CW,* 2:285.

21. Thomas Paine, "Address and Declaration of the Friends of Universal Peace and Liberty" (1791), in *CW,* 2:536. Paine alluded to Burke's *Appeal from the New to the Old Whigs* of 1791 when he argued on natural law grounds that human beings are subjects of their government and must accept their God-given place in society.

22. Burke, *Reflections*, 14.

23. Thomas Paine, "Answer to Four Questions on the Legislative and Executive Powers," in *CW,* 2:522.

24. See also [Paine], "A Serious Address," in *CW,* 2:285–87, and *Dissertation on the First Principles of Government*, in *CW,* 2:577–85, where he discussed equal rights.

25. Locke, *Second Treatise of Government*, 8.

26. Jonathan Israel, *Enlightenment Contested: Philosophy, Modernity, and the Emancipation of Man, 1670–1752* (Oxford: Oxford University Press, 2006), 561, who relates the link between natural and civil rights in Paine's

thought to Spinoza and the Spinozistic system, not Locke and Lockean ideas.

27. Paine to Thomas Jefferson, Feb. 1788, in *Thomas Paine: Collected Writings,* ed. Eric Foner (New York: Library of America, 1995), 368. The *CW* editor, Philip Foner, dates the letter from 1789, which, though inaccurate, was corrected by his nephew, Eric Foner.

28. Locke, *Second Treatise of Government*, 9.

29. Common Sense [Thomas Paine], "Candid and Critical Remarks on a Letter Signed Ludlow" (1777), in *CW,* 2:274.

30. Paine, *Dissertation on the First Principles of Government,* in *CW,* 2: 578, 579. See Bernard Vincent, *The Transatlantic Republican: Thomas Paine and the Age of Revolutions* (Amsterdam: Rodopi, 2005), 117–24.

31. Paine, *Dissertations on Government,* in *CW,* 2:372. The general will also played a major role in Paine's thinking on economic and social issues; see chapter 5 of this volume.

32. Thomas Paine, "An Essay for the Use of New Republicans in Their Opposition to Monarchy" (1792), in *CW,* 2:543. Jonathan Israel finds the roots of Rousseau's general will in Spinoza's concept of the common good, the *res publica,* "in terms of safety, freedom and the rule of law . . . providing a universal criterion of good and bad by which states, of whatever kind, can be appraised." Israel, "The Intellectual Origins of Modern Democratic Republicanism (1660–1720), *European Journal of Political Theory* 3 (2004): 30.

33. The principle banning "prior restraints" on the press was constitutionalized by the Supreme Court in the Pentagon Papers case of *New York Times v. United States,* 403 U.S. 670 (1971). The principle had been bounding around in American law since the 1735 trial of John Peter Zenger and in *Near v. Minnesota ex rel. Olson,* 283 U.S. 697 (1930). For Zenger, see Livingston Rutherford, *John Peter Zenger, His Press, His Trial, and a Bibliography of Zenger Imprints* (New York: Dodd, Mead, 1904), and *Freedom of the Press from Zenger to Jefferson,* ed. Leonard Levy (New York: Bobbs-Merrill, 1966).

34. Thomas Paine, "Liberty of the Press" (1806), in *CW,* 2:1011.

35. Merrill D. Peterson and Robert C. Vaughn, eds., *The Virginia Statute for Religious Freedom: Its Evolution and Consequences in American History* (Cambridge: Cambridge University Press, 1988).

36. [Paine], "A Serious Address," in *CW,* 2:285.

37. Although the Occasional Conformity Act of 1711 had prohibited a once-per-year practice of receiving the Anglican Communion, the ban was repealed eight years later, only to be replaced by the more hospitable Indemnity Acts after 1727. These acts preserved the independence of Dissenters as religious sects but did not aid them in their political aspira-

tions. See Michael R. Watts, *The Dissenters* (Oxford: Clarendon Press, 1978, 1985).

38. That Jefferson collaborated on the draft of the French Declaration is well known. See Jay Winik, *The Great Upheaval: America and the Birth of the Modern World* (New York: HarperCollins, 2007), 229. It is curious that Article X, if Jefferson influenced it as well, did not more explicitly guarantee religious liberty.

39. The debate over whether it also bound the states was not resolved until the doctrine of incorporation was enunciated by the Supreme Court, beginning at the end of the nineteenth century. The Establishment Clause was not incorporated until the case of *Everson v. Board of Education*, 330 U.S. 1 (1947). See Jefferson to Messrs. Nehemiah Dodge and Others, a Committee of the Danbury Baptist Association in the State of Connecticut, 1 Jan. 1803, in Peterson, *Writings: Jefferson*, 510.

40. There may be some objection to how central his passage was to his argument, given that Paine placed it in a note, and not in the body of his commentary.

41. [Paine], *Four Letters on Interesting Subjects*, 5.

42. For the argument that much of the Revolution debate was over language, see Steven Blakemore, *Burke and the Fall of Language: The French Revolution as a Linguistic Debate* (Hanover, NH: University Press of New England, 1988).

43. Jean-Jacques Rousseau, *On the Social Contract*, ed. Donald A. Cress (Indianapolis: Hackett Publishing, 1987), 154.

44. Thomas Paine, *Dissertations on Government; the Affairs of the Bank; and Paper Money* (1786), in *CW*, 2:369. On Paine and nature, see Jack Fruchtman Jr., *Thomas Paine and the Religion of Nature* (Baltimore: Johns Hopkins University Press, 1993).

45. Paine to James Monroe, 10 Sept. 1794, in *CW*, 2:1347.

46. See Paine, *Dissertations on Government*, in *CW*, 2:372–73, where he addressed his thinking concerning the meaning of "republic" in just these terms.

47. Paine to Jefferson, 1 Nov. 1786, quoted in Jack N. Rakove, *Original Meanings: Politics and Ideas in the Making of the Constitution* (New York: Alfred A. Knopf, 1996), 41. See Woody Holton, *Unruly Americans and the Origins of the Constitution* (New York: Hill & Wang, 2007), 196, for a brief discussion of the debate over property qualifications at the Constitutional Convention in 1787.

48. Rousseau rejected the idea of representation, however, because he argued that sovereignty was indivisible.

49. [Paine], "A Serious Address," in *CW*, 2:290.

50. Thomas Paine, "On Preserving the Life of Louis Capet," speech be-

fore the French National Convention during the trial of Louis XVI, 15 Jan. 1793, in *CW*, 2:553. Paine was referring to Louis XVI as Louis Capet as early as June of 1791; see Paine, "A Republican Manifesto" (1791), in *CW*, 2:518.

51. Thomas Paine, "On Bringing Louis XVI to Trial," speech before the French National Convention on 21 Nov. 1792, in *CW*, 2:548. Louis XVI was tried by the Convention, which first met in September of 1792 specifically to write a new republican constitution for France after the fall of the monarchy on 10 Aug. 1792; Paine was elected as a member from Pas-de-Calais and three other jurisdictions as well.

53. *CW*, 2:551.

53. *CW*, 2:552 (emphasis added).

54. Paine, "A Republican Manifesto," in *CW*, 2:517–19.

55. Paine, "On Preserving the Life of Louis Capet," in *CW*, 2:554.

56. Thomas Paine, "Shall Louis XVI Be Respited," a speech shouted at the French National Convention, 19 Jan. 1793, in *CW*, 2:557–58. On the one-vote margin in the convention in favor of the king's execution, see Winik, *The Great Upheaval*, 313.

5. From a "Hamiltonian" Spirit to Public Welfare

1. That the two thinkers shared views on virtue, commerce, and finance but possessed quite different ones on public credit and other economic matters is made clear in Michael D. Chan, *Aristotle and Alexander Hamilton on Commerce and Statesmanship* (Columbia: University of Missouri Press, 2006), who argues not that Hamilton was Aristotelian especially, but that he and Paine shared many financial and political ideas.

2. Quoted by Ron Chernow, *Alexander Hamilton* (New York: Penguin Press, 2004), 307.

3. Samuel Johnson, *Taxation No Tyranny!* in *The Yale Edition of the Works of Samuel Johnson*, ed. Donald J. Greene, 16 vols. to date (New Haven: Yale University Press, 1957–), 10:454.

4. Justice and Humanity [Thomas Paine], "African Slavery in America" (1775), in *CW*, 2:17, and Humanus [Thomas Paine], "A Serious Thought" (1775), in *CW*, 2:15–20. See also The Forester [Thomas Paine], letter 3, "To Cato" (1776), in *CW*, 2:82n.

5. Charlie Savage, *Takeover: The Return of the Imperial Presidency and the Subversion of American Democracy* (Boston: Little, Brown: 2007), esp. 14–22 and 124–27, where Savage identifies the quintessential contemporary Hamiltonian as former Vice President Richard B. Cheney.

6. Thomas Jefferson, *The Anas*, 4 Feb. 1818, in *Thomas Jefferson: Writings*, ed. Merrill D. Peterson (New York: Library of America, 1984), 670–71.

7. The first constitution created the National Assembly under the

king, that is, a constitutional monarchy. The second, as noted above, drafted in part by Condorcet, Paine, and the other committee members appointed by the National Convention, was designed to create a democratic republic for France. When the Terror ended, the Convention drafted yet a third constitution, in 1795, and Paine again worked and commented on it as a deputy.

8. John Ferling, *Adams v. Jefferson: The Tumultuous Election of 1800* (Oxford: Oxford University Press, 2004), 114, for both quotations.

9. The most authoritative works are Jack N. Rakove, *Original Meanings: Politics and Ideas in the Making of the Constitution* (New York: Alfred A. Knopf, 1996), and Carol Berkin, *A Brilliant Solution: Inventing the American Constitution* (New York: Harcourt, 2002).

10. Alexander Hamilton, *Report on the Subject of Manufactures*, in *Alexander Hamilton: Writings*, ed. Joanne B. Freeman (New York: Library of America, 2001), 647–734.

11. Chernow, *Alexander Hamilton*, 393.

12. Eric Foner, *Tom Paine and Revolutionary America* York: Oxford University Press, 2005), 191.

13. Thomas Paine, *Six Letters to Rhode Island* (1782–83), in *CW*, 2:352.

14. William Hogeland, *The Whiskey Rebellion: George Washington, Alexander Hamilton, and the Frontier Rebels Who Challenged America's Newfound Sovereignty* (New York: Scribner, 2006), 239. Hogeland's is the authoritative account.

15. Paine, *Six Letters to Rhode Island*, in *CW*, 2:333–66.

16. John Keane, *Tom Paine: A Political Life* (Boston: Little, Brown, 1995), 235–40, and Jack Fruchtman Jr., *Thomas Paine: Apostle of Freedom* (New York: Four Walls Eight Windows, 1994), 146–49. See the conclusion below, when Paine reiterated his disdain as late as 1802 for Rhode Island's failure to raise taxes to support the war effort.

17. Darren Staloff, *Hamilton, Adams, and Jefferson: The Politics of Enlightenment and the American Founding* (New York: Hill & Wang, 2005).

18. A point emphasized recently by both Joseph J. Ellis, *American Creation: Triumphs and Tragedies at the Founding of the Republic* (New York: Alfred A. Knopf, 2007), 196, and Jay Winik, *The Great Upheaval: America and the Birth of the Modern World, 1788–1800* (New York: HarperCollins, 2007), 487.

19. Chernow, *Alexander Hamilton*, 553–55.

20. Quoted in Gordon S. Wood, *Revolutionary Characters: What Made the Founders Different?* (New York: Penguin Press, 2006), 138.

21. Quoted in Chernow, *Alexander Hamilton*, 567. Vice President Adams's response was, "I don't know whether to laugh or weep," and then thought maybe Hamilton wanted to use his army to seize control

of the government with himself at the head to transform the U.S. into a British province. Quoted in Chernow, *Alexander Hamilton*, 568. For Miranda, see Fruchtman, *Thomas Paine: Apostle of Freedom*, 305–6.

22. Staloff, *Hamilton, Adams, and Jefferson*, 69, and Chernow, *Alexander Hamilton*, 156–60.

23. American customs duties, collected by Hamilton's Treasury Department, accounted for 90 percent of American revenues. Ellis, *American Creation*, 194.

24. Thomas Paine, "The Case of the Officers of the Excise" (1772), in *CW*, 2:3–15.

25. Marxist historians may argue that Paine's support of the exploited worker earning a bare subsistence wage and subservient to the owners of the means of production made him a proto-socialist. See Gregory Claeys, "The Origins of the Rights of Labor: Republicanism, Commerce, and the Construction of Modern Society Theory in Britain, 1796–1805," *Journal of Modern History* 66 (June 1994): 249–90, although Claeys is concerned with Paine's last great work, *Agrarian Justice* (1796). See also E. P. Thompson, *The Making of the English Working Class* (New York: Vintage, 1963), for the classic take on this subject.

26. Istvan Hont and Michael Ignatieff, eds., *Wealth and Virtue: The Shaping of Political Economy in the Scottish Enlightenment* (Cambridge: Cambridge University Press, 1983), remains the classic work, and see esp. John Robertson's essay, "The Scottish Enlightenment at the Limits of the Civil Tradition," in ibid., 137–78.

27. On Smith, see Donald Winch, *Adam Smith's Politics: An Essay in Historiographic Revision* (Cambridge: Cambridge University Press, 1978), and for Hume, see Duncan Forbes, *Hume's Philosophical Politics* (Cambridge: Cambridge University Press, 1975).

28. Thomas Paine, *Dissertations on Government; The Affairs of the Bank; and Paper Money* (1786), in *CW*, 2:404

29. See Foner, *Tom Paine and Revolutionary America*, 198, and Woody Holton, *Unruly Americans and the Origins of the Constitution* (New York: Hill & Wang, 2007), 113. Paine was careful to distinguish between "paper" in the form of contracts and bank notes, which people were not obliged to accept, and paper money as a means of exchange, which people are compelled to accept if they wish to engage in commerce, industry, or finance. Paine was joined in his sentiment by many Americans, such as George Mason, Elbridge Gerry, and Charles Cotesworth Pinckney, though none of these men went as far as he did in suggesting the demise of supporters.

30. Harvey Flaumenhaft, *The Effective Republic: Administration and*

Constitution in the Thought of Alexander Hamilton (Durham, NC: Duke University Press, 1992).

31. David Hume, *Essays Moral, Political, and Literary of David Hume,* World's Classics (London: Grant Richards, 1903), esp. "Of Public Credit," 355–61.

32. J. G. A. Pocock, "The Political Economy of Burke's Analysis of the French Revolution," in Pocock, *Virtue, Commerce, and History: Essays in Political Thought and History, Chiefly in the Eighteenth Century* (Cambridge: Cambridge University Press, 1983), 194–95.

33. The best summary remains Albert Goodwin, *The Friends of Liberty: The English Democratic Movement in the Age of the French Revolution* (Cambridge, MA: Harvard University Press, 1979). See also H. T. Dickinson, *Liberty and Property: Political Ideology in Eighteenth-Century Britain* (New York: Holmes & Meier, 1977). For a recent sweeping analysis of democracy's progress and foibles, see John Dunn, *Democracy: A History* (New York: Atlantic Monthly Press, 2005).

34. See Claeys, *Thomas Paine,* 96–101, for an illuminating discussion of this topic.

35. Isaac Kramnick, *Republicanism and Bourgeois Radicalism: Political Ideology in Late Eighteenth-Century England and America* (Ithaca: Cornell University Press, 1990).

36. Alfred Owen Aldridge, "Why Did Thomas Paine Write on the Bank?" *Proceedings of the American Philosophical Society* 93 (Sept. 1949): 309–15.

37. Paine to Robert Morris, 20 Feb. 1782, in *CW,* 2:1206.

38. The details are laid out in Foner, *Tom Paine and Revolutionary America,* 192–203.

39. Thomas Paine, *The Decline and Fall of the English System of Finance* (1796), in *CW,* 2:654–55.

40. *CW,* 2:656, 674.

41. Paine to Thomas Jefferson, 1 Apr. 1797, in *CW,* 2:1387. See also Paine to Jefferson, 1 Oct. 1800, in *CW,* 2:1413–14.

42. One of Paine's biographers noted that when this occurred, he "appeared to the world as an acute economic prophet." David Freeman Hawke, *Paine* (New York: Harper & Row, 1974), 318. More recently, John Keane says that the bank's action caused Paine to crow that his writings had contributed to "hastening the collapse of the Georgian monarchy." Keane, *Tom Paine,* 428.

43. Paine to Thomas Jefferson, 1 Apr. 1797, in *CW,* 2:1388.

44. Paine, *Decline and Fall,* in *CW,* 2:669.

45. Paine cited the *Social Contract* in the *Rights of Man.* For Rousseau's

democratic credentials, see James Miller, *Rousseau: Dreamer of Democracy* (New Haven: Yale University Press, 1984).

46. Paine, "An Essay for the Use of New Republicans in Their Opposition to Monarchy" (1792), in *CW,* 2:543. Paine is quoting from *On the Social Contract,* bk. 3:60.

47. Alfred Cobban, *Aspects of the French Revolution* (New York: W. W. Norton, 1968), 152. See, again, the Talmon citation above, Introduction, note 34.

48. In this sense, we can distinguish the "communal" views of Americans, as Shain defines them. Shain suggests that American communalism meant that Americans "believed that local intermediate (familial, social, religious, and governmental) institutions must play a prominent and intrusive role in defining the ethical life of individuals by lacing limits on individual autonomy." Barry Alan Shain, *The Myth of American Individualism: The Protestant Origins of American Political Thought* (Princeton: Princeton University Press, 1994), 48. The communalism that Paine espoused did not focus on what individuals must refrain from doing but on the responsibility of government to care for its less fortunate citizens, a very modern form of communalism not realized until the twentieth century.

49. Jean-Jacques Rousseau, *On the Social Contract* (1762), ed. Donald A. Cress (Indianapolis: Hackett Publishing, 1983), 24.

50. Carol Blum, *Rousseau and the Republic of Virtue: The Language of Politics in the French Revolution* (Ithaca: Cornell University Press, 1986), 71–72. Blum shows how Rousseau's thought permeated revolutionary France long after his death in 1778.

51. Rousseau, *On Social Contract* (1762), 19, 26.

52. Thomas Spence and Thomas Hardy come to mind. For Spence, see Marcus Wood, "Thomas Spence and Modes of Subversion," *Enlightenment and Dissent* 10 (1991): 51–77; Jack Fruchtman Jr., "Two Doubting Thomases: The British Progressive Enlightenment and the French Revolution," in *Radicalism and Revolution in Britain, 1775–1848,* ed. Michael T. Davis (London: Macmillan, 2000), 30–40.

53. Thomas Paine and the Marquis de Condorcet, "Answer to Four Questions on the Legislative and Executive Powers" (1792), in *CW,* 2: 533.

54. John Locke, *Second Treatise of Government* (1690), ed, C. B. Macpherson (Indianapolis: Hackett Publishing, 1980), 18–21. Marx would later use this concept in the development of his ideology. For the background, see Thomas L. Pangle, *The Spirit of Modern Republicanism: The Moral Vision of the American Founders and the Philosophy of Locke* (Chicago: University of Chicago Press, 1988), 141–71.

55. Thomas Paine, *Dissertation on First Principles of Government* (1795), in *CW,* 2:581.

56. Kramnick, *Republicanism and Bourgeois Radicalism,* and Foner, *Tom Paine and Revolutionary America.*

57. Jean-Jacques Rousseau, *Discourse on the Origin of Inequality* (1755), in Cress, *On the Social Contract,* 140.

58. Rousseau, *On the Social Contract,* in ibid., 27.

59. Again, an echo of Jefferson's comment that the earth belongs in usufruct to the living: Thomas Jefferson to James Madison, 9 Sept. 1789, in *Thomas Jefferson: Writings,* ed. Merrill D. Peterson (New York: Library of America, 1984), 959. See Bernard Vincent, *The Transatlantic Republican: Thomas Paine and the Age of Revolutions* (Amsterdam: Rodopi, 2005), 125–35, and his discussion of Paine's contribution to the contemporary doctrine of Basic Income Theory.

60. Again, the classic Marxist work remains Thompson, *The Making of the English Working Class.*

61. Paine, *Dissertation on First Principles of Government,* in *CW,* 2:580, 583.

62. *CW,* 2:583.

6. Public Spirit, Civic Engagement, and Evolutionary Change

1. Thomas Paine, *To the Citizens of the United States,* letter 3 (1802), in *CW,* 2:919–21, Paine to Samuel Adams, 6 Mar. 1795, in *CW,* 2:1376; Paine to James Madison, 24 Sept. 1795, in *CW,* 2:1379; Paine to Anon., 4 Mar. 1797, in *CW,* 2:1386; Paine to Thomas Jefferson, 1 Oct. 1800, in *CW,* 2: 1412.

2. One clear exception is his vociferous attack on George Washington, who he thought had done nothing to secure his release from prison by claiming him as an American citizen. James Monroe, then the American minister in Paris who had urged French authorities to free Paine, tried and failed to dissuade Paine from publishing the open letter. See Thomas Paine, *Letter to George Washington* (1796), in *CW,* 2:691–723. In my judgment, the letter contains no statements that could reasonably fall into a political philosophy.

3. Edmund Burke, *Reflections on the Revolution in France* (1790), ed. J. G. A. Pocock (Indianapolis: Hackett Publishing, 1987), 80.

4. Thomas Paine, "Prosecution of *The Age of Reason*" (1797), in *CW,* 2:743, 744. Back in America, Paine continued his vigorous defense of deism, especially in *Prospect Papers,* essays he wrote for the *Prospect,* a deist journal founded by Elihu Palmer, who wrote a work Paine considered to

be the "bible" of deism, *The Principles of Nature,* in 1801. For Paine's essays, see Paine, *The Prospect Papers,* in *CW,* 2:788–830.

5. Paine also developed a new or renewed interest in Masonry, which he saw as being ideologically close to deism. See his essay on the Theophilanthropists, the "Prosecution of *The Age of Reason,*" in *CW,* 2:745–48, and his short work, "The Existence of God" (1797), an address to the Society of Theophilanthropists, in *CW,* 2:748–56, and "Origin of Freemasonry" (1805), in *CW,* 2:830–41.

6. Thomas Paine, "Worship and Church Bells: A Letter to Camille Jordan" (1797), in *CW,* 2:757, 758.

7. Thomas Paine, *Dissertation on First Principles of Government* (1795), in *CW,* 2:587.

8. *CW,* 2:571.

9. *CW,* 2:573.

10. John Locke, *Second Treatise of Government* (1690), ed. C. B. Macpherson (Indianapolis: Hackett Publishing, 1980), 113.

11. The electorate grew from 409,000 to 814,000 in just one year. See Michael Brock, *The Great Reform Act* (London: Hutchinson, 1973). For the passage of the Reform Act of 1832 as a means to overcome perceived threats of revolution, see Robert A. Dahl, *On Political Equality* (New Haven: Yale University Press, 2006), 44–45.

12. Martin Malia, *History's Locomotives: Revolutions and the Making of the Modern World* (New Haven: Yale University Press, 2007), 6–8, and Malia, *Russia under Western Eyes: From the Bronze Horseman to the Lenin Mausoleum* (Cambridge, MA: Harvard University Press, 1999), 12–13.

13. The idea that the economy became increasingly backward as one observed the peoples from West to East, from Britain to Russia, was first considered by Alexander Gerschenkron, *Economic Backwardness in Historical Perspective* (Cambridge, MA: Harvard University Press, 1962). Though his analysis does not move into the twenty-first century, Malia, who died in 2004, may have considered twenty-first-century terrorism the natural outcome of this history of violence and radicalism.

14. Paine, *Dissertation on the First Principles of Government,* in *CW,* 2:572 (emphasis added).

15. *CW,* 2:573–74. For the view that the French Revolution was doomed from the very beginning to end in terror and violence, see the revisionist studies by François Furet, *Interpreting the French Revolution,* trans. Elborg Forster (Cambridge: Cambridge University Press, 1981), and Simon Schama, *Citizens: A Chronicle of the French Revolution* (New York: Alfred A. Knopf, 1989).

16. *CW,* 2:574–75.

17. This view does not comport with the American experience of in-

cumbency and the near-inevitable re-election of those in office, though the argument remains that Americans always retain the right to vote them out. Hence, the focus among some reformers in America on term limits.

18. Paine, *Dissertation on the First Principles of Government*, in *CW*, 2:587–88. Paine's reference to the constitution that should have been established "two years ago" is to the 1793 document he worked on with Condorcet and others, which was set aside by Robespierre.

19. On Paine's reelection, see Paine to James Madison, 24 Sept. 1795, in *CW*, 2:1378.

20. Thomas Paine, *The Eighteenth Fructidor: To the People of France and the French Armies* (1797), in *CW*, 2:595.

21. As we have seen above, Paine had begun to move toward accepting bicameralism as early as 1786, when he suggested that a single legislative branch should be divided into two parts to discuss issues but should vote together. See Thomas Paine, *Dissertations on the Government; the Affairs of the Bank; and Paper Money* (1786), in *CW*, 2:409, and "Answer to Four Questions on Legislative and Executive Powers" (1792), in *CW*, 2:525–27.

22. Paine to James Monroe, 10 Sept. 1794, in *CW*, 2:1350. Paine at the time was in the Luxembourg prison and hoped to convince Monroe, the new American minister to Paris, to work to get him out, thus arguing that he was a full-fledged American, not English.

23. Paine, *Eighteenth Fructidor*, in *CW*, 2:595.

24. Paine, *Dissertation on the First Principles of Government*, in *CW*, 2:588.

25. *CW*, 2:579.

26. See two classics: J. G. A. Pocock, *The Ancient Constitution and Feudal Law: A Study of English Historical Thought in the Seventeenth Century*, reissue with a retrospect (1957; Cambridge: Cambridge University Press, 1987), and Carl B. Cone, *The English Jacobins: Reformers in Late 18th-Century England* (New York: Charles Scribner's Sons, 1968).

27. Paine, *Dissertation on the First Principles of Government*, in *CW*, 2:582, 585.

28. *CW*, 2:581.

29. Thomas Paine, "The Constitution of 1795" (1795), in *CW*, 2:590.

30. Paine to the Council of Five Hundred, 28 Jan. 1798, in *CW*, 2:1403; Paine to Thomas Jefferson, 1 Oct. 1800, in *CW*, 2:1415–16; Paine to Thomas Jefferson, Oct. 1801, in *CW*, 2:1424–25; head note, in *CW*, 2:675; Thomas Paine, "To the People of England on the Invasion of England" (1804), in *CW*, 2:680; Paine to Thomas Jefferson, 23 Sept. 1803, in *CW*,

2:1450. For the comment about Napoleon, see 679; see also Thomas Paine, "Remarks on English Affairs" (1805), in *CW*, 2:686.

31. Paine to James Madison, 27, Apr. 1797 in *CW*, 2:1395.

32. Paine, "To the People of England," in *CW*, 2:682–83.

33. Paine to Thomas Jefferson, 23 Sept. 1803, in *CW*, 2:1449.

34. Paine to Thomas Jefferson, 2 Aug. 1803, in *CW*, 2:1441.

35. Ibid.

36. Paine to John C. Breckenridge, 2 Aug. 1803, in *CW*, 2:1446.

37. Richard Hofstadter famously coined the term *paranoid style* to analyze responses like Paine's near-hysteria to the Federalists' attempt to create a monarchy in America. See Hofstadter's *The Paranoid Style in American Politics and Other Essays* (New York: Alfred A. Knopf, 1965). See also Gordon S. Wood, "Conspiracy and the Paranoid Style: Causality and Deceit in the Eighteenth Century," *William and Mary Quarterly*, 3rd ser., 39 (July 1982): 401–41.

38. On the rise of party in America, see the classic work by Richard Hofstadter, *The Idea of a Party System: The Rise of Legitimate Opposition in the United States, 1780–1840* (Berkeley: University of California Press, 1970), and more recently, Stanley Elkins and Eric McKitrick, *The Age of Federalism: The Early American Republic, 1788–1800* (New York: Oxford University Press, 1993), esp. 257–302. See also Joseph J. Ellis, *American Creation: Triumphs and Tragedies at the Founding of the Republic* (New York: Alfred A. Knopf, 2007), 165–206.

39. Thomas Paine, *To the Citizens of the United States*, letter 8, June 17, 1805, in *CW*, 2:951. The background of the rise of the party system is to be found in Ellis, *American Creation*, chap. 5. For the impact of Paine's ideas on radicals who followed him, see Michael Durey, *Transatlantic Radicals and the Early American Republic* (Lawrence: University Press of Kansas, 1997).

40. Quoted by Philip Foner in his head note, in *CW*, 2:909, from "A Christian," *Philadelphia Aurora*, Mar. 26, 1803.

41. Paine, *To the Citizens of the United States*, letter 2, 22 Nov. 1802, in *CW*, 2:913.

42. Ibid., letter 8, in *CW*, 2:949, 951.

43. Ibid., in *CW*, 2:954.

44. Ibid., letter 2, in *CW*, 2:916.

45. Ibid., letter 8, in *CW*, 2:955.

46. Ibid., letter 6, 12 Mar. 1803, in *CW*, 2:936. The act, as Paine explained it, stated that "if any person should write or publish, or cause to be written or published, any libel [without defining what a libel is] against the Government of the United States, or either House of Congress or against the President, he should be punished by a fine not ex-

ceeding two thousand dollars, and by imprisonment not exceeding two years" (*CW,* 2:938). Pickering's disloyalty came from his association with Hamilton, who advocated more than anyone, including Adams, an actual war with France. Pickering has largely been ignored, except for Garry Wills, *"Negro President": Jefferson and the Slave Power* (New York: Houghton Mifflin, 2003), esp. 19–34 and 186–92.

47. Paine, *To the Citizens of the United States,* letter 7, 21 Apr. 1803, in *CW,* 2:939. Paine thought the first Washington administration was on the right track insofar as the president attempted to form a neutral government, giving positions to both Hamilton and Jefferson, but that he fell prey to evil Federalist influences after his reelection to a second term.

48. Paine included the text of the treatise in letter 7, in *CW,* 2:940–45.

49. Captured in Paine's infamous open *Letter to George Washington,* 30 July 1796, in *CW,* 2:691–723, which includes his sharpest attacks on the Jay Treaty and contains mostly vitriol.

50. William Hogeland, *The Whiskey Rebellion: George Washington, Alexander Hamilton, and the Frontier Rebels Who Challenged America's Newfound Sovereignty* (New York: Scribner, 2006), 240. See Wills, *"Negro President,"* 127–39, for Pickering's plans for New England's separation from the republic.

51. Four years earlier, power had passed from Washington to Adams peacefully, but they were both Federalists.

52. Paine, *To the Citizens of the United States,* letter 3, 29 Nov. 1802, in *CW,* 2:918–19.

53. Thomas Jefferson, First Inaugural Address (1801), in *Thomas Jefferson: Writings,* ed. Merrill D. Peterson (New York: Library of America, 1984), 493.

Conclusion

1. Thomas Paine, "To John Inskeep, Mayor of the City of Philadelphia" (Feb. 1806), in *CW,* 2:1480.

2. Paine, *To the Citizens of the United States,* letter 8, in *CW,* 2:956.

3. Thomas Paine, "Remarks on Gouverneur Morris's funeral Oration on General Hamilton" (1804), in *CW,* 2:962.

4. Paine to George Clinton, 4 May 1807, in *CW,* 2:1487. Clinton at the time was vice president of the United States.

5. Gouverneur Morris to Thomas Jefferson, 21 Jan. 1794 and 6 Mar. 1794, in *The Gouverneur Morris Papers,* Library of Congress, Washington, DC. Morris lied to Jefferson, who had just resigned as secretary of state the previous December, telling him that he had indeed applied to the French government for Paine's release when in fact he never did. Paine was only released after James Monroe, in replacing Morris, applied to

the French government, with President Washington's approval. Recall, too, that the French jailed him for being "English."

6. This is contained in "My Private Thoughts on a Future State" (1807), in *CW*, 2:892. See also Thomas Paine, "Predestination" (1809), in *CW*, 2:894–97, reputedly, according to Philip Foner, the last words written by Paine (head note, 894).

7. Samuel Adams to Paine, 30 Nov. 1802, in *CW*, 2:1433.

8. For the best description of the events surrounding the Religion of Reason, see Mona Ozouf, *Festivals and the French Revolution*, trans. Alan Sheridan (Cambridge, MA: Harvard University Press, 1988).

9. Paine to Samuel Adams, 1 Jan. 1803, in *CW*, 2:1436.

10. *CW*, 2:1437. Philip Foner says the letter can be found in *The Writings of Samuel Adams*, ed. Henry Alonzo Cushing (New York, 1908), 4:340–44.

11. Paine, "To John Mason" (1804), *Prospect Papers*, in *CW*, 2:815. (The "sir" is addressed to Mason, not Sam Adams, but the thought is the same.)

12. Paine to Samuel Adams, in *CW*, 2:1438.

13. For Paine's death and the disposition of his remains, see Paul Collins, *The Trouble with Tom: The Strange Aftermath and Times of Thomas Paine* (New York: Bloomsbury, 2005).

Appendix

1. Britons today typically claim Paine as an Englishman. See John Keane, "Démocratie républicaine, nation, nationalisme: Repenser les "Droits de l'Homme de Thomas Paine," trans. Bernard Vincent, in *Thomas Paine, ou la république sans frontière*, ed. Bernard Vincent (Nancy: Presses Universitaires de Nancy, 1993), 137–58, and Keane, *Tom Paine: A Political Biography* (Boston: Little, Brown, 1995). See also Steve Tillston and Maggie Boyle, *All under the Sun*, a CD with the song "Here's to Tom Paine," with its refrain, referring to Paine as "Never a better born Englishman." Flying Fish CD, FF 663, 1996.

2. *Universal civilization* is a term Paine used in his 1782 *Letter to the Abbé Raynal*, in *CW*, 2: 256, and the phrase "citizen of the world" may be found in Common Sense [Thomas Paine], *American Crisis*, no. 7, 21 Nov. 1778, in *CW*, 1:146. For a recent assessment of the idea, see Michael Scrivener, *The Cosmopolitan Ideal in the Age of Revolution and Reaction, 1776–1832* (London: Pickering & Chatto, 2007).

3. Thomas C. Walker, "The Forgotten Prophet: Tom Paine's Cosmopolitanism and International Relations," *International Studies Quarterly* 44 (2000): 51–72, esp. 52; David Fitzsimons, "Tom Paine's New World Order: Idealistic Internationalism in the Ideology of Early Amer-

ican Foreign Relations," *Diplomatic History* 19 (Fall 1995): 569–82; and Mark Philp, *Paine* (Oxford: Oxford University Press, 1989), 68–70.

4. Ian Dyck, "Local Attachments, National Identities, and World Citizenship in the Thought of Thomas Paine," *History Workshop Journal* 35 (1993): 117–35. Two older studies are still useful: A. Owen Aldridge, "La Signification historique, diplomatique et litéraire de la lettre à l'Abbé Raynal de Thomas Paine," *Etudes anglaises* 8 (1955): 223–32, and Darrel Abel, "The Significance of the 'Letter to the Abbé Raynal' in the Progress of the Thought of Thomas Paine," *Pennsylvania Magazine of History* 66 (Apr. 1942): 176–90.

5. Franklin to Joseph Galloway, 25 Feb. 1775, in *The Papers of Benjamin Franklin*, ed. Leonard W. Labaree et al., 39 vols. to date (New Haven: Yale University Press, 1959–), 21:509.

6. Common Sense [Paine], *American Crisis*, no. 1, 23 Dec. 1776, in *CW*, 1:50.

7. Ibid., 56.

8. Common Sense [Paine], *American Crisis*, A Supernumerary Crisis, in *CW*, 1:237–39.

9. Paine to Anonymous, 1789, in *CW*, 2:1297 (Philip Foner is uncertain about the date of this letter).

10. For his citations of Rousseau, see *Rights of Man*, 94; "Essay for the Use of New Republicans in their Opposition to Monarchy," 26 Oct. 1792, in *CW*, 2:543; *Dissertation on the First Principles of Government* (1795), in *CW*, 2:570–88. See also Jack Fruchtman Jr., *Thomas Paine and the Religion of Nature* (Baltimore: Johns Hopkins University Press, 1993), 147–50, and A. Owen Aldridge, *Thomas Paine's American Ideology* (Newark: University of Delaware Press, 1984), 137–46.

11. Paine to James Monroe, 20 Oct. 1794, in *CW*, 2:1367.

12. From a letter dated 16 Mar. 1790, quoted in Moncure Daniel Conway, *The Life of Thomas Paine*, 2 vols. (New York: G. P. Putnam's Sons, 1792), 1:271.

13. Paine to James Monroe, 18 Aug. 1794, in *CW*, 2:1342–43.

14. Paine to James Monroe, 20 Oct. 1794, in *CW*, 2:1367 (emphasis added).

15. Thomas Paine, *Letters to the Citizens of the United States*, letter 4 (1802), in *CW*, 2:926. Note this comment Harvey Kaye made as late as 2005 about Paine's Americanness when Paine resettled in America in 1802: "Returning to the country he admired, loved, and *considered his home*, Paine, now almost sixty-six years old, would receive at best, a mixed reception." See Harvey J. Kaye, *Thomas Paine and the Promise of America* (New York: Hill & Wang, 2005), 89 (emphasis added).

16. See note 3 in this appendix for the full Walker citation. For the

most recent articulation of this position, see "A Citizen of the World," in Kaye, *Thomas Paine and the Promise of America*, 64–90, though see note 15, above.

17. See the citations in notes 2 and 3 of this appendix.

18. Paine to the Marquis de Lansdowne, 21 Sept. 1787, in *CW*, 2:1265.

19. Thomas Paine, "Reasons for Preserving the Life of Louis Capet" (1783), in *CW*, 2:552.

20. In the course of his accusation that Deane was war profiteering at the expense of the new United States, he unwittingly revealed the Americans' new alliance with France before the government announced it. For details, see Craig Nelson, *Thomas Paine: Enlightenment, Revolution, and the Birth of Modern Nations* (New York; Viking, 2006), 126–45.

21. Paine to Thomas Jefferson, 4 Oct. 1800, in *CW*, 2:1417.

22. *CW*, 2:922.

23. Wilson Carey McWilliams, *The Idea of Fraternity in America* (Berkeley: University of California Press, 1973), 170.

24. Paine to Anonymous, 4 Mar. 1797, in *CW*, 2:1385; Paine to James Madison, 27 Apr. 1797, in *CW*, 2:1394; Paine to Anonymous, 12 Thermidor, Year VIII, in *CW*, 2:1406; Paine to Thomas Jefferson, 1 Oct. 1800, in *CW*, 2:1412.

25. Paine to Kitty Nicholson Few, 6 Jan. 1789, in *CW*, 2:1276.

26. Thomas Paine, *Prospects on the Rubicon, or an Investigation into the Causes and Consequences of the Politics to be Agitated at the Next Meeting of Parliament* (1787), in *CW*, 2:632.

RECOMMENDED READING

Aldridge, A. Owen. *Thomas Paine's American Ideology*. Newark: University of Delaware Press, 1984.

Claeys, Gregory. *Thomas Paine: Social and Political Thought*. Boston: Unwin Hyman, 1989.

Foner, Eric. *Tom Paine and Revolutionary America*. 1976. Updated ed. New York: Oxford University Press, 2005.

Fruchtman, Jack, Jr. *Thomas Paine and the Religion of Nature*. Baltimore: Johns Hopkins University Press, 1993.

Hawke, David Freeman. *Paine*. New York: Harper & Row, 1974.

Hitchens, Christopher. *Thomas Paine's "Rights of Man": A Biography*. New York: Atlantic Monthly Press, 2006.

Kaye, Harvey J. *Thomas Paine and the Promise of America*. New York: Hill & Wang, 2005.

Keane, John. *Tom Paine: A Political Life*. Boston: Little, Brown, 1995,

Larkin, Edward. *Thomas Paine and the Literature of Revolution*. Cambridge: Cambridge University Press, 2005.

Nelson, Craig. *Thomas Paine: Enlightenment, Revolution, and the Birth of Modern Nations*. New York: Viking, 2006.

Paine, Thomas. *Collected Writings*. Edited by Eric Foner. New York: Library of America, 1995.

Philp, Mark. *Paine*. Past Masters Series. Oxford: Oxford University Press, 1989.

Vickers, Vikki J. *"My Pen and My Soul Have Ever Gone Together": Thomas Paine and the American Revolution*. New York: Routledge, 2006.

Wood, Gordon S. *Revolutionary Characters: What Made the Founders Different*. New York: Penguin Press, 2006.

INDEX

Adam (Biblical), Eve and, 45
Adams, Abigail, 105
Adams, John, 1, 21, 57, 152; bicameralism and, 51, 53; fear of democracy and, 38–39; fear of Hamilton and, 109, 193–94n20; Paine and, 2–3, 6, 29, 146–50
Adams, John Quincy, 147, 149
Adams, Samuel, 21, 29, 51, 154–55, 177n10; *Common Sense* and, 59, 65
Aitken, Robert, 21
Aldridge, Alfred Owen, 116–17
American Revolution. *See* Revolution, American
Anglicanism (Church of England), 23
Annet, Peter, 24
Antichrist, the, Protestant theology and, 31–32
armies, standing, 149
Arnold, Benedict, 33
Articles of Confederation, 12, 38

Babeuf, Gracchus (François Noël), 170n17
banking, 106, 109–10, 116–19
Bank of England, 119
Bank of New York, 109
Bank of North America, 13, 110, 116–19
Bank of the United States, 13, 109, 116
bargaining, collective, 112–13
Bell, Robert (printer), 59, 184n5
bicameralism, 6–7, 51–54, 141–42, 152–53, 199n21
Blount, Charles, 175n23

Blum, Carol, 122
Bolingbroke, Henry St. John, Lord, 38
Bonaparte, Napoleon, 136, 144–45
Boudinot, Elias, 70
Burke, Edmund, 4, 119–20, 126, 135–36; economy and, 113–14; on English Revolution, 71; language and, 97; Paine and, 24, 32, 42–43, 143, 189n21; *Reflections on the Revolution in France* (1790) and, 57, 77, 81–83; and theory of prescription, 42–43, 82–83, 87; and theory of property, 79

Calvinism, the Elect Few and, 35
Capet, Louis. *See* Louis XVI
Chalmers, George ("Francis Oldys"), 173n3, 176–77n3
Charles I (king of England), 17
Christianity, Paine's attack on, 28–30, 34–40, 93
Church of England, religious establishments and, 94–96, 135
civilization, universal, 77–78
Claeys, Gregory, 4, 189n14
Clinton, George, 201n4
Cobban, Alfred, 121
Collins, Anthony, 24
commerce, 6, 107–8
Committee on Foreign Affairs, Paine and, 12
Condorcet, the Marquis de, 79, 126, 140
Constitution, American, 1, 91, 94, 141–42, 147–48
constitution, ancient, 71